Lars Rudebeck, Olle Törnquist and Virgilio Rojas (*editors*)
DEMOCRATIZATION IN THE THIRD WORLD
Concrete Cases in Comparative and Theoretical Perspective

Howard Stein (*editor*)
ASIAN INDUSTRIALIZATION AND AFRICA
Studies in Policy Alternatives to Structural Adjustment

International Political Economy Series
Series Standing Order ISBN 0–333–71708–2 hardcover
Series Standing Order ISBN 0–333–71110–6 paperback
(*outside North America only*)

You can receive future titles in this series as they are published by placing a standing order. Please contact your bookseller or, in case of difficulty, write to us at the address below with your name and address, the title of the series and one or both of the ISBNs quoted above.

Customer Services Department, Macmillan Distribution Ltd, Houndmills, Basingstoke, Hampshire RG21 6XS, England

Institutionalizing Development Policies and Resource Strategies in Eastern Africa and India

Developing Winners and Losers

Martin Doornbos
Professor of Political Science
Institute of Social Studies
The Hague
The Netherlands

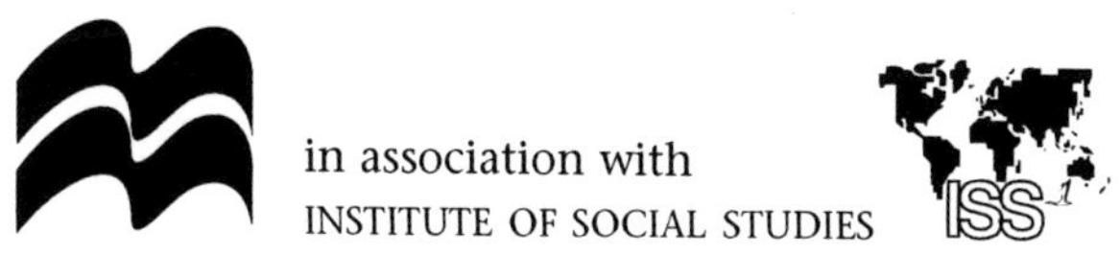

in association with
INSTITUTE OF SOCIAL STUDIES

 First published in Great Britain 2000 by
MACMILLAN PRESS LTD
Houndmills, Basingstoke, Hampshire RG21 6XS and London
Companies and representatives throughout the world

A catalogue record for this book is available from the British Library.

ISBN 0–333–68772–8

 First published in the United States of America 2000 by
ST. MARTIN'S PRESS, INC.,
Scholarly and Reference Division,
175 Fifth Avenue, New York, N.Y. 10010

ISBN 0–312–22737–X

Library of Congress Cataloging-in-Publication Data
Doornbos, Martin R.
Institutionalizing development policies and resource strategies in
Eastern Africa and India : developing winners and losers / Martin
Doornbos.
   p.   cm. — (International political economy series)
Includes bibliographical references and index.
ISBN 0–312–22737–X (cloth)
1. Africa, Eastern—Economic policy.   2. India—Economic
policy—1980–   I. Title.   II. Series.
HC860.D66   1999
338.954—dc21   99–32871
                                                                    CIP

This book is printed on paper suitable for recycling and made from fully managed and sustained forest sources.

10   9   8   7   6   5   4   3   2   1
09   08   07   06   05   04   03   02   01   00

Printed and bound in Great Britain by
Antony Rowe Ltd, Chippenham, Wiltshire

To Wicky

Contents

Part 4 Dairy Aid and Dairy Development in India: Institutions and Resource Strategies

List of Tables and Maps

Tables

Maps

Acknowledgements

This collection of essays results from a long-standing curiosity about the effects of the *institutional factor* upon the success or failure of development policies and the social and political processes they generate. The studies concerned have emanated from involvement in a range of different research projects and networks. Several of these engagements have been quite different in purpose and focus, ranging from discussions on state formation and institutional incorporation to questions of resource conflicts about access to land and boundary disputes, or again from the development of ranching schemes in Uganda to the institutionalization of dairy development in India. Yet a common thread has throughout been an interest in the social and political effects of institutional arrangements in development policy and interventions – effects that may be anticipated or actually designed, or which are unintended but no less consequential, as the case may be.

This monograph thus owes a major debt to several research contexts and networks which over successive periods have provided stimulation and relevant feedback for the studies presented here. To begin with, there was the privilege of being associated, in the mid-1960s, with the then newly established political science research unit directed by the late James S. Coleman at what is now the Makerere Institute of Social Research in Kampala, Uganda. This involvement, together with the links maintained with colleagues at Makerere University during subsequent years, provided the initial impetus and research base not only for the case studies included here on issues of *land tenure*, the politics of *ranch allocations* and the role of *kingship* in Ankole, Uganda, but also for reflection on several wider questions of *political and institutional development*. On the Uganda front I have incurred lasting debts to many individuals, but I should like to single out here Tibamanya mwene Mushanga, now Ugandan Ambassador in Bonn, and the late Dan Mudoola, former Director of the Makerere Institute of Social Research, for their continuing support and friendship.

Several of the interests first developed in Uganda could be pursued further in other fora during subsequent years, including the informal Dutch-based research network initiated by Hans Claessen on early state formation; various African studies ventures in The Netherlands, commonly in conjunction with the African Studies Centre at Leiden University and in constructive dialogue with Wim van Binsbergen, Peter Geschiere, Gerti Hesseling and other colleagues; the stimulating recurrent workshops on Uganda organized by Holger Hansen and Michael Twaddle in Roskilde, Denmark; several special seminars organized by the Working Groups on Rural Development and on Aid Policy and Performance of EADI, the European Association of Development Institutes, led by Herwig Palme and Olav Stokke respectively; and last but not least, various venues at the Institute of Social Studies, which throughout has served as a dependable, if demanding, intellectual home base. Several of the studies comprised within this volume have benefited greatly from discussions within the ISS Rural Development seminars and State and Society seminars, as well as in various courses within the Institute's post-graduate programmes in development studies, most notably that focused on the Politics of Alternative Development Strategies. Also at the ISS, the long-standing editorial association with the journal *Development and Change* has been a continuous source of stimulation. Friends at ISS, past and present, to whom I owe intellectual debts reflected in this book are just too many to mention, though I should like to make an exception for Jan Breman, Richard Brown, Kurt Martin, Wicky Meynen, Mohamed Salih, Jan Aart Schotte, Nico Schrijver, Brian Van Arkadie, Joan Verloren van Themaat and Peter Waterman.

Another involvement that has left its imprint on the present collection has been the collaborative research project, under the auspices of the Indo-Dutch Programme on Alternatives in Development (IDPAD), on different aspects of the major *Indian dairy development* programme, Operation Flood. This research project, with the fascinating insights it yielded into the politics of evaluation and other dimensions of the institutionalization of power – and the power of institutionalization – kept the active attention and engagement of a widening group of Indian and Dutch researchers from the early 1980s till the early 1990s, resulting in two joint volumes and a large number of articles on the social and economic dimensions of dairy aid and dairy development, two of which are included here. Collaboration in this context with B. S. Baviskar, Frank van Dorsten, Manoshi Mitra, K. N. Nair, Piet Terhal and several others has throughout been a highly stimulating learning experience on the phenomena of *institutionalizing development policies*. Further engagement in analysing food aid issues came in the context of the Advisory Group for the Netherlands Ministry of Foreign Affairs Evaluation Unit's study of the effectiveness of Dutch food aid (1990), and more recently in conjunction with the EADI Working Group on

Aid Policy and Performance's project on *Food and Human Security: The Role of Food Aid and Finance for Food* (1998). An opportunity to appraise alternative institutional approaches relevant in this connection, notably in crisis contexts, was obtained through association with the War-torn Societies Project, in particular Matthias Stiefel, at the United Nations Research Institute for Social Development (UNRISD), Geneva, between 1996 and 1998.

A final area of research-networking of relevance to the concerns of this book consists of ongoing project involvements on issues concerning *the state and pastoralist communities*, with special reference to the Horn of Africa. On the pastoralist front, collaborative contacts with John Markakis of the University of Crete, with Mohamed Salih at ISS, and with Abdel Ghaffar M. Ahmed at the Organization for Social Science Research in Eastern Africa in Addis Ababa, have been of prime relevance in this connection. The chapter included here on issues of pastoralism and the state reflect part of this ongoing work.

Earlier versions of the materials presented in this volume have been part of the proceedings of various workshops and conferences or were published in preliminary form elsewhere. Thus, Chapter 1 is based partly on a paper on 'State and Society in the Third World: Changing Perspectives' presented at the *International Symposium on Challenges to the Third World in the 1990s*, November 1992, in Beijing, organized by the Chinese Centre for Third World Studies of the Chinese Academy of Social Sciences. The second section of the chapter is based on my 'Foreword' to the special issue of *Development and Change* on 'Emancipations: Modern and Postmodern', which came out in 1992. An earlier version of this chapter was published in *No Easy Way Out: Essays on Third World Development*, edited by Annelet Harts-Broekhuis and Otto Verkoren, Utrecht, 1994. Chapter 2 is an only slightly revised version of an article first published in *Development and Change*, 1 (1), 1969, then a largely unknown journal. Chapter 3 is a revision of a chapter which was published in Olav Stokke (ed.), *Aid and Political Conditionality*, London: Frank Cass, 1995. An earlier Dutch version of this paper appeared in *Antropologische Verkenningen*, 12 (4), 1993. It drew on insights I had gained as invited chair for a panel on 'good governance' at the World Bank's 1991 Annual Conference on Development Economics, where the concept was first launched and discussed. Chapter 4 is a revision of 'Incorporation and Cultural "Receptivity" to Change', published in Wim van Binsbergen, Filip Reyntjens and Gerti Hesseling (eds.) *State and Local Community in Africa*, Brussels: CEDAF/ASDOC, 1986, based on a Belgian-Dutch workshop in African Studies held in

Antwerp, December, 1994. An earlier version of Chapter 5 on the fate of Ankole kingship appeared as 'Institutionalization and Institutional Decline' in Henri J. M. Claessen, Pieter van de Velde and M. Estellie Smith (eds.) *Development and Decline: The Evolution of Sociopolitical Organization,* South Hadley, Mass.: Bergin and Garvey Publishers, 1985. A postscript has been added which reflects on the resurfacing of the kingship issue in Uganda in the mid-1990s and its special implications for Ankole. Chapter 6 is a reworked version (with a 1998 postscript) of an earlier article entitled 'Land Tenure and Political Conflict in Ankole, Uganda', which appeared in *The Journal of Development Studies*, 12 (1), 1975. Of Chapter 7 an earlier version was published as part of a collection edited by Michael Lofchie, *The State of the Nations: Constraints on Development in Independent Africa*, Berkeley and Los Angeles: University of California Press, 1971. Again, a 1998 postscript updating recent developments around the scheme has been added. Chapter 8 was first presented as a paper at a colloquium at the University of Aberdeen in 1990 on *Pastoral Economies in Africa and Long Term Responses to Drought*, and published in its proceedings edited by Jeffrey Stone in 1991. Part of this paper was based on my 'Pasture and Polis: the Roots of Political Marginalization of Somali Pastoralism', in John Markakis (ed.), *Conflict and the Decline of Pastoralism in the Horn of Africa*, Basingstoke: Macmillan, 1993. Chapter 9 is a revised version of an article which first appeared in *Development and Change*, 19 (3), 1988, broadly covering the ground of the above mentioned research project on Operation Flood. Chapter 10, published earlier in *The Journal of Development Studies*, 30 (4), 1994, takes this further in discussing the major conclusions of this research on the institutions of Indian dairying. Chapter 11 represents a preliminary version of a contribution to a collection on *Food Aid and Human Security* being prepared by Edward Clay and Olav Stokke on the basis of the 1998 EADI Workshop on Food and Human Security, held in Lysebu, Oslo. In several cases, a trading of sections has taken place between chapters. Permission to use these various materials for purposes of inclusion in reworked form in the present volume has been generously granted by the respective editors and publishers concerned, along with several co-authors, and is herewith gratefully acknowledged. Grateful acknowledgement is also made to the University of California Press for permission to redesign maps from Michael Lofchie, *State of the Nations: Constraints on Development in Independent Africa*. Patricia Aeilkema-Schor, Jane Pocock and Teresa Waldin provided valuable assistance in preparing the manuscript for the press.

Last but not least, I thank Yusuf Bangura, Des Gasper and Liana Gertsch, and particularly John Markakis and Wicky Meynen, for their critical and constructive comments on earlier drafts of the Introduction and Conclusion, and Tim Shaw for his helpful feedback and encouragement throughout the course of this project. None of them should, of course, be held co-responsible for the views and arguments I put forward.

The Hague   MARTIN DOORNBOS

List of Abbreviations

AMUL	Anand Milk Producers' Union Limited
CCP	Committee on Commodity Problems
CED	Centre for Education and Documentation
CFA	Committee on Food Aid
DC	District Commissioner
EADI	European Association of Development Institutes
EC	European Community
ECA	European Court of Auditors
EEC	European Economic Community
EPRDF	Ethiopian Peoples' Revolutionary Democratic Front
EU	European Union
FAO	Food and Agriculture Organization
GNP	Gross National Product
GOI	Government of India
IDPAD	Indo-Dutch Programme on Alternatives in Development
IDC	Indian Dairy Corporation
IGAD	Intergovernmental Authority for Development
IMF	International Monetary Fund
KDCMPU	Kheda District Co-operative Milk Producers' Union
NCA	National Commission on Agriculture
NCDF	National Co-operative Dairy Federation of India
NDDB	National Dairy Development Board
NGOs	Non-Governmental Organizations
NICS	Newly Industrializing Countries
NRA	National Resistance Army (Uganda)
NRM	National Resistance Movement (Uganda)
OAU	Organization of African Unity
OECD	Organization for Economic Co-operation and Development
OF	Operation Flood
PC	Provincial Commissioner
SMP	Skim Milk Powder
TPLF	Tigray People's Liberation Front
UN	United Nations
UNICEF	United Nations International Children's Emergency Fund
UNDP	United Nations Development Programme
UNEP	United Nations Environment Programme

UNFPA	United Nations Population Fund
UNHCR	United Nations High Commission for Refugees
UNRISD	United Nations Research Institute for Social Development
UPC	Uganda People's Congress
USAID	United States Agency for International Development
WFP	World Food Programme
WSP	War-torn Societies Project

Glossary of non-English terms with reference to Ankole, Uganda

Bagyendanwa	Royal Drum
Eishengyero	District Council
Ekyikari	Enclosure
Enganzi	Chief Minister, Ankole
Engure	Headband
Gombolola	Sub-County
Kihimba	Administrative Secretary
Lukiko	Council
Mailo	Square miles of land
Mugaba	Palace
Nkore	Pre-colonial kingdom from which the name Ankole was derived
Omubiki	Treasurer
Omugabe	King
Omujasi	Head of Ankole askaris
Omuramuzi	Chief Judge
Omwigarire	Queen
Saza	County

Notes on Co-authors

Liana J. Gertsch is currently Programme Specialist at the Asia-Pacific Desk of the Bernard van Leer Foundation, The Hague, The Netherlands. Earlier, she was a Research Associate at the Institute of Social Studies and had worked on Operation Flood and some of its political dimensions in the context of her research towards a M.A. degree in Development Studies.

Michael F. Lofchie is Professor of Political Science at the University of California, Los Angeles (UCLA), and a former Director of the UCLA African Studies Center. He has written extensively on agricultural development in Eastern Africa as well as on broader issues of African economic development. He is presently involved in a World Bank research project on government–business relations in Ghana.

John Markakis is Professor of African Studies in the Department of History and Archaeology at the University of Crete and a Visiting Professor at the Institute of Social Studies, The Hague. He has previously taught at the University of Edinburgh, the University of Zambia in Lusaka, the University of Botswana and Swaziland, St John's University in New York, Addis Ababa University and at Brooklyn College. His major publications include *Ethiopia: Anatomy of a Traditional Policy; Class and Revolution in Ethiopia; National and Class Conflict in the Horn of Africa;* and *Resource Conflict in the Horn of Africa.*

Manoshi Mitra is currently working as Social Development Specialist with the Asian Development Bank in Manila, Philippines. Dr. Mitra is an economic historian by background and the author of *Agrarian Social Structure: Continuity and Change in Bihar, 1786–1920.* In recent years she has done considerable research on gender and development issues, on which she has published widely.

Pieter van Stuijvenberg is an economist with a background in both development-related research, with a special emphasis on India, and management consultancy. He has co-authored (with T. M. Thomas Isaac and

K. N. Nair) *Of Modernisation and Employment: the Coir Industry in Kerala (1992)*. At the moment, he is Managing Director of BMB Management Consulting, which offers consultancy services on issues of public, private and social sector development in Eastern Europe, Asia, Africa and Latin America.

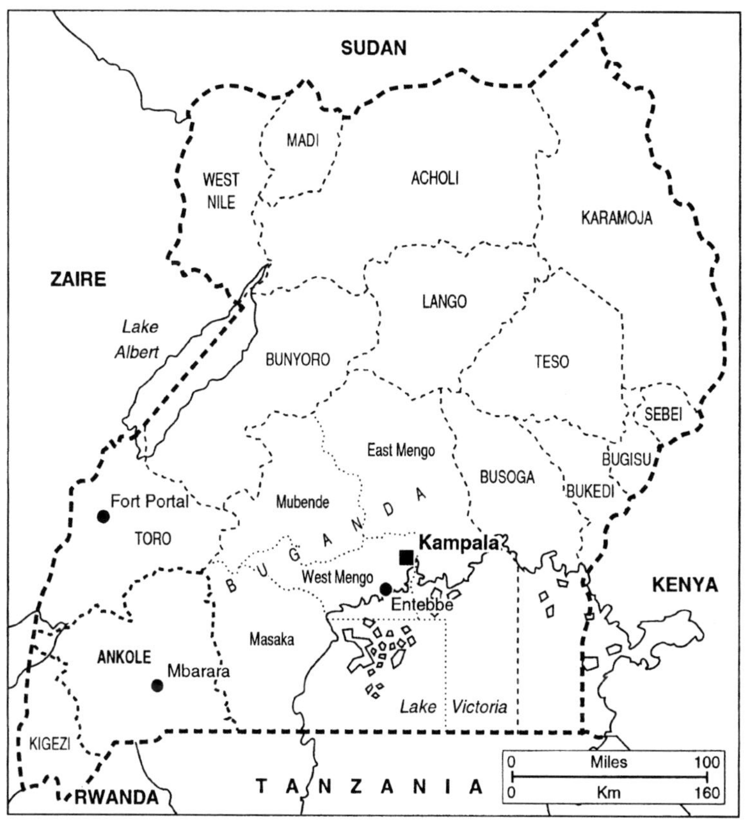

Map 1. Uganda: district boundaries until 1973

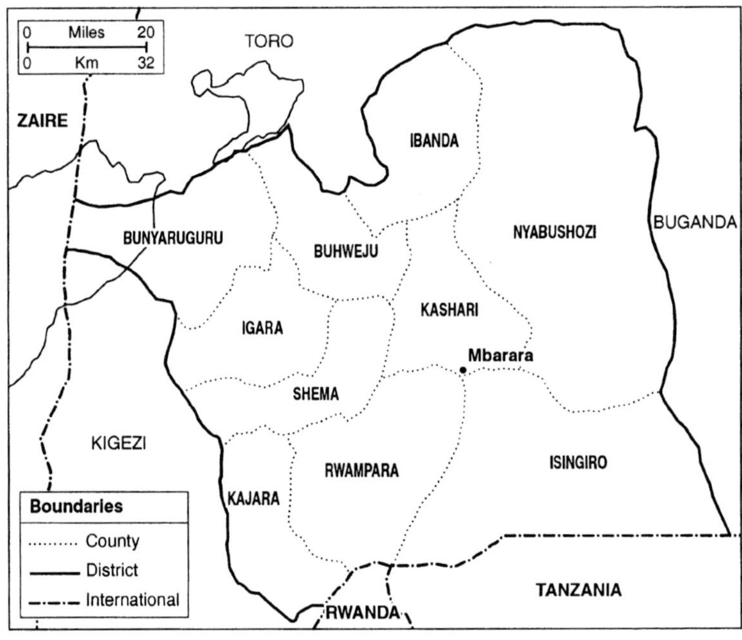

Map 2. Uganda: district boundaries after 1973

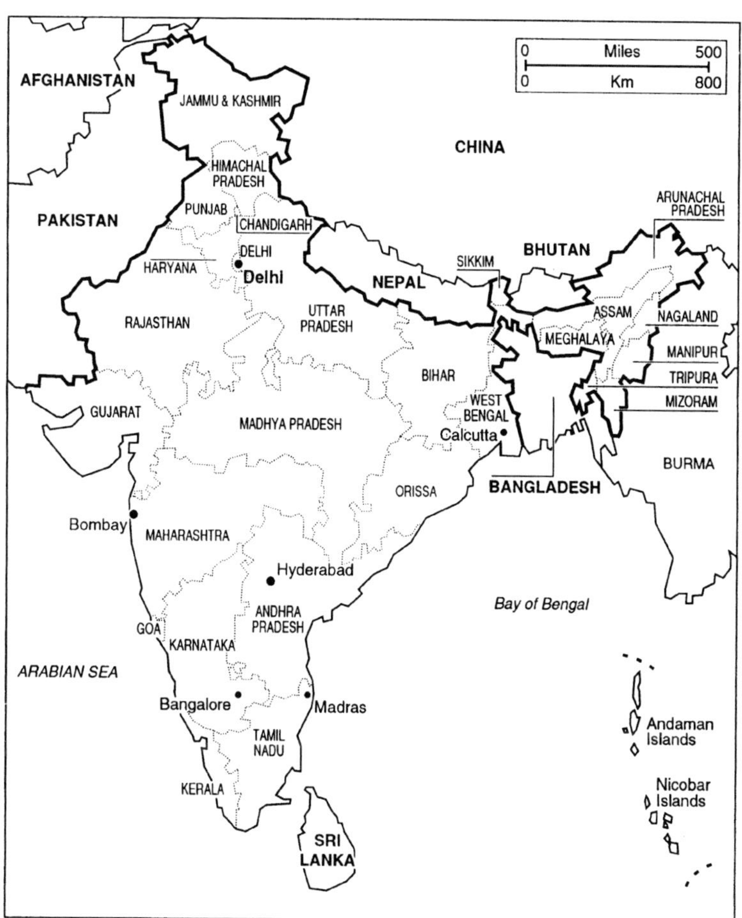

Map 3.   Map of India, 1987

Introduction

'Laws are like sausages.
It is better not to see them being made.'
Otto von Bismarck, Chancellor of Prussia

Do institutional structures matter? More specifically, do project designs, organograms, constitutional provisions and other institutional arrangements make a difference to political and administrative processes, or do they only represent one-dimensional, if not caricature, representations of reality? In studies of political processes, especially in regard to less developed countries, it is widely held that descriptions of formal jurisdictions are a highly inadequate, even deceptive, guide to an understanding of the 'real stuff' of politics, of actual political processes, and state-society relations. This point, often reiterated, has attained the status of a 'given' in political studies. In a recent formulation, for example, James Manor writes that 'the informalities of politics are usually more important than formal laws, rules and structures in shaping state-society relations' (Manor, 1996).

This assumption is an old one indeed, dating back to the time when political science first emerged as a distinct field of study and, pointing to behavioural rather than formal dimensions of political processes and structures, thereby emancipated the study of politics from constitutional law as one of its parent disciplines. Obviously, there is much to be said for this insight. We are all familiar with the phenomena of informal power relations, intra-bureaucratic politics, and manifold personality, cultural and other variables affecting political behaviour. Common parlance expressions like 'dead rules', 'the power behind the throne', 'kitchen cabinets', 'the corridors of power' and numerous others indicate awareness of layers of political reality other than what the rules on the books appear to describe or prescribe. In the Third World, discrepancies between the formal and informal are often very substantial, as even the most cursory perusal of constitutional provisions in Congo or Liberia will reveal. Clearly, it would be naïve to negate any such realities.

And yet, all this presents at best only one side of the picture. No matter how instructive it is to highlight how 'real' political processes elude formal structures, the reverse – namely how (formal) institutional structures give rise to distinct, yet no less 'real', patterns of political, social and economic relations – is of equal significance; or perhaps even more so. Self-evident as this logic would seem to be, though, it has not always received the attention it deserves.

Many years ago, the anthropologist Lucy Mair made it a point to emphasize that legal frameworks of political activity are more than formalities, and potentially have an effect on political behaviour; even though the same rules may well be understood differently from one situation to another (Mair, 1967). More recently, Thelen and Steinmo in a *'historical institutionalism'* approach, addressed the same point when arguing that 'Institutional analyses do not deny the broad political forces that animate various theories of politics . . . Instead, they point to the way that institutions structure these battles and, in doing so, influence their outcomes' (Thelen and Steinmo, 1992, cited in Fox, 1993:22). State-society relations, indeed, certainly in the Third World, are shaped through innumerable institutional interventions from which they derive their distinctive features and patterns, though this in no way implies that the practices they give rise to follow strictly formal contours. In many development contexts, *institutional interventions* have been of central prominence, and a focus on the form and impact of institutional arrangements placed at the nexus of state-society relations may help unravel some of the latter's key dimensions and unresolved questions.

For a better understanding of the kind of political conflicts that may arise in various instances, such as issues of resource management and utilization, it will be instructive to look into the specific institutional interventions, and into the implicit *design* of social and political relations that these tend to further. In this connection, there is a wide range of different agencies and arrangements, constituting a virtual universe of development institutions, that deserve attention for their role in the politics of resource mobilization, allocation and extraction. This category includes land development programmes, resettlement schemes, co-operative unions, credit schemes, marketing boards, welfare agencies, irrigation projects, forestry departments, local governments, various other government branches and non-governmental organizations (NGOs). Not a few of these institutions find themselves at one time or another addressing resource conflicts of various kinds, either as a party or arbiter or, who knows, as both – though quite conceivably in several such instances their own set-up and structuring might well call for some closer scrutiny with respect to the allocation of powers, resources and rewards they entail.

Critical assessment of development policies and initiatives, therefore, requires examining the institutional instruments and processes that give shape to particular patterns of interaction, relations of power and distribution of burdens and benefits, and calls for special attention to the politics of institutional design. It goes without saying that it is important to comprehend these patterns not only within the organizational space internal to the institutions concerned, but especially with reference to the broader sectors and contexts that fall under their jurisdiction and intervention. It is in order to highlight and examine these issues that the essays in this volume have been brought together.

Analysing development institutions

Briefly, the argument underlying this volume might be summed up as follows: *Development is about interventions, interventions involve institutional arrangements, and institutional arrangements impact on socio-economic processes, but differentially so, creating 'winners' and 'losers'. By implication this causes the role of many development institutions to become contested terrain, perceived in highly contrasted terms by sponsoring bodies, intermediaries and different categories among the 'target' groups, all of whom may develop different stakes in them.*

In essence this pattern has been basic to the formulation and engineering of innumerable novel organizational forms, resource allocation structures, rules of access to public services and other institutional innovations through which the development-oriented state and other actors, including donor-agencies and NGOs, have been pursuing their mission. It has also been the recipe for the innumerable instances of unequal resource allocation, at times of fierce resource conflicts, the by-products of constructed realities engineered through development interventions. Such results were not necessarily intended (though often enough they were), but in all cases they provide support for a conception of politics defined as 'who gets what, when and how' (Laswell, 1936). What remained to be added, though, was: 'and who does not get, why not', and, 'for how long?'

In the light of these observations, one key concern for political analysis remains that of tracing how the design of institutional arrangements actually comes to be determined, and what implications this carries. What this calls for is an effort to unravel what often tends to be the profoundly political element in the way they give shape to socio-political relationships and processes, define the parameters for coping with conflicting demands, or tend to privilege specific client categories through key selective criteria.

A focus on *the political dimensions of institutional infrastructures*, or on *the political implications of institutionalizing development policies*, however, opens up an extremely wide and amorphous field of enquiry. This must be cut down to manageable proportions through relevant questions on selected issues and aspects. Specifically, it will be important to enquire into the manner in which institutional arrangements embody control over resources, human as well as material, and what power relationships lie at the basis of any such patterns, or tend to emerge from them.[1]

Chapter overview

The remaining part of the Introduction will be devoted towards developing an agenda for institutional analysis in the above perspective. The chapters that follow highlight several issues connected with the analysis of *institutions and institutional interventions in development contexts*, both theoretical and praxis-oriented, and will be particularly concerned with the often implicit *political dimensions* of their design and role. The volume is organized in four main parts. The first two are focused on some conceptual and theoretical issues which need to be addressed when trying to get a proper understanding of *the institutional factor*, of *the politics of institutional design*, and of *processes of institutionalization*. The latter two parts are devoted to detailed analysis of various specific projects and programmes of *institutional intervention*. These are largely concerned with issues involved in the use of environmental resources and resource competition in Eastern Africa and India, particularly regarding land and livestock utilization.

Part 1, on *Development Discourses and the Institutional Factor*, explores the angles from which some of the broader conceptualizations of development and development strategies have viewed the institutional factor, that is, what roles and significance have been implicitly or explicitly assigned within their frameworks to various institutions and processes of institutionalization in the context of development processes and programmes. Questions about the conceptual and epistemological linkages concerned recur at several levels. Thus, Chapter 1 is addressed to broadly changing perspectives on state and society in the Third World, asking to what extent one can justifiably speak of paradigmatic changes in this regard, and what implications these could have for perspectives on the role and the analysis of development institutions and interventions. To the extent that such broad shifts are indeed occurring, it is submitted that institutional analysis may basically come to constitute a more autonomous area of enquiry, that is, one within which the agenda and criteria for evaluation become important in their own right, and with respect to which the question about the place for social priorities and criteria of equity in the context of institutional strategies and performance will need to be freshly addressed.

Chapter 2 further pursues this line of enquiry and argument, adding a historical dimension and perspective to it. Going over some debates that ran a few decades ago, the chapter may add to our sociology of knowledge though its review of the ingredients and criteria once proposed to define *'political development'*. It is interesting to see from a present-day perspective which of the criteria then debated now look dated and obsolete, while others have retained their relevance or have even grown in relative importance. Specifically, the critique of the institutionalization thesis as a yardstick for 'political development' essentially appears still valid today. Chapter 3 is focused on the recent international preoccupation with criteria of *'good governance'* in less developed countries, and probes into some of the factors that have prompted the re-launch of the concept, its intrinsic links with the earlier concerns with 'institutionalization', and its connections with a new generation of proposed *'political conditionalities'*.

Part 2, on *Institutional Incorporation and Cultural Diversity*, shifts the discussion to the receiving end, or at least to perceptions of it. It first offers, in Chapter 4, a critical reappraisal of debates on *'cultural receptivity'*, submitting that attributions of predictable, culturally determined dispositions *vis-à-vis* incorporation into new institutional arrangements more often than not have failed to give adequate recognition to new patterns of interest politics and interest orientations, prompted precisely by the new propositions concerned. Chapter 5 shifts the discussion to another dimension of processes of state formation and institutional incorporation, namely the potential loss of relevance that a once meaningful institution may incur upon its incorporation within a new political framework. The discussion proceeds via a conceptual juxtaposition of notions of institutionalization and *institutional decline*, the latter being based on an examination of the neo-traditionalization of Ankole kingship.

Part 3, on *Land, Pastoralism and the State in Eastern Africa: Institutional Interventions*, reviews several instances illustrating the political implications of various institutional interventions in patterns of land utilization and competing resource claims. Thus, Chapter 6 provides a detailed analysis of the differential impacts and the deepening political controversies emanating from two institutional modifications of land tenure arrangements introduced in the former Ankole district of Uganda, namely the *mailo* and the *individual land titles* schemes. Each of these schemes had the effect of sharpening conflicts over environmental resources, and of creating categories of winners and losers in the process. Complementing these analyses, Chapter 7 offers a review of the interest politics focused on the formulation of the institutional arrangements, specifically regarding the eligibility of absentee ranch-owners, which laid the basis of another land utilization project in the Ankole area, namely the *Ankole Ranching Scheme*. The early politics around the design of the Ankole Ranching Scheme were of particular significance and consequence in view of the involvement of USAID in the project and the bilateral controversies that arose concerning the criteria of rancher selection.

Following this discussion of a specific intervention in pastoralist livestock utilization patterns, Chapter 8 takes up the more general question of the nature and premises of state policies *vis-à-vis* the *pastoralist mode of existence* as manifested in the Horn of Africa, though with specific reference to the evolution of policy interventions in the Somali context. Virtually irrespective of regime type and constituency, it appears that the predicaments of pastoralism have steadily been aggravated as a result of institutional interventions by most governments of Eastern Africa, with dire consequences for the prospects of environmental security and the course of resource conflicts.

Lastly, Part 4, on *Dairy Aid and Dairy Development in India: Institutions and Resource Strategies*, shifts the terrain to the operations of the mega-institutions governing the interventions in a different kind of livestock utilization pattern, namely that of the *Operation Flood* programme for *dairy development* in India. Here, the key dimensions of the politics and the design of the interventions concerned have been markedly influenced by the strong ties to various sources of international aid, which enabled the programme to take off the way it did. Both the shape of the institutional structure, the claims of success made for the programme, and the element of increasing *dependency* within a context of globalization of marketing arrangements it appears to have engendered, have given rise to a considerable amount of analysis and debate. Chapter 9 reviews the general premises and impacts of the Operation Flood programme in the context of a discussion of the evolution of strategies of international dairy aid, and in conclusion takes up the question of institutional interests and the politics of evaluation. Chapter 10 examines the various debates which the Operation Flood programme has given rise to in an extensive literature, with a particular focus on the compatibility of corporate interest, technological innovation and sustainability of the resource basis. Throughout the analysis, particular attention is given to the way in which the design of institutional interventions tends to give rise to and address certain categories of programme beneficiaries, as well as prioritize particular patterns of resource utilization. Winners and losers have tended to emerge at several levels, among different categories of producers and consumers, among Indian states, and among the protagonists of different resource strategies.

While Chapters 9 and 10 focus on some of the institutional implications at the receiving end of food aid linkages, Chapter 11 has been added to this Part as it examines the role of the institutional factor in shaping policies and programmes at the 'giving' side of food aid. As the availability of surplus commodities in the North for distribution as food aid is becoming less assured at the present time, the chapter discusses the 'threat' to the institutional interest represented by the core agencies involved in keeping a continued role in food aid disbursement and developing food aid programmes.

In the Conclusion, an attempt is made to draw some lessons and place the foregoing analyses in a broader perspective. First, on the basis of the discussion in particular in Part 4, a re-visit to some broad theoretical propositions – about *corporatism, dependency,* and the *relative autonomy of the state* – is proposed concerning the role of political institutions in development processes, though now at a sectoral level rather than that of the state. Following this, the field of *changing forms of organization of collective activities* that can be noted in connection with patterns of global restructuring in many parts of the world is taken up for discussion. The implications of these transitions for the nature of institutional interventions are far-reaching, and need to be taken account of in institutional and political analysis.

Institutionalizing development interventions

A widely variegated range of institutional forms has emerged historically to shape state-society relations. Power and authority patterns are crystallized into institutional structures, subject to never-ending challenges and potential reversals. Control over resources becomes institutionalized through legal provisions, open to renegotiation within (or outside) established procedures. State policies and interventions must be given institutionalized form and expression – in projects, departments or other organizational constructs – for implementation to become possible in the first place. Civil organizations seek to institutionalize their own areas of involvement, either in collaboration with state agencies, or as an alternative. Institutionalization, *the process of translating power configurations and policy intentions into tangible, structural forms,* thus figures as one of the most basic and pervasive facts of social organization. If one were interested in elementary truths, one of them might be that there are no alternatives to institutionalization, save utopian ones.

As already noted, though, there is a tendency for institutions to assume a life of their own and become political actors in their own right. Moreover, institutional arrangements may raise vexed questions as to whether they actually, or accurately, reflect policy intentions. Discrepancies between declared purposes and pursued aims constitute political facts of a kind, which in turn invite scrutiny of what happens when policy objectives are concretized in institutional forms. How are such translations into 'real' terms made, and by whom? What agencies, with what specific agendas, are entrusted with these tasks, or put themselves forward for the purpose? A basic question is whose policy, and whose interests, are at stake in the first place?

There are important dynamic dimensions to these processes. Some institutions are set up with the best of intentions and the best of provisions, yet after some time they stultify into routine operations blocking innovation, or even degenerate into abusive instruments of power in the hands of dominant groups. The latter problem preoccupied Roberto Michels when he wrote his classic *Political Parties* early this century on the prospects of party structures remaining genuinely democratic (Michels, 1915/1962). In the 'iron law of oligarchy', he put his finger on a problem which remains basically unresolved. Examples of institutional self-preservation abound; they include cases of NGOs in the field of humanitarian intervention deliberately presenting over-dramatized pictures of victim destitution to safeguard their own survival (De Waal, 1997). Still, there are instances where an oppressive institution finds itself challenged by demands for equity and in the end is forced to become more open and democratic. Occasionally there are instances of subordinate groups successfully having recourse to legal provisions which had long been deemed closed to them. 'Weapons of the weak', as James Scott might agree, are not employed in losing battles only (Scott, 1985). Thus, notwithstanding all the weight of negative experience with institutionalized power, one might still postulate a cautious 'neutrality' to institutional structures in principle, leaving more categorical judgements to depend on who uses them, how and for what purposes. By implication though, such neutrality cannot be attributed to highly discriminatory or oppressive institutions whose structures have been specially designed for such purposes.

The issues raised above have particular relevance in the assessment of development policies. This is first of all due to the greater vulnerability of institutional structures in developing countries to the impact of global processes and demands. Especially in Africa, state structures have dwindled to modest proportions and have become highly dependent on external support and direction. In many instances of structural adjustment, the role of the state, once expected to act as the 'prime mover' in the development front, has been reduced to a nominal one, leaving space to a host of other actors, and to neo-liberalism as the guiding ideological perspective (Doornbos, 1990). In these conditions, development policies and projects are increasingly 'prefabricated' elsewhere through close consultation among key donor agencies, multilateral organizations and international NGOs. *Policy co-ordination* in fact appears to be more a matter of concern and convenience to the various outside agencies, than an instrument in the hands of the national government. Though closer inspection would show that donor co-ordination in practice is often less than optimal, this hardly gives national governments control of their own affairs.

In such contexts, the institutional infrastructure takes on very unconventional shades of grey indeed. With a range of different agencies putting forward their own profile and distinctive policy priorities, institutionalization may show traces of not a few externally conceived interests and demands. New *aid regimes* are emerging, with the potential, in a Foucauldian sense, to 'discipline' institutional and political processes in particular directions.

Many project and policy interventions in development contexts are initiated *de novo*, without involvement of the targeted groups which lack the capacity to respond. Actually, in a good number of cases the target is not these communities themselves but the resources – land, mineral, other – they happen to sit on. Also, there is a stronger chance of dominant interests getting a better hearing – and a better follow-up. This is partly because in many 'development' contexts there will be relatively few well-organized and alert bodies within *civil society* in a position to react on behalf of vulnerable sections. Indeed, there are greater dangers of non-represented interests and groups being overlooked here, at times quite deliberately so, at times simply because the interest at stake has not been adequately identified, let alone found a suitable defender

(Balbus, 1971). Thus, while various social groups are vulnerable to externally conceived interventions, dominant interests and outside bodies have better chances to influence policies and programme designs. It is noteworthy, nonetheless, to record instances in which weak 'target' communities counter such moves through recourse to legal action, demanding protection of their rights and interests on the basis of relevant national legislation (Lynch and Talbott, 1995). Also, various NGOs are taking up the cause of marginalized communities in various countries, and at times are able to help give these groups a stronger voice (e.g. Jones, 1998).

Institutionalization of development policies and programmes in numerous instances is concerned with *issues of resource management*: laying down a particular allocation of resources, or order of priority in resource utilization; establishing monopolies of resource use, either for the state or for other bodies; fixing or amending the status quo on property or labour relations, and thus bolstering the prevailing social framework. By implication, development institutionalization comprises manifold ways of extending a given political order, including the elaboration of particular rules for representation and participation in decision making that may be negotiated as part of the social contract concerned. In the most fundamental sense, development institutionalization represents the extension of a *frontier* of sorts: the replacement of remaining socially-specific patterns of resource allocation and control by institutional mechanisms with new claims to primacy and universal validity. However, parallel trends towards *de-institutionalization*, including the neglect or destruction of institutional capital embodied in hitherto functional institutions, may constitute the obverse side of these same processes. Contemporary variants of this occur as de-institutionalization of various public social services in the wake of pressures for privatization, structural adjustment and the general weakening of state functions in the current global context, though it is interesting to note that they may sometimes create conditions for radical policy reform (cf. Hutchful, 1997).

Given the interests at stake, it is hardly surprising that virtually any institutional intervention runs a chance of eliciting quite divergent reactions: high expectations of anticipated pay-offs on the one hand, and concern for the side-effects and implications for affected third parties on the other, thus prompting a replay of the recurrent contradictions that institutional arrangements tend to throw up. In this volume I will note several instances of such differential responses and their prior determination through *policy design*. Notably, Chapters 6 and 7 will be dealing with the determination of the controversial rules and regulations applied in the *allocation of resources like land and ranches* in Uganda, while Chapter 8 revisits the premises on which similarly disputed *pastoralist development policies* were determined in the Horn of Africa.

Political institutions and institutional politics

Exploring the kind of questions alluded to above requires entering the institutional zone between 'state' and 'society', and between 'public' and 'private'. This zone deserves more attention from a political economy and political sociology perspective than it has been accorded. Some aspects of it have often been ignored, on the premise that they are mainly concerned with the routines of administrative and bureaucratic praxis; as contrasted to the 'really' important issues played out in the realm of high politics and the state. Closer inspection would show this to be a mistaken and reductionist conception requiring correction. There are important dimensions of essential politics running right through the heart of the seemingly colourless zone of institutional infrastructure: such as the translation of changing power balances into new institutional arrangements; the emergence of powerful institutions with vast powers over economic and social domains; the strategic support and resources that specific 'bureaucratic' institutions may offer to political coalitions, and vice versa; or the competition for power and pre-eminence that large institutional bodies, national or international, may engage in.

Generally, within this institutional sphere one may also detect the entire ensemble of political manoeuvring at work associated with what was once so eloquently phrased as *the authoritative allocation of values* (Easton 1965, p. 53); i.e. the processes of determination, as to which recipient bodies or categories will qualify to benefit from particular kinds of public resources – and, by implication, who will not. Such moves and counter-moves will be present irrespective of whether or not the wider polity within which they occur might be called democratic or not. Representative democracy no doubt affects the style and manner in which interest politics will be manifested, but it will certainly not put an end to it. Nor would most authoritarian regimes, except for truly utopian ones.

Within virtually any organization and not least within public bureaucracies, one is also bound to find salient 'political' processes, such as the politics of bureaucratic patronage and intra-bureaucratic conflicts, which are all to be associated with competition for power rather than with any routine administrative praxis. Predictably, these have given rise to a 'politics within bureaucracy' field of enquiry among sociologists and political scientists, which has become a respectable tradition of critical analysis (Peters, 1987; Heaver, 1982). But surely there is more to the political process within bureaucracies than the petty politics of the bureaucrats, and one should not let the larger picture be eclipsed by the petty one.

Sometimes institutional arrangements may represent accurate approximations of what the policy intentions had been to begin with. At times, however, significant discrepancies may occur. These may be due to the appreciable autonomy enjoyed by the key political or institutional players within the grey zone, to ongoing struggles over the determination of priorities in resource allocations even after general policy guidelines have been laid down, or to the tendency for policy implementation to take its own course within (or beyond) the margins of interpretation of institutional rules. Therefore, indeed, it seems worth paying attention to institutionalization processes and their outcomes in order to learn not only who gets what, when and how out of the process, to borrow again Laswell's phrase, but also who does not and why.

A better understanding of actual political processes – specifically those connected with resource struggles and competition for control over particular spheres and interests – may be derived from probing into the realities of policy formulation and implementation, while having particular regard to the mode of their institutionalization. Researchers pursuing this line of enquiry are likely to find that the institutional sediment of many policy initiatives and project proposals will provide illuminating indicators of the actual distribution of power in the policy area, and of the constituencies earmarked for special attention or privileged access. As we will see, however, many development institutions are peculiar in the sense that even though they may thus be situated in the heart of the state-society nexus, they may nonetheless be viewed in strikingly contrasted or even apolitical terms, depending on the perspective and a priori preoccupation of their observers.

Contrasting perspectives

When trying to grasp the role of various development institutions, one encounters several notable contrasts and riddles, which complicate the task of developing a proper analytical hold on them. Among several paradoxes besetting the analysis of institutions, developmental or otherwise, the central one undoubtedly stems from the highly contrasted angles from which they can be viewed and understood. From one key perspective, that of *political sociology*, institutions of various kinds are essentially regarded as belonging to the world of politics, of power and the state itself, and deriving their significance from that context, directly or indirectly. For a second major perspective, one that is common in studies of *public policy and administration*, institutional structures are seen as part of the universe of administrative practices and routine management, to be judged primarily by the norms and standards prevailing in this universe.

If these two perspectives differ as to what institutions are about or how they ought to be assessed, this has everything to do with the diverse intellectual roots and expectations informing them. The first perspective is essentially analytical, placing primary emphasis on understanding the role and relevance of institutional structures within their particular social and political contexts. The second is basically praxis-oriented and normative, putting a premium on adherence to a generally accepted administrative norm, and reflecting a mission that is largely self-defined as instrumental. In addition, the public policy and administration perspective tends to look at institutional arrangements as being 'context-free', and generally aspires to deal with universally valid categories.

Clearly, there are potential tensions between these different perspectives and their related sets of expectations, and it should not be surprising that such differences have often led to confusion and conflict, especially if the same institution happens to be assessed from contrasted angles. While in one perspective particular importance is attached to contextual analysis and to the variation of institutional roles and relevance in different contexts, the primary concern in the other is with assessing institutional performance in accordance with universal norms. It is thus not too difficult to imagine that even one and the same institution might be evaluated as an example of successful performance in one, but as an exemplar of failure in another.

These contrasts tend to reappear in several guises. Thus, one question often raised is about the *replicability* of 'successful' projects or programmes in different cultural and socio-ecological contexts (cf. Paul, 1982; Ostrom, 1992). International development agencies generally are keen to identify successful projects that might be candidates for replication elsewhere. Sceptical analysts, however, tend to dispute the scope for emulation of such models, arguing that particular local circumstances usually play a decisive role in determining success or failure. This question played an important role, for instance, in contrasting assessments of the large-scale Indian dairy development programme *Operation Flood*, discussed in Chapters 9 and 10 of this volume. Here, as well as in other similar examples, the contradiction boils down to an assumption, on the one hand, that the 'secret' of success is internal to the institutional formula developed, and is thus in principle replicable in other contexts. A contrary assumption is that successful development in a given instance is more likely due to the interplay of particular contextual variables, cultural or otherwise, as to anything else and therefore does not warrant assumptions of general, let alone universal, validity of the model.

Such contrasting perspectives can be reconciled only if one recognizes that the variables they highlight and represent are engaged in continuously interactive and 'competitive' processes: institutional models designed for wider application will seek to re-fashion specific social patterns or political and cultural processes into particular, 'uniform' directions, homogenizing them as part of wider regimes. In turn, specific contextual variables will seek to mould the operations of such newly introduced institutional structures in ways that are familiar and consistent with known socio-political or cultural patterns and practices, thus attempting to reappropriate or reabsorb them into the local context and social structure.

The age-old universalizing mission and strategies of the Roman Catholic church presents a case in point: all embracing as it has been on the basis of several key tenets and institutional principles, in different world regions it has nonetheless had to accommodate itself to different cultural patterns. Indeed, in the process of establishing itself it has at times sought to incorporate such elements in order to build on them. In contrast, McDonald's institutional formula for global reach today seems much tighter and less compromising. Its popularity in 'remote' places like Beijing and Cairo, however, may partly be explicable by the 'exotic' touch it tends to represent there with its products.

A common experience with 'standard' institutions, therefore, is that they may take on notably different roles and meanings in different socio-cultural contexts. They may, though there is no certainty: the extent to which this will happen, and why, will depend on the relative strength of contending variables. It is the tension involved in the confrontation of these different variables which deserves attention when studying institutional processes and interactions. Institutional arrangements may fail and potentially collapse if they remain maladjusted to the context in which they are set up. At the level of development projects this may be illustrated by the fate of the *Ankole Ranching Scheme*, discussed in Chapter 7. Similar patterns and outcomes are manifested at the level of the state. The recent example of *state collapse* and initial ill-conceived, albeit 'humanitarian', external intervention in Somalia (Doornbos and Markakis, 1994; Lyons and Samatar, 1995), provide illustrations of such contradictions.

In other instances, the interactions of institutional arrangements with their environment are studied not for these institutions' failures and lack of grip on social processes, but for their impact on social groups and relations at the receiving end. Such impact has often been vast and pervasive, and analytical perspectives that seek to highlight cultural differentiation or non-formal processes may give this insufficient attention. In reviewing some earlier debates on *institutional incorporation and cultural 'receptivity' to change*, Chapter 4, stresses this point, arguing, that, for all the need to understand differentiated cultural response patterns, one should not overlook the basic impact of the interventions themselves.

Related differences in perception may apply when the institutional formula does not concern a development project or programme, but other kinds of institutional intervention or networking. Certain approaches towards conflict resolution and rehabilitation, for example, which seek to involve former rival combatants and political actors in the identification of common development goals, may indeed succeed in initiating constructive dialogues. However, whether they will succeed or not, and how, may have at least as much to do with whether the post-conflict context is receptive to having a bridge between two opposing sides, as with the bridge's intrinsic capacity to reconcile opposing parties. Beyond the semantics lie basic differences in perspective on the role and capacity of different institutional formulae.

At least as noteworthy as the contrasted responses which different institutionalized development interventions may evoke in the field, is an apparently parallel divergence on the academic side with respect to the role of institutions and the notion of institutionalization as such. Within several theoretical perspectives there is an a priori inclination to underwrite the idea of institutionalization *per se*; that is, understood as the routinization and formalization of power and property relations, to perceive it as a positive development in its own right, irrespective of the actual balance of benefits and relationships it might inaugurate. As will be highlighted in Chapter 2, institutionalization then tends to be viewed as the essential anchor point for social stability and 'development'. In conceptualizations of 'political development' in the late 1960s and 1970s, 'institutionalization' was thus viewed as the final yardstick of development. From other vantage points, in contrast, new institutional arrangements may be treated with indifference or a fair amount of caution. Indeed, institutionalization has often been associated with patterns of domination, unequal powers, political oppression and oligarchy. Yet other, more liberal or emancipatory perspectives expect institutional arrangements to create conditions of equity and neutrality, or even to provide protection for vulnerable social categories. Paradoxically, institutions and institutionalization may thus be perceived as the codification and entrenchment of human rights and civil liberties within some perspectives, but as the extension, consolidation or refinement of the reach of dominant institutions in others.

Such different expectations will commonly have their basis in historical experience, and in the particular interpretation people have developed of this experience. One sobering lesson of history, though, is that the striving for 'just' institutions, once they are established, all too often is followed by disappointment over their actual performance, and by growing misgivings over their positioning and political orientation. These experiences can give a Janus-face quality to institutions, which they may come to share with the state more generally.

Contrasted notions of institutionalization may also shed light on the perceived relevance and fate of historical institutions. Thus, in some perspectives a certain premium is attached to the perpetuation of institutions, more or less irrespective of their particular role or societal value. Chapter 5, dealing with the *neo-traditionalization* of kingship in Ankole, raises general questions for analysis in this connection. Institutionalization in the sense of the elaboration of formal and ceremonial functions and features is juxtaposed here with the notion of *institutional decline*, potentially applicable when societal roles and responsibilities of a given institution appear no longer to be valid. The case of the Ankole monarchy is of particular interest in this connection, in the light of the recent restoration of the institution of kingship in other parts of Uganda, though not in Ankole, where its relevance was strongly disputed (Doornbos, 1993).

Lastly, we should note one more cluster of contrasting perceptions about institutions. From a conventional management of public affairs perspective, institutions are seen as instruments of policy implementation, whether in compliance with 'higher' directives, or in accordance with basic grassroots ideologies or charters. In reality, institutions often manifest a virtually irresistible tendency to lead a life of their own, to incrementally increase their scope of autonomous action and, in the end, to redefine or write their own terms of reference.

Thus, when exploring the depth and rationale of the institutionalization of development policies and programmes, one should not fail to give due attention to the nature and behaviour of institutions found at the core of these processes. It is not uncommon for these core institutions to constitute a dominant interest themselves, and to actively pursue strategies of self-preservation, aggrandizement, and multiplication of functions that do not arise from their founding mandate. Institutional maintenance itself may then become an overriding concern, potentially eclipsing the purpose for which the institution was set up to begin with.

In such instances, institutional maintenance may prompt more overt political roles by its leadership in a wider political arena, national or international, largely to secure continued political support. These tendencies can be particularly pronounced in the case of development institutions whose core function may not have been crystal clear from the start, or whose mandate was not envisaged to be an indefinite one. It is not uncommon in such circumstances to see a tendency, not least in the case of large interventionist organizations, to become very sensitive especially about external evaluations, for fear that the myth of ongoing success on which their continued funding is premised might be jeopardized (Doornbos and Terhal, 1993). One may thus often find a kind of *politics of evaluation* syndrome occurring in the wake of major international aid and development programmes, characterized on the part of the institutions concerned by efforts to retain full control over all aspects of evaluation – whether internal or external, official or unofficial, and to challenge any outside critical review of one's programmes (Wenger, 1987; Carlsson *et al.*, 1994). In the final analysis, this syndrome results from the inclination of various institutions to chart their own, autonomous route, and thus from one of the key recurrent contradictions alluded to earlier in this discussion.

Recognizing these tendencies necessarily leads us back to the 'realist' perspective about the emergence of non-formal political and institutional processes noted above. The point worth reiterating is that the design of many institutional and political interventions implicitly carries the germ material for institutional development in particular directions, potentially initiating interactions with contextual variables that will be shaping distinct patterns of access to power, resources and control.

Exploring alternative approaches

To gain a better understanding of the effects and implications of institutional interventions, it is not only useful to reconsider, as in the above, different ways in which institutions and processes of institutionalization may be perceived. It is equally important to explore alternative modes of institutional analysis that can help unravel complex questions about the processes concerned. Here, there are several current alternative approaches which it may be helpful to look at for comparative purposes, even if only briefly at this point, in an effort to delineate relevant parameters for institutional analysis.

Access

First, as for the kind of enquiry envisaged here, it should be noted that the focus in this volume on institutionalization and institutional design has been significantly influenced by the innovative research on problems of *access to public services*, pioneered by Bernard Schaffer some two decades ago (Schaffer, 1975, 1980; Schaffer and Lamb, 1981; Wood, 1986). The common ground shared with that line of enquiry is one of a primary analytical interest in the implications of rules of differentiation and inequality of access that are written into ostensibly neutral, public charters. Schaffer's contribution in opening up the realm of the provisioning mechanisms by state bureaucracies for critical analysis remains extremely valuable. It rests on the analysis of modes of access to public services through its useful focus on queues, counters, and other differentiating concepts, illuminating the interface of bureaucracy-client encounters.

It is useful to link access analysis to patterns of institutionalization. Notably, institutional incorporation will often involve a kind of negotiated inequality, though this will commonly be couched in egalitarian terms (Schaffer, 1981; cf. also Hall, 1988). Indeed, where incorporation chains are extended and contracted, the developmental benefits, participatory rights, and the protective shield offered by the incorporating body are likely to be stressed. By the same token, emphasis on the benefits which programme authorities or political centres themselves expect to derive from such incorporation, is less likely. The same holds for the importance attached to the curtailment of the joining units' autonomy. Even less is said of the risk and potential losses to new member-units or of the implications of marginalization of those left out. A widened form of access analysis can illuminate such literally 'in-built' discrepancies. Moreover, the distinction, and addition, to the access approach that is proposed here is to try and probe into the processes and mechanisms through which these differentiating rules of access come about, while at the same time attempting to better appreciate the different kinds of constituencies and excluded segments that are being created or re-created.

A different and useful complementary notion of 'access' and '*institutional access routes*' comes from Jonathan Fox (1993). Taking distance from notions of the state as homogeneous entities, he points out that 'when state actors decide how to deal with social actors, their preferences are conditioned in part by their institutional environments ... Different agencies "feel" social pressure differently [due to their] varying administrative or entrepreneurial tasks, institutional ideologies, vulnerability to electoral pressures, recruitment patterns and bureaucratic structures... Social forces thus face different access routes in pursuing their interests with the state' (Fox, 1993:31). Thus, in contrast to Schaffer's differential, and differentiating, access channels which are the products of deliberate institutional design, the institutional access routes which Fox refers to are rather the involuntary products of history, though they are no less real for that matter.

Entitlement

In terms of substantive interests and orientation, the approach focusing on institutionalization and institutional design also shares some common ground with what in recent years, following Sen, has been called *entitlement analysis* (Gasper, 1993; De Gaay Fortman, 1990; Leach *et al.*, 1997; Sen, 1981). Certainly, the interest in attempting to utilize the notion of 'entitlements', to grasp how institutionalized inequities or 'entitlement failures' in resource allocations come about and may generate discontent, is addressed to key issues in the dynamics of resource conflicts, the importance of which can hardly be underrated. However, it remains uncertain whether the concept of 'entitlements' as such, the possible meanings of which continue to occupy a good part of the debate among scholars seeking recourse to it, is actually more of a help or a hindrance in searching for the causes of unequal resource claims (cf. Leach *et al.*, ibid). Issues of social exclusion, privileged access, and the institutionalization of unequal power positions can be, and have been, fruitfully addressed without first having to negotiate the complexities of the 'entitlements' concept. Besides, even if different 'entitlements' could be adequately mapped out – which is what another level of the debate is addressed to – then the key question still remains as to what institutional provisions and mechanisms, and what specific policy or programme designs, actually give rise to them. And lastly, 'entitlement' analysis, through its sheer focus and chosen entry point, may have acquired a somewhat mechanistic quality that hampers its coming to grips with some of the less tangible dimensions and determinants of power, control and distribution processes.

Actor-oriented approaches

A third mode of analysis that addresses questions of some shared concern has been referred to as the *actor-oriented approach* in recent studies of development policy, notably by Norman Long (1988, 1992), working from the general structuration framework of Anthony Giddens (1979, 1984). In an effort to avoid overly deterministic explanations of the nature and direction of agricultural policy and its impact on peasant communities and farming systems, actor-oriented approaches as proposed by Long focus on the interface created by the encounter between state agents, farmers and other local actors. In doing so, these approaches seek to leave room for policy outcomes being shaped at the level of these encounters, with the active imput of farmers and others involved, rather than viewing these outcomes as pre-determined 'givens'. This intention not to prejudge what will happen at the interface is to be appreciated. However, a principled openness can become delusive if it fails to recognize that actors coming to the interface commonly do so with notably unequal powers and resources for negotiation or confrontation. Power to control and power to resist must enter the equation, but the fact is that in many cases (admittedly not all) the equation has already been worked out well before the encounter takes place.

Institutional design

These comments lead us back to the need to try and capture the elements that shape policy and its institutionalization – and thus 'entitlements' or differential access that may follow from it – closer to source, at any rate much further 'upstream' than where the outcomes may eventually surface. Each of these foregoing approaches tends to focus on the outcomes side of public policies, though in the case of actor-oriented approaches one might perhaps better speak of the downstream end of public policy. This is not to suggest that policy 'design' will always be equalled by policy 'outcomes'. Nor is it to assume that the institutional designs which result from policy debates would reflect single undivided 'visions'. All too often, the institutional outcomes of such contestations still carry the marks of confrontation and compromise. But recognizing the broader field of forces within which policy is being conceived and eventually implemented, will undoubtedly help in grasping the intricacies of confrontation at the encounter stage. It is in that sense that having a clearer picture of the 'design' that may have gone into policies and their institutionalization is highly relevant – if only to better understand why they may be resisted or fail in certain situations, or to grasp why one particular kind of confrontation rather than another might come about at the implementation stage. Potentially useful could thus be, for example, to have more of an actor-orientation at the point where institutions are being shaped or re-shaped, allowing a closer understanding as to which actors and factors, and with what agendas and expectations, have an influence on the institutional design concerned.

A final observation in this connection is that the specificity of the various approaches discussed here lies particularly in their *different vantage points*. None of the approaches – access, entitlement, actor-orientation, or institutional design – is strictly theoretical in the sense of representing a full-fledged explanatory *theory* of political and institutional behaviour; even though from time to time we may encounter references to the 'theory of access' or 'entitlement theory'. What matters is that while they share a fair amount of common ground or common interest, each approach chooses a different vantage point from which to survey the entire field. While all vantage points potentially allow a useful contribution to be made, in the end the question is which has the capacity to yield the fuller or more relevant perspective. That in turn is partly a matter of purpose: whether one wants to better understand bureaucracy-client encounters in the field, differential privilege and access enshrined in bureaucratic formula, the basis for 'legitimate' claims to elementary provisions, or more generally the question as to what happens at the design stage where real or imagined conflicting interests are being 'accommodated' into institutional frameworks and/or from where the institutional formulae adopted will begin to have their differentiating effect.

There is definitely every reason to recognize the value of a clearer appreciation of access venues, of entitlements, or of the nature of actor encounters in our efforts to get a better view on relevant dimensions of public policy. The intriguing question, however, remains how in fact do these different policy outcomes come about, what or who shapes them, what is the hidden or overt design that is being followed or developed, and, last but not least, what effects do they have in terms of future patterns of co-operation or contestation, or the emergence of winners and losers, out of the arrangements concerned? A focus on the contents and interactions in institutionalization processes suggests itself as a way to gain a better understanding of these issues.

In conclusion, though, there are two caveats. One is that reiterating these final questions just above assumes a generally positive answer to the question raised in the beginning of this introduction, namely, 'Do institutional structures matter?' – a question in regard to which, hopefully, the analyses that follow will affirm why and how, generally speaking, they do. Second, there is an even prior question, namely, why is all this important and why would we want to know? The twofold reason is quite basic, namely, first, to try and gain a better understanding on how and why social inequities and particular patterns of interaction come about, and to make this visible, and second, if one wants to influence processes and outcomes, to have a better idea at which end to begin and where one might be most effective.

Note

1   It is not too difficult to empathize with Bismarck's reluctance, cited above, to watch the process of sausage-making. Nor is it difficult to extend his law-making analogy to that of institutionalization processes, at least not where the institutionalization of development policies is concerned. Still, if one has a consumer's interest in seeing the quality of sausages being improved, an occasional re-visit to their manufacturing might be a useful step to undertake.

Part 1

Development Discourses and the Institutional Factor

1
Changing Perspectives on State and Society in the Third World

Introduction

Today, at the end of the turbulent 1990s, there are profound changes with respect to prevailing outlooks on Third World politics and development. This area of intellectual interest in fact has lost a good deal of the relative stability it had known during the initial post-independence decades. Major perspectives and concepts, associated with 'modernization' and 'dependency', have been losing their currency, or have been said to be doing so, while alternative visions and projections are being proposed. In particular, these shifts in perspective have entailed a move away from a central focus on the state, present both in 'modernization' and in 'dependency' theory, to give more attention to the role of autonomous institutions, social movements and configurations within the wider society. The rapidly spreading interest in what is viewed as the emergence or re-emergence of *civil society* in the Third World and in Eastern Europe is one indication of this shift of focus.

Generally, such changes of perspective as are at issue here are unlikely to be unrelated to changing political realities, specifically those of global political alignments and internal dynamics of power. To be sure, it would be wrong to assume too readily a one-to-one relation between these different levels, let alone to infer causalities in this regard. Still, one cannot but be struck by the coincidence of the calls for academic attention for the dynamics and pluriformity of political culture on the one hand, and on the other hand the advocacy, and increasingly the reality, of a retreat of the state and the encouragement of 'privatization' by international circles and organizations. A further parallel is that in both spheres – that of political 'reality' and that of 'perspectives' – there has been growing uncertainty as to the nature and direction of future trends.

This chapter is concerned with the second level of these changes; namely, perspectives on state-society relations in the Third World, and the shifts in the premises and criteria with which analysts would set out to assess ongoing dynamics of Third World politics and development. First, it considers the critique offered on the 'political development' and 'dependency' perspectives. This is followed by a discussion on the main ingredients of a 'rethinking' perspective and its affinities to post-modernism. Lastly, the question is raised whether or not changing theoretical perspectives can still be expected to accommodate an emancipatory dimension and what implications this has for institutional analysis.

'Political development' and 'dependency' theory

In the introduction to a collection of essays by a distinguished panel of political theorists, entitled *Rethinking Third World Politics*, James Manor wrote, 'The study of Third World politics is in disarray' and then proceeded to account for this state of affairs by pointing to the 'severe difficulties encountered by the two paradigms or schools of thought which have dominated the study of Third World politics in recent memory' (Manor, 1991). The two paradigms he referred to are, of course, the familiar 'political development' school – traditional political science's home ground within the broader spectrum of modernization studies – and the 'dependency' school, comprising a range of radical and neo-Marxist analyses of the determinants and dynamics of Third World politics. The purported decline of the currency of these paradigms and their increasing inability to account for a number of trends in Third World politics, in the view of Manor and his colleagues, lie at the root of the 'disarray' evident in the study of the politics of development. The collective effort of these authors represents an attempt to find a way out of this impasse, which gives an a priori interest and significance to their work, even though not all contributors appear to share the same agenda.

Rethinking Third World Politics is in no way an isolated attempt at reorienting the study of the 'politics of development'. Other analyses which have recently been initiated similarly seek to illuminate and interpret the symbolic and experiential dimensions of Third World political realities, which for a long time had been ignored if not suppressed. For example, in a contribution to another 'rethinking' exercise, a special issue of *Political Studies* devoted to 'Prospects for Democracy', Bhiku Parekh (1992) critically examines the universalist claims of liberal democracy, reducing them to a validity primarily limited to the Western sphere of provenance. It seems reasonable to expect many more instances of such reorientations on Third World politics to follow, and in their collective emphasis on specificity and pluriformity to inaugurate important new patterns and perspectives.

These 'rethinking' efforts to break new ground in political analysis are related to the much wider wave of post-modern reorientations which have been emerging with respect to the study of culture and society. Post-modernism has been singularly difficult to define (Appiah, 1991; Nederveen Pieterse, 1992; Slater, 1992), except perhaps in the negative – which curiously may explain some of the popularity it has been gaining. Nonetheless, its characteristic ingredients have tended to include a basic resistance to all-encompassing visions and theory, a virtual celebration of pluriformity, and a seemingly principled negation of normative judgement. In consequence, 'post-modernism' appears more easily 'depicted' than 'defined'. Some publishers have in fact attempted to do this through the presentation of apparently random selections of (Latin) typeface in some of their (post-modernist) book titles, each of them originating from a different typographical design, and collectively suggesting arbitrariness, pluriformity of style, and seemingly an absence of any priority of norms.

To appreciate better the new emphases and directions which various authors propose for a rethinking of Third World politics, it will be useful briefly to note what they consider to be essential points and shortcomings of the two waning paradigms, 'political development' and 'dependency'. Much of this is familiar ground, so much so that the phrase 'stale litanies' has been gaining currency with reference to them (Harriss, 1992). For decades, the two paradigms have coexisted and dominated the field in an essentially competitive fashion, largely paralleling each other in time, although 'dependency' had basically emerged in reaction to what it saw as the flaws of the 'political development' school, not least in the light of 'real' world realities (Randall and Theobald, 1985). Increasingly, the two schools had also served as inspiration for opposite political projects, and in some degree as justifications in the struggle for hegemony by the key global powers.

Of the two, 'political development' theory was basically concerned with the institutional implications and demands of a transition from 'tradition' to 'modernity' which it had postulated as being basic to the situation of post-colonial societies in the Third World. Requirements formulated for 'nation-building' stood very central in its analysis: creating effective and acceptable authority structures, integrating diverse institutional patterns and social segments into common politico-legal frameworks, and instilling into it all a sense of common identity and destiny which would fill the political space with fresh meaning and purpose (Binder *et al.*, 1971). There were, of course, many different elements and emphases within this broader perspective, including some that would prove of more intrinsic and enduring quality than others. Certainly, the questions of legitimate power and political identity that were key concerns in the 'political development' school continue to command prime attention today, although from radically different vantage points. Initially, however, there was already a basic lack of clarity or consensus, or both, as to the criteria that should be used in defining 'political development'. This is traced in greater detail in Chapter 2 of this volume.

In its perception of the relation between state and society, the 'political development' school's focus was firmly placed on the side of the state; that is, of the ensemble of institutional arrangements that were seen as requisite for the 'building' of viable political systems. The 'society' part of the equation received far less attention, except as part of a general notion that it was largely based on 'traditional' relationships. But it was precisely that quality which made it the raw material for 'modernization': as 'traditional' patterns presumably were bound to be transformed anyway, modernization and political development theory basically had little intrinsic interest in the specificities or evolution of particular social configurations. Hence the radically different concern with 'identity' from that which may be found today: 'modernization' and 'political development' were understood as requiring the conscious construction of new, integrative identities befitting modernizing political entities, and assumed the shedding of 'traditional' identities standing in the way of such new 'national' projections. 'Tradition' in this perspective might be called upon only to supply suitable ornamentations for newly constructed, essentially secular political frameworks.

However, as Donal Cruise O'Brien, one of the contributors to *Rethinking Third World Politics*, already pointed out in an influential 1972 article, the political development school's own political orientation tended to shift from a liberal, democratic stance to an authoritarian bias fed by primary preoccupation with the maintenance of 'order' (Cruise O'Brien, 1972). In the course of time, this particular quality would indeed increasingly gain a centrality in the school's image of and about itself.

In contrast, although 'dependency' theory shared a strong orientation towards the role of the state with the 'political development' school, the functions it attributed to the state, current as well as alternative, differed diametrically from those in the 'political development' perspective (Doornbos, 1990). Again, while it is difficult to summarize the multi-layered dependency debate without distorting it, the least that can be

said about it is that it addressed the extent to which structural determinants in the world economy which are controlled by hegemonic powers
restrict the room for manoeuvre, policy options and growth potential of
Third World economies. With only a narrow scope for manoeuvre, it saw
the role of the state in Third World countries as one essentially facilitating such dependency relationships, with ruling groups typically assuming a 'comprador' role in collaboration with international capital and
hegemonic powers. In response, 'dependency' theory focused on the scope
and means for 'delinking' from international capitalism, and for initiating alternative development strategies stressing equality, autonomy and
internal resource mobilization, among other things. To achieve these
ends, a large, albeit alternative, role in theory was again reserved for the
state, which was expected to be engineering an amorphous, victimized
but pliable society to new and progressive futures.

If 'political development' theory dissipated over time through its loss
of credibility at the hands of its own narrowing of focus and the critique
from 'dependency' theory, 'dependency theory' in turn ran into difficulties when, contrary to its logic, various countries, especially in East Asia,
proved it was possible to get out of a situation of economic and political
dependency, without actually featuring any 'alternative' power structures. Also, the experience with alternative strategies defended by some
dependency-theorists proved not very promising, a fact which, with a
curious twist, has sometimes been held against dependency theory as
such. This is curious because failures to combat dependency situations
can hardly be held to render the enduring reality of such unequal political and economic relationships, and thus their analysis, any less significant in many countries.

The 'rethinking' perspective

If 'political development' theory was equilibrium-oriented, with insufficient attention for prevailing contradictions within society, 'dependency'
theory, in the view of current critics, was overly preoccupied with international economic forces and class variables, ignoring the cultural specificities and hybrid social formations which have emerged in many Third
World countries. Both perspectives, in the view of Manor and others,
have tended to underrate the diversity and importance of historical and
cultural experiences, and in their teleological and agenda-setting orientation have tended to distort a proper understanding of actual realities, the co-existence and interplay of contradictory elements in these
realities, and the significance of the imaginary dimensions in political

discourse and institutions. Thus, Manor proposes to redress these short-comings by adopting a deliberately detached and eclectic view *vis-à-vis* all paradigms, by refraining from an urge to engage in prescriptions or even from a prime preoccupation with public policy. Instead, it is proposed to approach Third World political configurations in a more open-ended manner, with particular attention given to the historical dimensions, cultural diversity and institutional variations (Manor, 1991: Introduction). Such reorientations should allow a better understanding of the variations in the relations between state and society in different regions of the Third World, and also a better appreciation of the social actors and forces constituting civil society.

This, then, is essentially a *postmodernist agenda* (though postmodernists usually say they have no agendas). To be sure, in more than one way this represents an important new departure in the study of state-society relations in the Third World. As an emerging perspective, it has several strong points in its favour, and it is likely to become more manifest as a way of looking at Third World politics. Notwithstanding many basic insights which have resulted from the dominant intellectual activities and confrontations of the earlier two major schools, there had been too strong a degree of straitjacketing of the variety of Third World political confrontations into standard vocabularies, either of 'political development' or 'dependency' terminology. This has tended to eclipse important variations and, possibly, explanations of particular courses of events in different countries and cultural contexts. A deeper historical understanding of the trajectories of political conflict in particular had been long overdue in the world of the two paradigms and perhaps the most important shortcoming of the two schools was their relative disinterest or inability to interrogate longer-term historical processes and dynamics. And to try and come to a better understanding of the symbolic meaning and expressions of identity hidden in the more theatrical dimensions of politics in the Third World and elsewhere, is also a laudable objective, though perhaps not exactly as novel as Manor, for example, would seem to suggest (cf. Hobsbawm and Ranger, 1983).

A few qualifying observations, however, appear to be in order. One is simply to note that paradigm shifts do not take place overnight but are more likely to evolve as a matter of gradual transition. What seems to be more abrupt may be the explicit statements by various theoreticians in the field declaring that, in their view, a shift of paradigm has occurred, is occurring or is about to occur. Such signals may 'officially' confirm and sanction that certain shifts have taken place, and/or serve to change the beacons for future research. Among other things, a change of beacons may mean a change of focal points, emphases and indicators and particularly, perhaps, of conceptualizations and terminology. Fads and fashion are not entirely unrelated to such changes, especially not to the last-named two. Moreover, it is even more important to recognize that, even though there has been an important impetus towards conceptual 'rethinking', it would be naïve to expect this to signify the eclipse of the essence of the modernization and Marxist positions. Rather, one should expect an active 'rethinking' both of modernization theory and of Marxism to follow in the wake of the current challenge and impasse (e.g. Post, 1997; Saul, 1997).

Interestingly, meanwhile, during any perceived 'paradigm' shifts other factors may come to light as well. One, for example, is the possible recognition that various scholars for a long time had already been pursuing the kind of interests and priority concerns which are now declared *bon ton* under a change of paradigmatic flags. In the present case, for example, this would apply to the emphasis now advocated for longer-term historical processes and culturally specific analyses. Researchers who had been pursuing such lines may now find their endeavours recognized and in retrospect 'legitimated'. Other kinds of discrepancies are likely to occur in future: just as in the world of high fashion, a change of paradigmatic signals may not necessarily result in wholesale adoption of newly recommended attires. Nonetheless, this does not reduce the wider significance of major conceptual shifts, including the ones that we now appear to be witnessing with respect to the study of Third World politics.

Innovative and appropriate in a number of respects as the latter departures may be, however, they also raise some serious questions and problematic issues. Probably the most basic question thrown up by what appears to be the post-modernist position derives from the wish to stay clear of normative theory. One may recognize and appreciate the reservation against a priori normative analysis that has for long characterized both modernization and dependency theory. Yet a determination to avoid such fallacy can easily translate itself into its logical opposite; namely the advocacy of a kind of 'a-normative' theory. In the end, this could mean taking cultural pluriformity and relativism to their extreme and, by implication, accepting instances of social injustice or grossly exploitative relationships at face value as they might be viewed as the products of distinctive 'pluriform' cultural patterns.

The emancipatory dimension

One basic question raised by inclinations to abstain from normative positions is whether the paradigm changes that we seem to be witnessing today will still allow for an emancipatory dimension in social theory and theorizing, specifically with respect to development theory. Whatever their faults, both modernization and dependency theory had such an emancipatory dimension: in the end both postulated a 'better' world to come. To better appreciate this question, a few preliminary observations may be useful.

As times change, we can see a never-ending succession of people's collective projects, priorities and paradigms. Such changes are also true for the broader processes and structures that comprise shifting patterns of hegemony and incorporation on the one hand and the searches for autonomy and a decent existence these engender on the other. As patterns of domination reshape themselves in the wake of changing priorities and justifications, so do the foci and strategies of emancipatory movements, or in fact all social action seeking to define liberation, equality, and social justice. Thus, state and civil society today increasingly compete with capital and class for primary attention, as part of an unending chain of subtle but definite shifts in the foci and rationale of modes of maintaining 'order' on the one hand, and of efforts at preserving or enlarging social 'space' on the other. But whereas opposite foci – such as power versus freedom – may change in tandem, opposition *per se* and the relevance of the counterpoint in socio-political processes will remain. Continuous change equals no change in this fundamental respect. The processes will never be completed. *That* would mean the end of history.

At a juncture such as the present one, when major visions of an alternative future society have dimmed while there is also a rapidly shifting ground at the level of ideas and of perceptions of reality, the question as to what conceptions of emancipation remain or are emerging seems particularly pertinent. Is post-modern also to be understood as post-emancipatory; that is, does post-modernism signify the dwindling and denial of emancipatory projects and ideals? Or does it instead offer an uneasy but compelling grounds for radical rethinking of emancipation? What is the paradigmatic significance of the 'new' social movements – feminism, ecology, non-party political movements – in this context? And what content is there for the concept of 'development', if this is still to be a relevant signifier? These and other related questions are of a kind of first order magnitude at the present time, which accounts for their being raised and debated in a whole range of centres of social and philosophical enquiry in the North and in the South.

In this movement of enquiry and debate, it is important to address the crucial question of emancipation in conjunction with any rethinking of Third World politics, and to engage in a critical inventory of our concepts of liberation. Indeed, in the midst of multiple concurrent streams of reflection on macro and micro processes of social transformation, it will be necessary to seek an increased understanding of the implications of the present paradigmatic shifts in social theorizing for current emancipatory thought and praxis generally. Are these shifts to last? If so, what lessons should one draw from them and in what ways, if at all, should we revise our perspectives on social processes, politics and alternative development strategies in the light of them? Second, in the specific area of Third World politics, one would be especially interested in coming to a critical juxtaposition and reappraisal of notions of emancipation and development. Are they still valid? Can they still be related? If so, in what ways? To what extent, for example, have the implications been thought through of what appears to be a shift away from a primary focus on poverty alleviation in current discussions on developmental strategies to one on the (re)creation of 'civil society' and the formation of middle cadres? Are these both, and equally, to be viewed as 'emancipatory' intervention strategies?

Implications for institutional analysis

In the light of current shifts away from previously dominant paradigms, and of new queries as to the future trajectories of emancipatory and critical development thinking, it is of special interest to try and bring out the underlying notion or concept of emancipation which so often is kept hidden behind the 'if only' element in social analysis: 'if only this or that basic structural constraint could be overcome, vistas of emancipation would more readily unfold themselves'. Or would it no longer be the case that there is an image of a better world implied in contemporary social theory – if only? Such probing might give us a clue as to whether or to what extent emancipatory thinking is still intrinsic to social theory, and in what directions it appears to be evolving. The aim of such exercises, however, should not necessarily be an attempt to promote the construction of any new consensus. Indeed, a bouquet of differently coloured and structured conceptualizations of emancipation would seem to be quite meaningful. In that case, there would not necessarily be a contradiction with the post-modern orientation. While we may have to get used to thinking in terms of emancipations in the plural, corresponding to the pluriformity of power configuration in the real world rather than emancipation *per se*, one would hope to see that the scope for emancipatory thinking as a basic ingredient of social theory is upheld, and, who knows, even widened in a vastly changing intellectual context.

Back to a more pedestrian level, what would this mean in terms of analysis of rather more concrete matters like development projects, interventions, policies or institutions? Or, related to this, to our understanding of various kinds of struggles, as in instances of increasing competition around institutional resource allocations? Significantly, although any institutional constructs may have their own continuity of existence, and perhaps their own rationale and *modus operandi*, the way we normally tend to look at them, judge them and appreciate them would vary markedly depending on the broader paradigmatic perspective from which they are considered. Thus, various kinds of interventions, institutional arrangements or actual resource struggles are likely to be understood quite differently if they are seen in the context of, and illuminated by, a dependency paradigm, a political development perspective, or any other overarching – if not overpowering – grand projection. By implication, the same is true for the criteria institutional analysis would propose for evaluating the performance and merits of particular institutional set-ups. While within a modernization perspective, for example, institutions and institutionalization might be seen as constituting key elements enabling and promoting the unfolding of an ostensibly liberal socio-political order, from a dependency perspective existing institutional arrangements and interventions might rather be viewed as the linchpins upholding state or non-state systems of domination and extraction.

By the same token, though, if and to the extent that the larger paradigms are indeed losing their broad explanatory and interpretative appeal and relevance, one implication of far-reaching importance suggests itself: institutional interventions, either at the level of projects, programmes or policy designs, are then likely to be drawing increasing attention in their own right and should increasingly come to be judged on their own merits. In that event, evaluative criteria are likely to become 'internalized' as well; that is, to be addressed to the intrinsic qualities of institutional constructs or policy measures rather than being derived from 'external' paradigmatic norms, as has so often been the case. In turn, the question of criteria may reassert its primacy, though now at a level of concrete issues, institutions and interventions in the context of particular development strategies, rather than in any more abstract forms. In that connection, the questions raised earlier on the social and emancipatory dimensions of policy interventions and about their status as an ingredient in social theory and human development, would similarly come to reassert their significance – underscoring the relevance of assessing institutional arrangements on the basis of their added value in terms of equity as much as efficiency.

Last but not least, the latter considerations give us a hint as to how we might begin to derive criteria by which to assess the relevance of institutional design and interventions – whether by state agencies, NGOs or any other actors. The significance of this – that is, of employing a 'social benefit' yardstick – is plain, but can be easily underrated from an assumption that would treat institutional and organizational formula in essence as technical, apolitical or neutral, and thus fit to be handled only outside political discourse. Reality, of course, often is different. Institutional and organizational formulas have political dimensions that often remain implicit, though potentially having far-reaching implications.

But there is a second, related implication: within a changing paradigmatic context many institutional constructs bridging the state-society nexus are likely to assume increasingly pivotal roles in and of themselves. Quite possibly they may come to embody political dimensions, or acquire political leverage, in novel fashions which might be insufficiently recognized as such. In various contexts already we find in fact an important grey area emerging between public and private spheres, displaying novel mixes of political and non-political accountabilities, representation and substantial policy making powers. Political and institutional analysis must recognize this, and will need to develop new approaches to better grasp these changing realities. If it accomplishes this, the gain might not only be that of more meaningful assessments made of institutional constructs and interventions, now being analysed on their own merits and from relevant social criteria, but also of a field of analysis that recognizes the need to adapt and extend its own conceptual boundaries.

2
'Political Development': The Search for Criteria

Political scientists have claimed their own share of the development discourse. Whether or not the term describes anything about reality, in their field 'political development' has become a fact. The developmental orientation has assumed a central place, leaving few political scientists unaffected by its impact and appeals. A plethora of studies has been undertaken under the heading of political development, encouraging drastic changes in analytic approaches and the conventional division of labour within the discipline. A considerable amount of theory building has been stimulated through the political development orientation, which has also provoked an ongoing debate on its contents and criteria. Exactly how profound and lasting this impact will be remains to be seen. While few contemporary political science terms compare in frequency of usage with 'political development', virtually no other term is equally ridden with ambiguities. That it has become commonplace to state this fact indicates the semantic and definitional problems faced by political science in this regard. If there is any agreement, it seems to be that, for all the conceptualization to date, the question as to what constitutes political development can still validly be asked. It is also evident, however, that the political development orientation will be sustained only if meaningful answers to this question can be generated.

This chapter, based on a 1969 article in *Development and Change*, is concerned with the criteria which are to be attached to political development as an operational concept. It is beyond its scope to discuss the empirical factors and intellectual trends which have shaped political development as an area of interest, or to survey the vast array of subject matter and theoretical approaches which have come to form part of the developmental orientation in political science (Eckstein and Apter (eds), 1963: Introduction; see also Finkle and Gable (eds), 1966). These issues will only be touched upon in so far as they immediately bear on the ingredients of the political development concept. The procedure of this chapter is that of a review of different usages of the term, both as to content *per se* and technical construction. However, rather than undertake an extensive coverage of available definitions, the discussion will be limited to some major approaches. Identification of the principal conceptual bases of these approaches may enable a closer appraisal of the criteria that would be required to make political development a concept of adequate analytic power.

Development, political science and political development

It seems plausible enough that the political development orientation emerged in response to the notion that the problem of development involves certain specifically political aspects. A corollary assumption is that these aspects are conceptually distinguishable and allow themselves to be set apart for analytic purposes. However, this idea is not as self-evident as it may appear. Another, though not necessarily congruent, clue may be equally significant, namely, that political development provides political scientists with a convenient arena for a discussion of development issues. As a discussion ground, political development allows political scientists to theorize about development on their own terms and in their own vocabulary, facilitating their exchange of views and corresponding with organizational divisions of labour within universities.

The same point can be looked at from a somewhat different perspective. It is in the nature of the scientific process that analyses are made from specific angles, no scientist being capable of developing a method by which to grasp total reality. Inevitably, holistic problems must be broken down into components, even if this means artificial and to a certain extent arbitrary incisions. If one accepts this, the only relevant question is whether the incisions are meaningful.

The reason for raising this matter is that it implies a burden on political science to substantiate the relevance of political development. If there is a 'whole' development problem, then even such conventional subdivisions as are designated by the labels 'economic', 'social' and 'political' should be required to interpret significant aspects of the whole. In other words, while it may not be realistic to challenge approaches which flow from particular academic traditions in the absence of other cross-cutting foci, it is legitimate to expect a proposed mode of analysis to uncover important dimensions of a complex area of interest.

This demand is raised with special force in the study of politics. While many would argue that the political process involves certain ends in and of itself, only few people would hold that it can be meaningfully evaluated without reference to its effects on other aspects of society. This implies a special burden on political science. Its task cannot be limited to elucidating interrelationships between variables within the political superstructure of society, since it is expected that its concepts also be relevant and testable in terms of wider societal processes.

Recent trends within the discipline have increasingly reaffirmed this requirement. Traditional political science is often, if somewhat exaggeratedly, charged with having been preoccupied with political institutions and, in the extreme case, with studying these structures without regard for the environment in which they function. During the last decade or two, however, concern with reciprocal effects between political processes and other aspects of society has become much more dominant. This trend has partly been prompted by interest in the politics and societies of Third World countries, which emerged when the field had just begun to reorient itself on its basic foci and methods. The new demand to interpret the politics of the new states strongly expanded the number of variables used by political scientists and added many which traditionally would have been considered non-political (see, for example, Macridis, 1955).

It is obvious, then, that the construction of a concept of political development whose criteria are restricted to characteristics of the political superstructure would be an exercise of limited utility. Political development will be of wider and more intrinsic relevance as a concept if it specifies political conditions which can be related to more generalized notions of development. The issue is, therefore, whether such criteria can be attached to the notion of political development as will make the term useful as an analytic construct and relevant to social reality.

Meanings of political development

The direction in which construction of the concept of political development initially evolved, can largely be traced through two inventories which have been made of usages of the term. The first is by Robert A. Packenham who, in his article 'Approaches to the Study of Political Development' (Packenham, 1964:108–20), offers a taxonomy of five basic approaches which were current in the developmental literature until the early 1960s:

1 *Legal–formal.* According to Packenham, writers who follow this approach consider political development to be 'primarily a function of a legal–formal constitution that prescribes such features as equal protection under the law, the rule of law, regular elections by secret ballot, federalism, and/or the separation of powers'. As Packenham remarks, this approach is no longer as common as it used to be.

2 *Economic.* This comprises the more widespread view that 'political development is primarily a function of a level of economic development sufficient to serve the material needs of the people and to enhance a reasonable harmony between economic aspirations and satisfactions'.

3 *Administrative.* Political development is here considered as 'primarily a function of the administrative capacity to maintain law and order efficiently and effectively and to perform governmental output functions rationally and neutrally'.

4 *Social system.* This approach is based on the idea that 'political development is primarily a function of a social system that facilitates popular participation in governmental and political processes at all levels and the bridging of regional, religious, caste, linguistic, tribal or other cleavages'.

5 *Political culture.* Political development is here seen as 'primarily a function of the political culture – that is, the set of attitudinal and personality characteristics that enable the members of the political system both to accept the privileges and to bear the responsibilities of a democratic political process'.

This taxonomy is instructive in more than one sense. In each approach, political development figures as the dependent variable while the respective studies are concerned with its conditioning factors. Judging by the numerous studies reviewed by Packenham, these notions of political development as resulting from other conditions prevailed until at least the early 1960s. Moreover, in the studies under review, political development was seen as the result of one or the other of the five conditions. Packenham states that some studies could actually have been classified under more than one heading; however, 'each tends to emphasize one approach more than the others' (Packenham, 1964:109). In the 1950s and early 1960s (the main period covered by the survey) there was therefore at least implicit disagreement about criteria, although the field manifested widespread consensus that there was a dependent variable which could be referred to as 'political development'.

This paradox is of more than merely academic interest. It is also indicative of the way in which actual trends tended to be viewed in the recent past. In the period immediately before and after the independence of the new states, expectations were that this marked the starting point for progressive improvement of the conditions of political life. Nationalism was often regarded as the spiritual foundation stone for new political communities; on the basis of the consensus it supposedly created, it was thought that the next stages of political development would involve the establishment of institutional frameworks for regular political processes. Such expectations were perhaps somewhat unrealistic, but their existence had considerable effect on the fortunes of the political development concept. Its origin would not have been conceivable without this earlier confidence. As the dependent variable was known, all that seemed necessary was a specification of the determining conditions to round off the term. Consequently, the dialogue was mostly in the nature of 'my criterion is better than yours', but beyond this there was a rather pervasive agreement that in reality there was an end-result called political development.

This picture has changed. Subsequent patterns of political affairs raised doubts at a practical and theoretical level. Over the years disappointment grew with the performance of many of the new states, for whose systems the term was first developed. Sceptical voices had never been absent, but what had begun as a basically optimistic determination to elaborate and refine the meaning of political development now made room for an increasingly critical disposition to question the meanings attached to the concept, and indeed to query whether it stood for anything at all. Admittedly, the quarters from which these tendencies emanated have also shifted; what was a conservative critique a decade ago is the gist of many radical commentaries at present, such as the reservations in regard to élite performance. Many political structures which were earlier postulated as the proper vehicles for development are now challenged on the basis of apparent dysfunctionality. Precisely why in the new states political development did not come off the ground as was expected became the subject of much speculation. Numerous factors have been suggested, such as lack of skilled leadership, inadequate motivational attitudes, want of communication systems, ambiguity of role allocation, structural constraints in other respects, and so on. Each of these factors, however, as Willner has pointed out, has been derived through a procedure by which one first posits a prerequisite and then discovers the corresponding gap (Willner, 1964:472).

Scholars' disenchantment when actual trends did not meet their expectations transpires from titles of later articles: 'Authoritarian and Single-party Tendencies in African Politics' (Kilson, 1963), 'Demagogues and Cadres in the Political Development of the New States' (Shils, 1965: 64–77) and 'Breakdowns of Modernisation' (Eisenstadt, 1964:345–67), are cases in point. Certainly, it had become less obvious that reality showed signs of political development. It is worth asking how this new awareness should itself be interpreted: was there stagnation after a take-off of real development, or was the presumed initial development basically a misperception? Whatever it was, political development, which first seemed a highly promising concept and a term full of relevance, tended to become the object of terminological concern and apologetic interpretation. Doubts as to whether the term could be descriptive of reality in turn enhanced the need to scrutinize its criteria if it was to be of use as an analytic tool.

Some of these changed perceptions are evident in a second inventory made of the concept, by Lucien Pye. In his article 'The Concept of Political Development' (Pye, 1965:1–13), Pye lists ten different approaches to the notion. Unlike Packenham's classification, Pye's survey, which does not give explicit references, seems not so much based on trends in the literature of preceding years, but rather gives an impressionistic picture of the notions entertained in about the mid-1960s. This has the effect of telescoping the time difference between the two inventories and tends to reflect the increasing divergences and uncertainties in the conceptualization of political development.

While some approaches overlap, Pye's listing illustrates the expanding range of meanings of political development. This range of indicators analyses political development (1) as the political prerequisite of economic development; (2) as the politics typical of industrial societies; (3) as political modernization; (4) as the operations of a nation state; (5) as administrative and legal development; (6) as mass mobilization and participation; (7) as the building of democracy; (8) as stability and orderly change; (9) as mobilization and power, and (10) as one aspect of a multidimensional process of social change (see Table 2.1). Content-wise, each of the ten notions under review has its own merits and limitations. Pye's comments on these definitions are instructive. He introduces his article by suggesting the need to clear up the confusion around the concept. This confusion is twofold: (1) it is manifested in the considerable variety of substantive contexts given to the term; (2) apart from actual content, it results from the widely different terminological usages of the concept. Pye's concern has been with the first of these sources of confusion.

Table 2.1   Taxonomy of definitions of 'political development'

Definition	Dependent/ independent variable	Level of achievement process	Restricted/ universal scope	Focus on political superstructure/ wider social context	Prescriptive/ descriptive usage	Teleological/ open-ended
Political development as the political prerequisite of economic development	Independent	State of affairs	Universal	Viewed in relationship to other aspects of society	Prescriptive	Alternative patterns allowed for
Political development as the politics typical of industrial societies	Dependent	State of affairs	Geographically restricted	Wider context	Mixed	Teleological
Political development as political modernization	Dependent	Process	Universal	Wider context	Purports analytic content	Teleological
Political development as the operations of a nation state	Dependent	State of affairs	Universal	Wider context/ concentrates on specific governmental qualities	Prescriptive	Teleological

Political development as administrative and legal development	Dependent	Process		Focus on superstructure	Prescriptive	Teleological
Political development as mass mobilization and participation	Both	Process	Universal	Wider context	Mixed	Open-ended
Political development as the building of democracy	Both	Process	Universal	Implicit linkage to wider context	Prescriptive	Teleological
Political development as stability and orderly change	Independent	State of affairs	Universal	Wider context	Prescriptive	In principle open-ended
Political development as mobilization and power	Dependent, though the stress on capacity implies a view of the political system as the independent variable	Mixed	Universal	Wider context	Prescriptive	Open-ended
Political development as one aspect of a multi-dimensional process of social change	Dependent	Process	Universal	Wider context	Analytic	Open-ended

However, the conceptual and epistemological differences in the ten usages are equally important and are indicated in Table 2.1, in which each definition is considered on a number of terminological aspects.

It is clear, then, that the range of definitions soon became very complex. The various concepts reflect more and more dimensions of reality affecting, or affected by political development. By the same token, conceptual inadequacy became abundantly clear in that shortage of vocabulary was causing at least ten different matters to be identified by the same two words.

Pye's inventorization is guided by a wish to derive a more comprehensive notion of political development than was offered in the approaches under review, which all stressed specific aspects. The final alternative – political development as one aspect of a multi-dimensional process of social change – seems to be his partial answer to the confusion. Reviewing the entire list, Pye further suggests that three core elements emerge from among the ten notions of political development, namely, an emphasis on equality, on differentiation, and on capacity. While recognizing that tensions may occur between these three elements, he considers that together they lie at the heart of the development syndrome. In his terms, problems of equality are related to the political culture and to sentiments about legitimacy and commitment to the system; problems of capacity are related to performance of the authoritative structures of government; and questions of differentiation touch mainly on the performance of non-authoritative structures and the general political process in society (Pye, 1965:12–13). The emphasis on these three components as key elements in the political development complex is shared by many political scientists; some of their implications will be discussed further.

The use of a concept

The inventories by Packenham and Pye show that ambiguities regarding the content of political development did not induce clarity about technicalities of the term. On the contrary, a lack of consensus, explicit disagreement or mere confusion about the concept appears to have been operative at various levels. Even when disregarding the complex connotations of each of the words 'political' and 'development', the term 'political development' clearly acquires very different meanings if it is employed to denote a problem area, a geographically-bound phenomenon, a certain level of achievement or a process. Further differences occur through its usage as either a descriptive or a prescriptive term, or as a mixture of the two. Underlying these divergencies is the issue of criteria proper, even if this would only mean, at a minimum, that to distinguish the concept from other notions some kind of yardstick is necessary.

Choice of usage is generally not a matter of arbitrary option but rather a terminological dilemma in which losses in certain respects need to be incurred to obtain gains in precision in others. Thus, certain preferences have also been followed over the years, in keeping with the changing perceptions of the problems in the real world. At first, when political development was usually taken to mean a particular level of political performance, the criteria for such a state of affairs were not at all certain, but conviction was widespread that it found its closest resemblance in certain Western political systems. Hence, political development was a teleological concept; it postulated, implicitly if not explicitly, certain end goals. Similar to suggestions made regarding other fields such as economics, it was held that there were distinct levels of political development. On this basis, certain systems, particularly those of the United States and Britain, usually came out on top of the list (e.g. Almond and Verba, 1963). Other writers have not wanted to put this as explicitly as did Almond and Verba. However, to refer instead to the spread of 'world culture' is, as Mazrui pointed out, a euphemism with an essentially similar ethnocentric bias (Mazrui, 1968:68–83).

Thus, the use of the concept as a level of performance rested on two related convictions: (1) that Western political systems, and a few in particular, represented the optimal form of political development; and (2) that processes of state and nation-building which had been or would be set in motion would in due time cause 'underdeveloped' systems to approximate the model. From these assumptions followed two further characteristics of the concept as a measure of achievement, namely, a definite geographic basis and a strongly prescriptive quality. However, despite the firmness of these assumptions, there was no consensus whatsoever on the actual prerequisites of political development, as evidenced by the multitude of conditioning factors offered.

As noted, divergent developments from the postulated course tended to make the assumptions basic to the notion of political development as a level of achievement increasingly questionable. Political scientists became alerted to the possibilities of (1) stagnation or regression rather than development; and (2) alternative avenues of political development, not necessarily leading to one and the same model or along one uni-linear track. In addition, in the post-war era, awareness has grown of various ways in which the so-called developed countries might not be as politically developed as had been assumed. The poverty problem of the United

States, the quality of the political process in Italy and parochial attitudes elsewhere in the West, all suggest themselves as indices of less than optimal levels of political development. In any case, if greater conceptual precision is desired, not to put 'developed' systems to the same test as the 'underdeveloped' would seem rather futile. Rather than prejudge the question by letting the former stand as model for the latter, it would seem more profitable to leave a decision on what is politically developed until systems have been analysed on the basis of a comparative yardstick.

These issues have caused a recurrence, although in other terms, of the debate on the existence of a non-Western political process (Pye, 1958: 468–86; Diamant, 1959:123–7). Just as in respect to that term, uneasiness has grown regarding a concept of political development which is delineated by geographic rather than analytic boundaries and whose premises serve more as a legitimization of Western polities than as a tool with which to understand developmental processes both in the West and non-West. Hence, the tendency has been to search for a concept of political development which (1) is global rather than geographically limited in its application; (2) is essentially analytic/descriptive rather than prescriptive; (3) focuses on actual processes rather than on the state of affairs which would come as the end-result of any such processes; (4) is open-ended in respect to the direction of these processes and therefore does not a priori start from, or exclude, any ideological basis.

In addition, a concept of political development which is to have any possibility of application must be broad enough to encompass a wide range of relevant political data, yet precise enough not to become an amorphous concept lacking in meaning. In other words, if the term must mean more than mere political change and not be used to condone any *coup d'état*, rearrangement of political structures, manipulation of the masses or indulgence in prestigious symbolism, stringent criteria must be attached to the concept.

Dimensions of political development

Paradoxically, one significant effort towards more precise conceptualization of political development has moved away from, rather than come closer to, the issue of criteria. This is the formulation by the Committee on Comparative Politics of the Social Science Research Council, whose role within the development orientation in political science has been a central one. The Committee conceives political development as a broadly embracing term, encompassing six major dimensions. It is this attempt to bring as many relevant variables as possible under one heading that makes its contribution of interest. By implication, however, the issue of criteria has been shelved in this approach; political development, viewed broadly as an organizing concept, designates no more than a problem area and does not offer guidelines by which to decide what is or is not political development. Nonetheless, the aspects subsumed by the Committee on Comparative Politics are worth considering in some detail; within their scope, they are likely to comprise the ingredients for a more operational concept of political development. The six crisis dimensions, as they are known, are concerned with problems of *identity, legitimacy, penetration, integration, participation and distribution*, and form the subject of a collaborative volume by the members of the Committee (Binder *et al.*, 1971). An easily accessible formulation of this crisis model can also be found in Pye, 1966 and Almond and Bingham Powell, 1966). The components of the crisis model have become common currency among many political scientists, even though each writer tends to give them his/her own value. Inevitably, this will also be the case with the present interpretation.

Political identity

The problem of identity has often been mentioned as the main issue of political development (Geertz, 1963:105–57; Pye, 1962). This is based on the view that a major condition for the emergence of a coherent national community is a sense of common identity, as expressed in identification with the territorial system. A nation is usually distinguished from a state by virtue of feelings of belongingness and common destiny. Accordingly, a state only qualifies as a nation if it is such in the minds of its members. In many countries, not least in new states, this idea is not very pronounced. The reference group with which people primarily identify may exist within a formal national context but not be coterminous with it, or may be divided among a number of states.

The problem of identity is thus that of tension between the political definition of society and the culturally and psychologically determined identification with subgroups recognized on the basis of common language, religion, culture, custom, race or historical connection. The orientations which these subsystems generate are often viewed as essentially subjective and sentimental, whereas the national context tends to be associated with more pragmatic and rational orientations.

Nonetheless, some qualifications are in order when speaking of an identity crisis. Above all, the issue should not be regarded as necessarily presenting itself in diametric opposites. Almost anywhere in the world, people can be categorized in more than one reference group, with which they may identify simultaneously. In most cases, no acute problems are implied; just as people may be Friesian as well as Dutch, so a relative harmony may exist between Kikuyu identity and Kenyan nationality. It is true, however, that in Third World countries, identifications are often stronger at a sub-national than at a national level, whereas in most European countries a feeling of national identity is more pronounced.

Furthermore, it is often when a government attempts to create a stronger notion of unity that open conflict and crises tend to emerge. In situations of linguistic heterogeneity, for instance, it would obviously be desirable to have a bridging communication medium. But the selection of one language as the official vehicle for communication in many respects affects existing relationships. Not only the prestige of the languages concerned is then at stake, but important benefits are involved for those for whom the chosen language is the mother tongue. A similar dilemma was demonstrated by Hussein Adam in his discussion of the selection of a script for the Somali language (Adam, 1968). Alternatively, the prospect of a group's language being placed at a relative disadvantage or, in the extreme case, suppressed, bears immediate sensitive consequences for psychologically determined certainties which underlie collective and individual identities. Thus, when attempts are made to create one national identity in lieu of a multitude of attachments, chances are that a crisis of identity will wax rather than wane.

Lastly, it should be noted that the issue of identity, however important, may only be indirectly of political relevance. Firstly, the issues dividing individuals and groups are usually not differences in identity *per se*, but tend to be correlated with differences and conflicts about other questions, mainly those of political and economic advantage. More often than not, identity as an issue seems to be the symbolic expression of conflicts about more pragmatic matters. Thus, basic solutions to the identity problem frequently require the solving of underlying conflicts, the main factors of which seem to be inherent in problems of participation and distribution. Secondly, identity problems are not only indirect in a derivative sense, but their relevance tends to be indirect in their political consequences. Politically, identity problems come to be translated as either support of or resistance to the political system, either of which lies at the heart of the question of legitimacy.

Legitimacy

The notion of legitimacy refers to the social acceptance of an authoritative structure. It implies that a population considers the existing political role division and the premises on which it is based to be essentially right. Problems of legitimacy may touch upon three levels or aspects of a political system, the most fundamental of which is the political community itself (Easton, 1965). At this level, the questions raised are closely related to those of identity; they consider, for instance, the extent to which different nationalities acknowledge the system which comprises them both as being legitimate. Beyond the definition of the political community, further issues of legitimacy concern the regime, that is, the nature of the government structure and particularly the distribution of powers. A third set of questions concerns the incumbents, who may not be considered legitimate even if there is basic consensus on the definition of the political community and the political structure. Legitimacy, as compared to identity, refers particularly to the authority structure; its source therefore differs to that of identity. However, not only do legitimacy and identity affect one another, they are also affected by similar and even common processes of socialization. Hence, these processes constitute two dimensions of the creation of national unity, namely, the establishment of national consciousness and the acceptance of national authority. Despite its limitations, Max Weber's formulation of three types of legitimate authority (tradition-based authority; authority based on formal-rational rules; and authority deriving its acceptance from the charismatic qualities of a leader) continues to be heuristically significant in this regard. Problems of legitimacy tend to be particularly acute when shifts occur from one type to another, such as when tradition loses its lustre as justification of authority and orientations of legitimacy are directed to the person of a new leader (Apter, 1965).

Issues of legitimacy can occur in any political system. To speak of a legitimacy crisis in respect of Third World countries implies that political leaders need to establish a new basis of legitimate authority. Only in a few countries is legitimacy tradition-based, but even there it is only partly so. Charismatic leadership may at times be a bridging factor, as in the cases of Kwame Nkrumah and Fidel Castro, but it is inherently transient and must be routinized, either in a new tradition or through formalization in a rational-legal structure. Yet, for any of these transitions to be successful and to inaugurate a new basis of legitimacy, a government must generate confidence and support among the population through its general performance. To this end, it needs to successfully complete developmental and other welfare tasks and generally reach a satisfactory record of promoting prosperity. If this is achieved, a spill-over of legitimacy is conceivable from the leadership level to that of the regime and eventually to the political community.

In many countries of Africa and Asia, the legitimacy of the new structures was initially based on the fact that the political leadership emerged from the nationalist movement against colonialism. Although in many cases this only provided a limited basis for unity, it nonetheless created a certain fund of goodwill with which new governments could launch forth. More often than not, however, the earlier goodwill has tended to fade; when it is not followed up by new achievements, people tend to turn away from the regime. In many such situations one may validly speak of a crisis of legitimacy. However, the conditions underlying even these critical situations suggest that the acquisition of legitimacy is greatly dependent on achievements in other areas of government performance.

Political penetration

Penetration is a dimension of political development which focuses more directly on government performance. Although a somewhat elusive term, the concept of political penetration in the words of James Coleman refers to 'that ensemble of processes by which the political-administrative-juridical center of a new state (1) establishes an effective and authoritative central presence throughout its geographical and sectoral peripheries, and (2) acquires a capacity for the extraction and mobilization of resources to implement its policies and pursue its goals, however these may be determined' (Coleman, 1977:3). Emphasis is thus placed on enhancement of the managerial and administrative capacities of the governmental machinery. This involves the establishment of efficient channels of communication between the government administration and the population as a key condition for creating an effective political system. A basic assumption for the postulation of political penetration as a problem dimension of political development is that a system will only function reasonably well if contacts between bureaucracy and population are based on mutual understanding and acceptance and acquire a certain routinized quality.

In more practical terms, political penetration implies that a government develops a capacity to levy taxes and to extract other resources from the society, can command compliance with its laws and regulations, and generally becomes capable of directing social processes in ways conducive to the dual demands of greater institutional strength and increasing welfare. Creating this capacity also involves bridging the gap between central authority structures and local subsystems, in specific instances, the process by which peripheral communities are brought into the administrative framework of central government. A common observation is that a certain structural dichotomy between the centre and the periphery has persisted following (or due to) the introduction of colonial, later national, political frameworks in many Asian and African countries. Concern with closing this gap has been partly responsible for adding the 'crisis of political penetration' to political science vocabulary. Nonetheless, with different degrees of salience, the extractive and regulative processes implied in the concept are operative and in need of reinforcement in industrialized and non-industrialized societies alike. In any political system, the issue of penetration centres upon the requirement to forge rapport and to maintain effective institutional relationships between government and society at large.

Political integration

Closely related to the problem of penetration which focuses on centre-periphery relationships, is the issue of integration which refers especially to the need to establish institutional mechanisms for a regularized and coherent political process. While penetration presupposes integration and vice versa, the latter notion is essentially concerned with the integration of political functions into a single effective process. It thus posits the need to create and sustain suitable channels for such functions as the articulation of interests, rule-making, adjudication and other requisite tasks of a political system. It is further argued that these requirements should be met, as far as possible, on the basis of congruence between cultural norms and structural arrangements. Thus, the problem of integration as it is thus defined, is not that of reducing ethnic or other forms of pluralism through the encouragement of national homogeneity, nor does it refer to bridging the gap between élites and mass. In practical terms, the issue of integration is largely that of fostering compatibility and coherence among different administrative organs and adapting them to existing cultural prerequisites. As such, it is concerned with diminishing the inefficiency and waste inherent in duplication of bureaucratic activities and with reducing the lack of awareness and communication among administrative units about each other's activities. Pertinent to this, is the growing realization in development efforts that many failures to bring about economic and social change are often due to insufficient co-ordination, lack of clarity about administrative roles and, more generally, to maladjustment of the organizational machinery to the tasks it is required to perform. In the final analysis, the problem of integration is one of creating suitable mechanisms towards greater institutional strength.

Political participation

The problem of participation is that of meeting the rapidly growing demands for participation in the political process by broad layers of the population, commonly referred to as the 'revolution of rising expectations'. These demands are generated by processes of social mobilization, which are largely determined by such factors as education, economic development, urbanization and related change patterns through which new expectations and ideals tend to originate among wider groups in society (Deutsch, 1961:493–514). Hence, the crisis of participation is essentially concerned with the need to channel these demands. An additional aspect is the need to mobilize the population when developmental efforts require active popular involvement to have a chance of success. Thus, the issue of participation refers both to the need of creating channels for popular participation and to the stimulation of popular engagement.

In many newly independent states, however, this problem is greatly complicated by rapidly growing cleavages between élites and masses. These increasing gaps lend a new and critical aspect to the issue, tending to stimulate and at the same time frustrate desires for participation in the political process. Political élites are often apprehensive of participation for its possible effects on their own privileged positions. Only in a few states have political élites consciously faced up to the problems by trying to restructure society in the sense of creating greater opportunities for popular involvement.

Such purposeful policies have not often been chosen, however, and the attitudes adopted by some ruling groups can hardly be considered to facilitate a solution to this crisis. It is true that the problems confronting even the best-intentioned governments often appear to be of such magnitude and urgency that they prevent the initiation of constructive long-range policies. However, the attitude of many new élites appears to be one of *après nous le déluge*; in fact, some governments try to turn back the tide and quell growing demands for participation at their source: it is possible for a government to exercise a limiting and regressive influence on education which in time may act upon the volume of demands for participation. While such strategies may help perpetuate the system as it is, it is doubtful that they will lay conditions for development in any realistic sense. Instead, it is more likely that they will merely postpone more acute crisis situations.

Distribution

The distribution crisis is generated by claims to social and economic resources raised by social groups. Obviously this is closely related to the issue of participation, demands for political participation being frequently made as a way of laying increased claims on resources. Participation without distribution is of limited meaning to many people, but neither is greater distribution conceivable without greater participation having been achieved. Thus, while participatory demands may be made for the sake of participation itself, this does not reduce the importance of participation as a means of obtaining increased shares in social and economic welfare.

The distribution question is more easily posed than solved, however. Lack of natural resources often obviates the possibility of any spectacular long-term development. In many cases, shortage of suitable land and other resources, or a strategic economic position offering marketing advantages, simply puts a limit to the distributive potential which even the most obliging government can do little to change. Yet it is equally obvious that these circumstances do not correspondingly lessen demands for distribution. Claims for allocation of resources ('entitlement claims') only pose more critical burdens in situations of scarcity and thus strongly increase the obligation of governments to maximize possibilities within their resource potential. A capacity for increased distribution of economic resources obviously depends on the stimulation of economic development. It is clear, therefore, that in the end these are crucial factors in managing the distribution crisis and critically affect patterns of political development.

The crisis dimensions reconsidered

The categorization made by the Committee on Comparative Politics subsumes what is conceivably the broadest range of problem aspects of political development. Moreover, the formulation allows the search for interrelationships between various dimensions and may prove beneficial to the development of political theory. In particular it is possible, on the basis of the crisis model, to test the proposition that solution of one crisis will facilitate that of others. It is arguable, for instance, and in fact plausible, that if legitimacy is not at issue, problems of participation, distribution, integration, penetration or identity are more easily solved, or that a solution of the distribution crisis will mitigate problems of participation, penetration, identity and legitimacy. However, it still needs a good deal of research based on appropriate categories to test this out; for these purposes, the breakdown into six dimensions may prove a useful device.

The categorization throws up further questions regarding the conceptualization of political development as such. As noted, the term political development is rendered so wide by implication that it is at most a cover concept without any explanatory power of its own. This is further enhanced by the fact that most dimensions affect one another, either as prerequisites or as obstacles to the solution of other crises. Besides, by its very width, a concept which would embrace no less than six problem dimensions might dilute problems which are possibly more critical than others. Finally, even if all six are crucial problems worthy of the attention (and thus in that sense comparable), the various dimensions are of somewhat different order. Whereas identity and legitimacy refer to qualitative aspects of political systems, penetration and integration are essentially about the functioning and maintenance of systems, and participation and distribution about the social responsibilities toward social categories. Brought under one heading, the general concept thus derived would necessarily reflect and suffer from the heterogeneity of its various ingredients.

The question of criteria thus reasserts itself with full force and suggests the need to reconsider the six problems to see whether some of the proposed dimensions might be considered more intrinsic than others to a meaningful notion of political development. If we try our hand at this, then identity and legitimacy are clearly matters of considerable concern, both with regard to countries of Africa and Asia and those of Europe and America. Legitimacy can be enhanced or thwarted in many different situations, including those which might be labelled highly developed or relatively underdeveloped on other counts, such as economic indices. That fact by no means implies that legitimacy might not be an ingredient of a concept of political development. On the contrary, the universality of the problem of legitimacy is congruent with the scope which a meaningful concept of political development needs to have. The crucial point, however, is that the growth or decline of legitimacy tends to follow other factors in the political process, and is particularly dependent on the performance of government in its various policy spheres. Attempts to create legitimacy by means of symbolic extortion instead of by improving governmental performance usually produce meagre results and tend to be short-lived, even though governments may often resort to this strategy. Dependent as it is on other factors, it should be questioned whether legitimacy ought to be included as a component of the political development concept. To do so does not seem to offer any operational advantage, but tends rather to overburden the concept. It would be a different matter if the concept of political development as such was entirely focused on enhancement of legitimacy; this would certainly be justified by its significance. Even if this were so, however, the conditioning factors must necessarily be found elsewhere. It seems more advantageous, therefore, to be able to illuminate these more fully and directly.

Similar considerations apply in regard to identity which, as we have seen, can in some ways be brought under one category with legitimacy; together, the two clearly have a quality different to the other problem dimensions. Moreover, it has been noted that the question of identity becomes politically significant through its effect on legitimacy, while its own enhancement is also largely dependent on performance elsewhere in the system. Thus, some reservation again suggests itself as to whether the problem of identity ought to be a key component of the concept of political development. Let us see, therefore, whether political development can be formulated in such a way that it does not incorporate notions of legitimacy and identity, but nonetheless allows us to check the effect of other processes upon these aspects.

In regard to other dimensions, it has been seen that problems of participation and distribution are very closely related. This is so because participation is partly engaged in distributive purposes, while basic increases in distribution without participation are hard to conceive. In the long run, at any rate, participation makes little sense without at least the objective of redistribution. Thus, the two problems are essentially of a piece; it is proposed, therefore, that they be considered as one, and be further referred to here as 'participation'.

A similar overlap suggests itself with respect to the last two dimensions of political development: penetration and integration. They are both addressed to the problem of creating effective and coherent frameworks of government, and share an emphasis on institutionalization and strengthening of authoritative structures. For this reason, again, it is proposed to subsume them under one heading and to refer to them simply as 'penetration'.

As a concept, then, political development would be centrally concerned with matters of participation and penetration. This would immediately draw attention to two vital aspects of the political process and would almost certainly provide the ingredients necessary to assess whether we can speak of political development in any concrete situation. However, these are only ingredients and still not a working concept; if one holds that political development involves increasing political penetration and participation, the two might quite conceivably be opposed. Thus, the question of criteria has yet to be answered.

Institutionalization as criterion?

The conceptualization of political development by Samuel Huntington represents one possible position in regard to this question. Huntington has sharply criticized concepts of political development which comprise and sanction virtually anything that was earlier recorded as political history. His much-quoted article, 'Political Development and Political Decay', is essentially a plea for criteria (Huntington, 1965:386–430). It is necessary, he argues, to select such criteria as will enable the construction of a theory of political decay as well as a theory of political development. Without such a dual theory, it would not be possible to account for any form of regression; instead, one would be forced to deduce political development no matter what the actual trends in any situation.

Huntington's proposal is to use institutionalization as the yardstick for political development. On that basis, political development would be measured by the extent of institutionalization, as indicated by the adaptability of institutions, their complexity, autonomy and coherence. Adaptability, in turn, would be measured in terms of age: chronological, generational and functional (Huntington, 1965:394). Huntington's concept thus corresponds roughly with the ingredients of the term penetration as discussed above. This notion has the advantage of offering a firm basis: criteria would be based on concrete indices; it is relatively measurable; it has universal application both in time and scope; and it seemingly answers demands for empirical objectivity.

However, Huntington's proposition is not without its pitfalls. It raises some serious conceptual problems, not the least of which is an inherent bias towards the élite's capacity to stand firm regardless of contingent conditions within the political system at large. In situations of increasing distance between political élite and masses in particular, there is a potential danger of mistaking the élite's strengthened grip on the system, euphemistically referred to as increased capacity of the authoritative structures (institutionalization), for political development, although very little development may be forthcoming on the side of the populace. However universal a concept focusing on institutional strength may be, it is by no means value-free and may miss what is most relevant in the life experiences of political systems. Moreover, even if it is useful to have a cool, clinical look at institutions and to be able to say, for example, that some countries have strong institutions and others have not, it may very well be that in some such 'strong' situations a revolution is brewing which will one day dismantle the entire elaborate superstructure. Such an event would not fall under political development as defined in terms of institutionalization, if only because it would interrupt the longevity of the institutional structure. Yet not a few people might, on quite good grounds, want to consider that very transition as a moment of political development.

Yardstick versus relevance

Huntington's proposition well illustrates the difficulties encountered in the choice of criteria. The question is whether there is any conceivable standard by which the concept of political development can retain political as well as analytic relevance. The choice of criteria is clearly complicated by value-preferences, couched in arguments of 'yardstick' versus 'relevance', and has become especially acute due to centrifugal tendencies in the socio-political make-up of many countries, particularly new states. The questions raised by such situations basically concern the validity of firm yardsticks which may stress essentially formal features.

In the final analysis, the value issue cannot be avoided. Political scientists are constantly confronted with conflicting demands of scientific rigour and relevance to reality. Scientific rigour implies that their conceptual apparatus should be as objective as possible, and be based on measurable indices. Demands for measurability and objectivity are even particularly strong in political science due to the complexity of its subject matter and the difficulty of evaluation. Virtually all aspects of political reality are open to subjective evaluation. Political scientists have become quite sensitive to this, and in response have tried hard to develop value-free theories. The literature shows growing preoccupation with the use of measurable indices as a way of reaching objective analysis. In a field concerned with political reality, these indices are largely derived from concrete situations. However, if the most tangible elements in reality are relied upon as tangible measurements, this implies the danger that concreteness will be mistaken for empirical objectivity. The insistence on firm yardsticks may lead to the choice of criteria which, however concrete and measurable they may be, obscure possibly more relevant though less tangible aspects. While almost any choice usually shifts rather than eliminates the value-basis of theory, the pursuit of concreteness entails the risk of reducing the relevance of theory to reality.

Instead, it should be recognized that the subject matter of political science implies an inherent limitation to its capacity to reach objective measurement. Rather than try to overcome or wish away this problem, it is more realistic to develop theories with this limitation in mind. Less tangible, though perhaps more realistic, criteria should be selected if the analysis so demands. Instead of trying to reach value-free premises (which in any case is virtually impossible), the debate may well be carried into more meaningful directions if positions are made explicit. After all, many academic disputes are directed towards, and find their conclusion in, the discovery of another's paradigm behind a smokescreen of methodological niceties. A considerable time-advantage would be gained if debates could start from value premises. Such confrontations might lead to greater understanding and reconciliation of ends which, in turn, may benefit the discussion on means. For purposes of theory building, this suggests that we should try our hand at constructing what may be called 'shell concepts': concepts which allow scope for different interpretations of that part of their contents which seems intrinsically relevant but which is subject to different value judgements. An explicit provision for this would allow us to see how far the area of agreement reaches and at what point differences begin. Unlike more wholesale concepts, whose fate is either wholesale adoption or rejection, this approach enables the shell to be retained on account of its agreed relevance, while disagreement may be registered on the evaluation of content. An advantage is that elaboration of a common conceptual apparatus can proceed relatively unfettered by ideological disputes; the frameworks created in this way would allow the discussion of methodological and ideological issues to be conducted at appropriate levels. At present, a major reason why dialogues often end without insights gained on either side is that methodological arguments are used against ideological reasoning and ideological weapons against methodological ones. The problem can even be compared to that of the role of the university generally. Faced with conflicting demands to be socially relevant and scientifically rigorous, the university can only meet both if it serves as a marketplace where the two can be exchanged and related to one another. This, then, is as true for the academic universe as it is for its particles, its concepts.

What is politically relevant?

These points stress the need for a concept of political development which, among other things, does not necessarily sanction any overthrow of institutions, but which neither excludes it. At the same time, it is expedient that a concept of political development in some way focuses on institutions since they form an intrinsic part of political systems. However, there is no reason why criteria of political development should be based merely on their longevity, complexity or autonomy. Historically, the growth of institutions has often been equated with decay, especially if they did not prove particularly useful. Again, the dwindling of institutions may well correlate with development or with improvements in other aspects of political life. At all times, stagnating structures are in need of rejuvenation, which can be achieved either through adaptation, replacement or overthrow. In fact, the abolition of redundant institutions sometimes appears to be more functional than their adjustment; despite the stupendous cost and misery which so often accompanies radical breakdowns of institutional structures, there is no a priori ground to elevate the gradualist, adaptive pattern of institutional change as a norm applicable in all cases.

Rather than look for strength, differentiation or longevity of institutions, as in Huntington's approach, it seems useful to consider what they do for society, or in fact to consider their relevance. The old anarchist argument that government can be dispensed with, if sympathetic, is naïve. However, it has a point, namely, that many authoritative structures have little relevance. Anarchists share this persuasion with Poujadists and some other right-wing radicals. In their protest, both orientations tend to overlook that authoritative institutions, however structured, are necessary in any organization and in principle are established for purposes of regulation and promotion of common welfare. Yet the essence of their position may provide us with the key to a more meaningful concept of political development. It can be postulated that institutions which are geared to regulation and common welfare are functional. The test is whether their operation makes a contribution to the social process, conceived in development terms. This is more easily said than done, yet the procedure to be followed could simply be to hypothetically think an institution away and ask what difference its presence or absence makes to the welfare of the clientele it is supposed to serve. Basically, this amounts to a kind of cost-benefit analysis in broader than merely economic terms, admittedly no easy task. However, while any exactitude in this regard is impossible, this does not lessen the need to evaluate institutions by relating the tasks they perform to the social and economic costs of their upkeep. This would immediately draw attention to the price which society pays for its regulative cadre.

The issue can now be looked at in a more general way. To perform their functions, political élites manning the institutions extract resources from society. However, there seems to be an inherent tendency for the price to go up and the service to go down. Institutions then become parasitic, a problem noticed by Aristotle in his discussion on the perversion of monarchy into tyranny, autocracy into oligarchy and so on, and lamented upon in many different ways ever since. This problem applies to industrial and non-industrial societies, to countries of the West and East, and to ancient times as well as the present. Clearly, therefore, the question is not so much whether institutions have a long life but rather whether they are functional in terms of social relevance, in other words, whether the parasitic/exploitative tendencies of institutions outweigh their regulative/welfare functions or vice versa.

In this way, it will be possible to make the kind of judgements which would allow us to speak either of political development or of political decay. Operationally, this is no more nor less difficult than measuring legitimacy, integration, system capabilities or political culture, which have all become accepted areas of enquiry in political science.

It is important that this procedure not only places the political structure within a broader social context, but also takes institutional characteristics as the independent variable. This allows political scientists to make a valid, perhaps even practical, contribution to development studies and does not necessitate reliance on other social sciences such as psychology or economics to define the conditions of political development. Moreover, while prescriptive implications may be deduced, the notion is open-ended, both in time and application, to widely different forms of government. The ultimate test should lie with society and societal relevance. As ex-President Nyerere of Tanzania once put it in the face of many complex theorists, 'the truth is that development means the development of people. Roads-building, the increases of crop output, and other things of this nature, are not development: they are only tools of development' (Nyerere, 1968:2). Transposed into other terms, this implies that we must look for welfare, participation, distribution, security, benefits.

This is at the heart of the value problem, but it is also where basic relevance lies. Opinions will differ as to what is most conducive to general welfare, but few will disagree that social welfare is a valid goal and criterion. Thus, as a shell concept, political development might be taken to denote the establishment or enhancement of such institutional structures as will benefit society at large, or the removal or adaptation of structures which are irrelevant or detrimental to broad social goals. It follows, then, that penetration (or for that matter, institutionalization) by itself is neither intrinsically functional nor necessarily detrimental. It can only be judged by its relevance in terms of the other key dimension in political development, participation. This test will tell us whether we are dealing with a functional instrument or with a parasite.

3
'Good Governance', Political Conditionalities and Externally-led Institutional Reform

Introduction

External involvement with the processes of public policy formation in independent countries of the Third World has been present for a long time, usually from the very inception of the decolonized states concerned and thus virtually by definition. However, categorization as a distinct variant of modes of state formation, namely, state formation as a process evolving under external supervision and direction, now appears justified given the extent to which various forms of external, that is, international preoccupation with the *internal* policy frameworks and the structuring of political processes in formally independent Third World countries have come to be intensified and exemplified in recent years. These tendencies imply a crystallization of an increasingly explicit tutelage relation *vis-à-vis* the countries concerned. Discussion of these issues has developed largely around the recently rediscovered, though by no means unequivocal, concept of *governance* and the adoption of *political 'conditionalities'* by the global organizations and the major donor governments.

This chapter reviews the emerging field: it will look at recent modes of external intervention in Third World countries with respect to the structuring of their policy processes and institutional frameworks. Subsequent discussion considers the launch of the concept of 'good governance' and its relevance in a wider context. The chapter starts off with a note on the 'good governance' agenda, followed by a brief look at concepts of 'state formation'.

The 'good governance' agenda

In recent years, an important entry point into the debate about political and development institutions has been that of the 'good governance' agenda. 'Good governance' has currently become a priority interest in global circles involved in the re-thinking and praxis of development policy, and through the very nature of its focus becomes easily linked to institutional reform. It is interesting to reflect on why this came about at this particular time. The present chapter, addressing itself to the phenomenon of 'state formation under external supervision', traces some of the historical roots of this question.

One can hardly dispute that quality of government, in today's parlance 'good governance', merits serious attention, whether in connection with development policy or generally. It is interesting to note also that, following its recent 're-launch' in international policy circles, the concept of 'governance' has found its way back as a tool in scholarly analysis of state-society relations more generally (Bratton and Rothchild, 1992). Indeed, not a few scholars today might already find it difficult to enquire how one could do without it. Arguably, its relevance might be strongest not with regard to the analysis of power relationships covered by the traditional state-society dichotomy, but with respect to those resulting from current globalization trends, precisely because it does not prejudge the locus of actual decision-making (Hyden, 1992:6; Healey and Tordoff, 1995). Still, at the more mundane level of development policy and practice, the question remains what exactly is meant here by 'good governance', why was the concept introduced, and whose agenda does it represent?

Basically, if 'governance' refers to the management of public affairs, then 'good governance' evidently should mean sound or prudent management. However, this is to imply that there are known criteria by which one can judge this, which is far from certain. 'Governance' at any rate is understood to embrace a good deal more than the norms of administrative praxis. While including key components of administrative management, the concept 'governance' points to important political aspects as it is focused on the set-up of governmental institutions and the determination of their priorities and direction. With regard to the field of development praxis, questions about 'governance' are concerned with broad issues like the politics and mechanisms of macro-economic management and with specific aspects such as accountability and transparency in government operations. Thus the political component is actually never absent in current discourses about 'governance', even though in some contexts, notably that of the World Bank, there has been a tendency to perceive the concept more narrowly in 'neutral' administrative management terms (Gibbon, 1993).

Essentially, in donor parlance 'good governance' has to do with the nature and effectiveness of institutional structures and processes, allowing questions to be raised about their relevance in the context of overall development strategies. The 'good governance' theme has been closely related to strategies of institutional globalization. As I will discuss below, its re-launch appeared intended to provide a handle for the formulation of political conditionalities by external actors which previously did not dispose of such 'politically oriented' instruments for intervention and direction.

'Good governance' represents a novel route of approaching the field of development policy and policy studies through its emphasis on particular institutional capacities and relationships. It is noteworthy, though, that 'governance' in this respect figures as the latest in a whole series of akin concepts that have been proposed over the years to get a grip on institutional dimensions of state-society relations, and to give direction to interventions by international development circles. Precursor concepts include *capacity-building, institution-building, institutional development, institutional reform* and *institutionalization* as such, each representing the predilections of the day and meant to stress the particular nuances it was felt needed attention at the time, though nonetheless sharing a substantial degree of common ground (cf. O. P. Dwivedi, 1995). Recently, again, the World Bank in its *World Development Report 1997* devoted to 'The State in a Changing World', pays special attention to what it calls the 'challenge of reinvigorating institutional capability', now seen as including the task of bringing the state closer to the people, and of re-emphasizing the importance of adherence to institutional rules (World Bank, 1997).

Retracing earlier debates on the premises of some of these concepts, Chapter 2 has already highlighted notable continuities in the key concerns they convey. Specifically, *'institutionalization'* in certain perspectives was the key defining criterion of *'political development'*, though from other premises this remained at best an open question. From 'institutionalization' and 'institution-building', favourite themes in the development discourses of the 1960s and 1970s, there appears to be a direct link to the current preoccupations with 'good governance'. At the present time, though, the provenance of 'good governance' and its intellectual linkages to the inception of a new generation of 'political conditionalities', deserve particular attention.

Concepts of state formation

Concepts of state formation have comprised a wide range of meanings. In the first instance, state formation must of course refer to the processes through which the first ever state structures were shaped, and to the factors which appeared to have an impact on them. This area of interest has produced a rich and still growing literature (e.g. Claessen and Skalnik, 1978). The debate as to what constituted the original stimulus for the earliest processes of state formation continues, and has not only intrinsic historical but also contemporary relevance: what prompted or prompts the initial steps towards state formation, that is, towards the creation of a body politic with a distinctive identity; and what caused or causes some of these to develop staying power? Does the genesis lie with power-holders and power structures which create their own political domain, or does it originate rather with particular social and economic transformations which generate new modes of control and political structures? When considering recent state formation processes focused on and instigated by the European Union, for example, one encounters aspects and questions not fundamentally different from those raised in discussions on the origins of the earliest state forms. By the same token this is also true for various other contemporary and historical examples.

Contemporary examples, nonetheless, imply concepts of state formation which differ at least in one regard from those which refer to the earliest processes: once the idea of 'state' has emerged, its independent development is conceivable in some other locations, but otherwise its evolution is likely to be largely a matter of replication and elaboration of existing models or of posing alternatives to these (Doornbos, 1986). Generally, therefore, state formation processes almost by definition will also entail processes of incorporation and/or dismantling of pre-existing state forms which are superseded by new dominant structures. European as well as African and Asian history, colonial and pre-colonial, contains numerous illustrations of such patterns. In some cases this implies the establishment of new structures representing a direct, 'revolutionary' rupture with preceding forms, whereas other instances retain a certain degree of institutional continuity. The latter might obtain wherever – at least *vis-à-vis* the outside world – a façade of inherited formal structures is presented, but also where existing, culturally rooted patterns of social relations manifest themselves within changed institutional contexts, thus partly determining the content and subculture of the new state.

'State formation' based on replication thus refers to the formative processes of national states within Europe and subsequently beyond, and to the establishment of post-colonial states in the Third World as territorial political entities. However, the term 'state formation' may also refer more specifically to the creation, development and differentiation of state structures and institutions; to the crystallization and articulation of the role of the state and to corresponding manifestations of state power. It also indicates processes of incorporation of various social and political groupings and organizational networks within the overall state structure. In the latter sense 'state formation' must refer, among other things, to the dynamic aspects in the (changing) relations between state and society (Doornbos, 1990). Thus, in certain historical contexts the state emerges as a force overarching all other ranks and subdivisions, whereas in others one witnesses a loss or shedding of state functions and responsibilities. The latter may result from fiscal crises or from efforts to delineate more sharply the role of the state apparatus, as is in line with current persuasion today. As a multifarious and dynamic concept, state formation thus also comprises historical and contemporary instances of state *re*formation and *de*formation.

The changing nature of political conditionalities

In the light of the above, when we speak of 'state formation', we usually refer to the processes through which state structures are being generated and regenerated (Doornbos and Kaviraj, 1997). Institutional reform is an essential part of this. In principle this concerns autonomous processes, neither hindered nor aided by external factors, and protected under the principle of sovereignty. In recent years, however, externally led direction has become increasingly important in determining the manner of adjustment, orientation and organization of political structures, notably with respect to Third World countries and particularly within the African context.

For a proper understanding of such 'state formation under supervision' and its relation to the discussion about 'good governance', it should be observed that whereas this evidently touches on the problem of external involvement in the implementation of government policy, the two phenomena are not necessarily the same. The numerous French administrators engaged in the bureaucracies of francophone West African states, for example, might, at least in theory, execute policy that had been fully determined by the governments concerned. Their involvement in the execution and even in the *preparation* of policy need not affect the state structures or the direction of state formation processes. A similar qualification applies to dependency relations. Externally-directed state formation is derived from dependency relationships, and hardly conceivable without them. However, not every economic or even political dependency relation will inevitably lead to state formation under supervision. Examples abound of regimes which for many years faced no difficulty in qualifying for loans or other assistance simply by means of adopting a 'loyal' posture, especially during the Cold War, although their policy and political frameworks were never questioned in the process.

Nor should the new strategy of externally-led political reform be confused with earlier examples of external political pressures to demand a particular policy position. There have been numerous instances of this. The relations between the United States and Latin America over almost two centuries constitute a continuing chronicle illustrating the practice. Also, from the very beginnings of the phenomenon of development aid, it has been recognized that aid without strings attached is illusory. Aid-receiving countries have been expected to display loyal behaviour in the international arena, such as, with respect to voting patterns within the UN system, the granting of military facilities, or by safeguarding a receptive climate for foreign trade and investment. Moreover, setting conditionalities of appropriate economic management before new loan applications are discharged by the international financial institutions has been common for some time already. With the imposition of the IMF/World Bank structural adjustment programmes, these kinds of conditions have become very detailed and severe. However, the posing of demands on theoretically sovereign states regarding the manner in which they should organize their institutional apparata, policy-implementing procedures, and indeed their political systems, evidently goes a step further and touches on 'delicate issues', to use the phrase employed by World Bank President Connable when introducing the new Bank policy in this regard at the World Bank Annual Conference on Development Economics, 1991.

The 'classical' type of political conditionalities, therefore, are by no means a novelty: but conditionalities regarding the manner in which countries should be structuring the political and administrative framework, certainly are. Especially since 1989, the international donor community, led by the major international organizations, has begun to set increasingly specified conditions with respect to the formation of institutional structures of 'client' states. This is motivated, among other things, by the conviction that African states and their economies in particular have been suffering from 'overdeveloped' and inefficient state structures – a viewpoint, incidentally, previously advanced by critical researchers (Doornbos, 1990). It also reflects the simple belief that 'liberalizing' the market requires 'liberalizing' the state.

The complex mixture of externally-led initiatives towards restructuring government machinery and introducing political reform which is directed at Third World countries has meanwhile crystallized into formidable packages of policy prescriptions. Together they account for a significant impact on, and a new phase in, the state formation processes of the countries concerned, even if they are often less than effective or are having distorting or contradictory effects. The processes thus put 'under supervision' bear a qualitative difference from most historical examples of state formation, partial exceptions being the process of decolonization in a number of cases and the organization of regimes previously converted to the soviet model, adopting the latter's party and state structures. In this sense, therefore, it appears justified to consider this contemporary type of process as a novel variant of 'state formation', leaving aside whatever qualifications one might wish to attach to it.

The policy packages concerned generally rest on a twofold strategy. On the one hand, there is a supply side with a notably varied assortment of what might be termed 'political development aid'. This includes a range of positive measures designed to increase the effectiveness and efficiency of selected government bodies, although usually in trimmed down form: support for judiciaries and media, training programmes for legislators and key government officers, logistic assistance for elections, and so on. Concrete examples are legion, but the World Bank's *African Capacity Building Initiative*, itself a whole package of measures, may be specially mentioned in this connection (World Bank, 1990). On the other hand, the strategy increasingly rests on the imposition of punitive 'conditionalities' of political or institutional reform, which must be fulfilled in order to continue to qualify for financial assistance or economic co-operation. Thus for various Western governments the adoption of a 'pluralist' political framework has become one key conditionality for continued development co-operation, especially since the end of the East-West rivalry and the drying up of the possibility of alternative sources of support for the countries concerned.

A donor perspective on these matters was formulated in a World Bank staff paper in the following terms:

Since poor countries generally have fragile polities and weak systems of accountability, with few autonomous institutions and little countervailing power to that exercised by the government at the centre, external agencies are potentially key political players capable of exerting considerable influence in promoting good or bad governance. In raising the shortcomings of a country's governance, external agencies are calling into question its government's performance. Clearly, this goes further than a critique of a particular programme or project (generally regarded as a legitimate concern of a financing agency), to touch on the ability of a regime to govern effectively in the interest of its citizenry (Landell-Mills and Serageldin, 1991:13).

In the light of this perspective, conditions are being proposed by the major international organizations and the main donor governments which, if implemented, should together produce different, more flexible and open, and more efficient state organizations. Among other things, they encourage a reduction of administrative structures, privatization of government services and the use of non-governmental organizations in aid operations. There is advocacy of the establishment of autonomous, 'non-bureaucratic' organizations with wide jurisdiction over particular policy areas; and the engagement in 'policy dialogue' with donor representatives about the way policy is given shape in particular sectors. The term 'co-governance', pointing explicitly to a sharing of authority over specific project or policy matters, epitomizes some of the new thinking on these issues. There is also increasingly detailed specification of external instruments of evaluation and of instructions with respect to the formulation and elaboration of national budget chapters and policy priorities. Wide-ranging and substantial decentralization of government functions is encouraged, paralleled in several countries by donor policies to concentrate their aid efforts in specific 'adopted' districts or regions. There is a general call for measures to make government bodies more accessible, while simultaneously ensuring their accountability; and, last but not least, multi-party systems are being called for in order to promote effective mechanisms of political accountability and control.

The emphasis placed by donors on the adoption of this package of measures, in full or in part, has been motivated by a variety of factors, including: dissatisfaction with the role of governments in Third World countries generally; concern about the lack of institutional capacity for absorption of donor-initiated development programmes; a desire to enhance efficiency and effectiveness in the public sector generally; the determination – strongly increased since the termination of East-West rivalry – to reduce the influence of political factors, often considered arbitrary and in the last instance held responsible for failing government interventions and inadequate public policy; and, more generally, interest in the initiation of political reforms which might break the hegemonic control by particular political strata or coalitions. Within the general package of instruments and conditionalities for political reform, it is particularly the demands with respect to the adoption of multi-party systems and democratization which have attracted widespread attention.

Discussion of these issues, in particular the question of democratization as a conditionality, has evolved rapidly in recent years, closely following changes in policy and practice (see, for example, Anyang 'Nyong'o, 1992; Barya, 1992; Healey and Robinson, 1992; Moore, 1993; ROAPE, 1990, 1992; Sorensen, 1993). We will not discuss here the question of recipient governments' compliance with political conditionalities, nor of donors' problems and dilemmas in enforcing them. Suffice it to say that the record so far is a mixed one, especially as regards the demands for the adoption, let alone sustainability, of multi-party systems. It should be noted, though, that a positive correlation between political conditionalities and democratization has not as yet been demonstrated (Healey and Robinson, 1992; Sorensen, 1993). Moreover, there are very substantial differences with respect to the expectations and objectives in this regard between external actors on the one hand and a whole range of different democratization movements on the other (Rudebeck, 1992). The external interest generally appears to offer little or no support for democratization movements 'from below' and in principle keeps itself focused on one particular, that is, liberal model, on the simple assumption and criterion that a multi-party system holds the key to democratization.

From a donor's perspective, promotion of this model may be viewed as a way of complementing structural adjustment programmes, in which the 'rolling back' of the state and the creation of open markets are central objectives. A political-ideological element is thus added to the economic vision of a liberal capitalist society. Significantly, however, with a reduced role of the state, the actual role of political parties within multi-party systems must be expected to be quite a limited one, while at the same time it is likely to leave considerable scope for external influence and direction over various branches of the state machinery.

The role of the 'good governance' concept

The new departures with political conditionalities have inevitably thrown up key questions as to the propriety of externally imposed political norms and the likely effectiveness of the conditionalities concerned. The discussion has been conducted partly with reference to the newly rediscovered concept of 'governance', which points to qualities comprising more than just proper administration and organization (though certainly including these). Early on, Edgardo Boeninger, the Chilean minister responsible for political reform, formulated the concept in these terms:

> A concept that has recently attracted attention is the role played by 'governance'...(H)ere we refer to governance as, first, identifying economic and social objectives, and second, charting a course designed to move society in that direction. Governance can then be defined as the good government of society. Good government guides the country along a course leading to the desired goal, in this case, development (Boeninger, 1991:1).

'Governance', originally a legalistic concept, thus in principle acquires a political dimension, broadly oriented towards the way the political system might be organized and how it is to be handled. Precise conceptual delineations are more difficult to formulate. Landell-Mills and Serageldin observe in this connection:

> 'Governance' is not a word that has been used extensively in the past by political scientists, but its recent appearance in popular usage has not been very rigorous. It has become in many ways both an all-embracing and a vague concept...In essence, therefore, governance may be taken as denoting how people are ruled, and how the affairs of a state are administered and regulated. It refers to a nation's system of politics and how this functions in relation to public administration and law. Thus, the concept of 'governance' goes beyond that of 'government' to include a political dimension (Landell-Mills and Serageldin, 1991).

It is striking to note how rapidly the 'governance' concept in recent years has been assimilated as a household word in development parlance and beyond. Its popularity in donor circles is probably best explained by its focus which implicitly helps to place the onus for many failing development policies and projects on bad recipient-country management. By being able to refer to 'fault' governance as a cause of inadequate performance, donors have acquired a seemingly objective instrument and yardstick with which to call recipient country governments to order.

It is notable that recent discussions on 'governance' have focused partly on the question of what exactly the concept would or would not comprise. This may be indicative of a rather unscientific procedure, but at the same time it demonstrates the search for a conceptual category to accommodate an acute donor concern. Resolution of the question as to what should or should not be understood by 'governance' is not attempted here. The question itself is perhaps not particularly interesting. More relevant is the coincidence that against a backdrop of lack of clarity as to the concept's content – in particular the extent to which it should be considered 'political' – organisations such as the World Bank a few years ago began to determine their position regarding the formal adoption of criteria of 'good governance' – and if so, which criteria – in their package of conditionalities and directives. This coincidence may itself have had its 'useful' instrumental aspects: while there is conceptual ambiguity it may be a little easier in this controversial area to test how far any package of conditionalities should go. The World Bank itself faced a constraint in this regard, as its constitution prescribes an essentially apolitical banking role. Evidently the search has been for a conceptual demarcation which would nonetheless ensure an influence over the entire sphere of development politics, policy making and implementation, thus accommodating the political concerns and demands of donors, and making it possible to call for various concrete policy measures by recipient governments. As Peter Gibbon has pointed out, the decision ultimately adopted by the World Bank was an ingenious one: it opted for a concept of 'governance' oriented towards 'depoliticised' management and accountability as far as its own programmes were concerned, whilst claiming a strategic convening role in communicating the political concerns of lending countries to recipients and making continuation of its own aid programmes subject to observance of other donors' political preoccupations (Gibbon, 1993:55–6).

The World Bank has indeed adopted an increasingly prominent role in setting standards in these matters *vis-à-vis* various Western donors, while the latter have sometimes sought to articulate, however faintly, a position of their own within more limited margins (cf. Payne, 1992/93; Gibbon, 1993:35–6). This tendency is related to the near impossibility for individual donors of indicating precise criteria for political reform whose observance should ensure particular envisaged effects. Meanwhile, it has been observed, and probably not without justification, that while 'the bilateral donors at present often refer to the World Bank's statements on good governance, this is probably more a case of hiding in the skirts of an international institution than a demonstration of the impact, or quality, of the Bank's ideas' (Uvin, 1993:67).

Political conditionalities and political contexts

For all the heightened concern with the promotion of 'good governance' in Third World countries, it is quite conceivable that one effect of the various external initiatives and involvements in this regard is, paradoxically, to reduce rather than strengthen Third World governments' capacity for policy making and implementation. At the micro-level the externally induced creation of autonomous institutions for improved management often undermines local government capacity. Diversion of aid flows via NGOs similarly weakens government departments charged with responsibility for the areas concerned. Demands for compliance with contradictory instructions from different donors often results in confusion and distortions, in addition to overburdening qualified manpower which is in short supply. Above all, it is in the essence of conditionalities that the setting and assessment of standards of proper policy management is shifted to various donor headquarters across the globe. Finally, donor co-ordination increasingly sets limits and targets for national policy making, leaving the governments concerned without the space for autonomous action. The price of enhancing external accountability thus is the progressive erosion of national policy-making capacity, the most vital political function of any government. Notwithstanding the powerful thrust of these new strategies, Yusuf Bangura aptly observes that:

> Neo-liberalism has no theory of the state or of state formation and offers limited clues by way of policy on how to respond to the problems of de-institutionalisation and the erosion of local level expertise. State systems have tended to further diminish in quality and reach in most countries where free market reforms have been attempted. Economic reforms cannot be effective in situations where the state is incapable of carrying out its primary roles of regulation, mediation and social protection (Bangura, 1994:298).

From a broader epistemological perspective, too, the formulation of criteria of 'good governance' as a 'conditionality' raises questions and issues of wider implication. The strategy rests on the assumption that it is possible in principle to search for universally valid criteria of proper management and policy making: 'good governance is good governance', no matter where or by whom (or for whom). This presumption, however, touches upon increasingly controversial issues within organization theory, social philosophy, cultural history and other disciplines. Here, there is growing recognition that Western rationality-based premises of the phenomenon of modern bureaucracy represent discontinuity with other cultural traditions. Thus the question that asserts itself is whether it is possible to conceive of general standards of 'good governance' that would be shared by both external and internal political actors to begin with. This must be addressed, irrespective of the further question as to whether the imposed nature of the instruments concerned is acceptable to recipient countries.

At the same time, external insistence on 'universal' conditions and structures for policy management and political organization is bound to have a certain effect in concrete situations, although it will be difficult to predict the precise nature of its impact on the complex networks of political or organizational processes. It is just as conceivable, for example, that it will accentuate existing social tensions and conflicts, at least in the short run, as that it will assist their resolution. Whether there will be any 'positive' effects in the longer run remains a very open question. As to the specificity of the contexts concerned, questions concerning their characteristics will hardly figure in the formulation of conditions for 'good governance' – except as an assumption that they carry short-comings to be overcome. In sum, it must be expected that the amalgam of externally-initiated policy measures will generate its own momentum on processes of political and administrative development, but its overall impact is likely to remain indeterminate at best.

Two further caveats should be borne in mind. The first is that presently in many Third World situations there is an ongoing exploration of new modes of structuring relations between state and society, and of different ways to give them significance. Such processes at times are problematic and difficult but, above all, require space and occasionally some cautious support. It remains most uncertain whether the introduction of external models for 'universal' good government as conditionalities is helpful in such situations. The specific role and position of the state structure within or *vis-à-vis* civil society varies significantly according to societal and cultural context and it is only natural that in varying contexts there will be vast differences in the way these relationships are structured or restructured. In the words of Denis-Constant Martin:

> [T]here is no standard formula for fostering an acceptable level of state management and good governance; the road to such a destination is mapped out by cultural factors that vary considerably from place to place and are in no way unalterable; on the contrary, they keep changing under the pressure of both internal and external dynamics, which makes it all the more difficult to define them (Martin, 1991:15).

The current packages of 'universalist' policy prescriptions for 'good governance' appear to ignore these basic givens and fail to offer any answer to them. Again, this is why it is quite conceivable that externally devised and a priori standard models for organizing government structures, which by their nature cannot take into account specific state-society relations, may have a negative rather than a positive effect. 'All things considered, it is most unlikely that good governance can be introduced from outside' (Martin, 1991:20).

The second point concerns the nature of external preoccupations with the promotion of transparent organization and management. 'Good governance' is put forward as a way of providing an 'enabling environment' for 'development' ('development' in this context usually meaning the totality of donor-led development programmes). By implication, the basic responsibility for the lack of a favourable 'enabling environment' is placed with the governments of the developing countries concerned, ignoring the co-responsibility which international donor organizations carry. The inverse argument is kept entirely outside the scope of debate: namely, to what extent does a global 'enabling environment' support 'good governance' and what conditions should receive priority attention in this context? This is the question which was raised in the report of the South Commission (1990), in the Manifesto of the *Stockholm Initiative on Global Security and Governance, Common Responsibilities in the 1990s*, in the UNDP *Human Development Report 1992*, and in many other fora. It underscores the importance of subjecting the elaboration of the concept of 'good governance', and by implication the premises and direction of contemporary state formation processes in many Third World countries, to continuous critical assessment. The 'good governance' debate must not be de-linked from the emerging 'global governance' debate.

Conclusion

Discussion and practice of external involvement with the development of 'good governance' undoubtedly will continue to draw a good deal of attention in the years to come. Questions are likely to focus on the problem of developing specific norms by which to judge 'good' and 'bad' management of public affairs, and on the formulation and application of sanctions which might be attached to any such norms. Debate will no doubt also continue on the tension between externally initiated, 'universal' standards for political management on the one hand and the specificities of the role and position of state structures and cultural variations inherent in different contexts on the other. Significantly, ethical issues are increasingly being made explicit in this connection. In the final analysis, the question which connects these different issues is: what agents determine the direction of future institutional interventions and attendant state formation processes in various countries concerned, and on the basis of what moral ground? The outcome of this is likely to be decided through many contests taking place in the 'field', and on the basis of innumerable initiatives for new norms and adjustments that are being posed every day, but adding up to broader institutional dimensions of globalization.

The growing gap between politically strong and weak on a world scale inevitably adds an important dimension and sobering context to all this. To what extent and through what routes globalization will come about, therefore, will be determined largely by the outcome of the dynamic processes of confrontation between the power and logic of specific politico-cultural patterns on the one hand and the universal claims and demands of globally integrative structures on the other. Significantly, the questions raised by such confrontations are not unlike those that have been arising from incorporation processes at other, micro levels, towards which we will turn in Chapter 4.

Part 2

Institutional Incorporation and Cultural Diversity

4
Institutional Incorporation: Debating Cultural 'Receptivity' to Change

One key dimension of state formation refers to the *strategies of incorporation* aimed at achieving the progressive integration of various local and regional communities into the political and economic framework of organizing states. There are strong parallels in this respect between the basic policy objectives of the colonial and post-colonial African state (Doornbos, 1983). From the perspective of state authorities, such incorporation strategies largely signify the gaining of control over and access to resources – taxes, labour, and others. By implication, for village or regional communities, incorporation may entail a loss of autonomy regarding the determination of basic priorities and choices and the use of resources, though in varying degrees this may be offset, at least in their estimation, by the enlarged scope for market or political participation that the incorporative framework may seem to be offering. In the final analysis a trade-off between incorporation and autonomy will be evident at the level of the individual and the household, as somehow epitomized in the phrase of the 'capturing' of the African peasantry (Hyden, 1980).

Incorporation processes should be understood as establishing a kind of institutional chain, reaching all the way from the micro-individual to the macro-international level, in which more and more decisions about matters concerning production and other policy areas tend to get concentrated in fewer centres of power and control. Aside from the state *per se*, various other agencies and project authorities, including international donor organizations, play important roles in these 'penetrating' incorporation processes, often finding themselves confronted with similar kinds of questions as regards the aims and effects of their actions.

Naturally, incorporation strategies have been successful only in varying degrees. Some 'target groups' have resisted, or have opted for counter strategies of token incorporation which might ensure them a continued measure of autonomy and 'uncaptured' status with respect to areas of vital concern to themselves. Other groups, strata or individuals may opt for collaboration within the new frameworks, depending on the perceived opportunities the latter may seem to be offering them.

Not surprisingly, perhaps, state officials and project authorities have often been perplexed and at a loss to understand why groups or individuals in one instance tended to respond 'positively' to new opportunities offered through the incorporating framework, whereas in other cases they rather opted for avoidance or resistance. Nor should it be surprising that this has led to a good deal of speculation and theorizing, among the authorities concerned as well as among scholars, about the roots of resistance or collaboration to official policies.

As it happens, explanations of such differential responses have commonly been sought in the characteristics of the 'target' groups, frequently summed up as the 'cultural' variable. The interest in these discussions has not necessarily been with culture *per se*, but has evidently often had a praxis-oriented strategic dimension. From this perspective, in fact, the focus on cultural variables as a determinant of 'receptivity' to planned change has acquired a long and powerful tradition in African and other Third World studies. This chapter is addressed to this particular mode of explanation of processes of change and seeks to critically review its premises.

'Other cultures'

Among social scientists engaged in the study of small-scale social networks one persistent mode of theorizing has, traditionally, centred upon the structural and cultural features of 'traditional' societies. For example, scholars speculated and debated for decades on whether new bureaucratic procedures could more easily be established in societies with one type of authority structure or cultural values rather than another. This was particularly during the colonial period, when the dominant discipline in African and non-Western studies generally was anthropology, but there has been a considerable carry-over into later years. Today, the 'other cultures' premise, to use Beattie's (1964) phrase, is notably expounded by the governments of some of the newly industrializing countries (NICs) with reference to the 'Asian values' debate (Ghai, 1997). As anthropology was basically concerned with 'other cultures', its explanations were largely also sought in terms of this perspective, thus, indirectly laying the basis for much of the current critique on its preoccupation with 'otherness' (Said, 1978, Mudimbe, 1988). Thus, traditional social structures and values for long provided the key hypotheses in many anthropological analyses –

and tacitly the colonial bureaucracy was not seldom viewed as a 'neutral' variable. To be sure, analyses along these lines and the debates that went with them have stimulated various laudable case materials, yet if the objective was to arrive at sustainable generalizations and insights into the processes of interaction between external forces and local groups, then some key methodological and conceptual issues would have needed to be confronted. All too often, however, the analyses were based on notions of traditional societies as relatively self-contained, integrated structures of norms and relationships.

These notions, whose ancestry can be traced back to the functionalist school of social anthropology, are, of course, no longer representative of that discipline. Increasingly, anthropologists have stressed the need to analyse social action in terms of the wider field of relationships in which it takes place, rather than as something that is confined to the boundaries of the membership unit. Early on, Leach (1954) and Turner (1957) based their ideas on this principle (see also Mitchell (1966) and Van Velsen (1967)). Moreover, increased emphasis has been placed on the choices available in social structures to account for what people do, and correspondingly less emphasis on the effects, for instance, of values and beliefs *per se* on behaviour. Put differently, while the traditional engagement in trying to understand the functioning of pre-modern societies led anthropologists to gather information about the structural arrangements and value-patterns presumed to underlie the internal cohesiveness of these societies, this perspective has increasingly made place for, among other things, analysis of relationships with other actors and entities and the relevance of these for patterns of conflict and integration. All this has naturally signified profound changes of orientation.

Now, for non-anthropologists it may well be somewhat difficult to map out the preoccupations in that field with optimal accuracy. The least that can be said, though, is that although anthropology has often, and easily, been stereotyped as the preserve for people interested in the distinguishing features of 'primitive' societies (or 'anthropologists' societies), in actual fact it now comprises a wide variety of theoretical tendencies and innovations which would defy any such singular characterizations. Among this whole array, however, the approach which focuses on the characteristics of 'traditional' societies and tries to explain action and attitudes as basically derivative from their internal features, is by no means a matter of the past. It is thus not difficult to see that a certain tension should have arisen between this functionalist orientation and those which subsequently made their entry. Nonetheless, as anthropological materials are so often turned to for preliminary background on particular African societies, its mixed intellectual heritage has implications which potentially reach well beyond its own borders. This is often still in evidence and the likelihood of this appears to be enhanced by a kind of popular credulity with which the premise that traditional values and authority structures can explain orientation and actions tends to be accepted. Nor is the matter restricted to discussions of African societies and cultures. For example, Benedict Anderson made a similar comment with reference to the state of Thai studies:

> The irony is that for all the importance attached, in analyses of Thai politics, to the idea of a 'uniquely Thai culture', this culture has very rarely been studied in a critical and dispassionate spirit. Nor is its dynamic relation to Thai social and political life concretely explored . . . The anthropologists' experimental models and hypotheses have too easily been reified by non-anthropologists as the axiomatic, fundamental reality of Thai society (Anderson, 1978:227).

Similar kinds of observations have been made in respect to various other Third World contexts, notably as part of a recent wave of critical 'invention of tradition' analyses (Hobsbawm and Ranger, 1983; Das, 1992). Over and beyond the question of the academic merits of these 'traditionalizing' orientations, other implications they have in common are essentially political. In their contacts and dealings with various local and regional groups, government bureaucracies of African and Asian countries typically pose as 'centre' *vis-à-vis* a 'periphery', or 'peripheries'. In political and administrative terms, 'centre' and 'periphery' usually stand at opposite ends from each other, having unequal powers, resources and interests. Friction and conflict occurring in the context of the implementation of central government plans, or in the execution of extractive policies or routine administration, are by no means uncommon. One characteristic response on the 'official' side to such situations is to attribute any local opposition to the influence of the cultural patterns or the traditional values of the people concerned. Implicitly this serves to deny potential alternative explanations for the reactions and confrontations evoked, such as the possibility that they might have been provoked by the very nature of the centre's demands, or by the particular way in which central and local interests have been structurally related to one another. Thus, emphasis on the cultural theme to explain (away) reaction and resistance to government policies or project execution, may have unwarranted legitimizing functions, if not purposes. Closer enquiry into the premises and origins of this theme, therefore, remains essential.

Incorporation

In discussions on the introduction of new political and bureaucratic structures in colonial and post-colonial Africa, the approach which viewed traditional societies as self-contained cultural units, and placed primary emphasis on their internal characteristics to explain success or failure of accommodation, was based on two misconceptions. One was, quite simply, sheer neglect of the wider social and political context of which these societies became part as a result of their incorporation into a colonial, and subsequently a post-colonial state. Inevitably, the situational context which came to exist from the moment that 'traditional' units were incorporated into wider bureaucratic frameworks was itself of paramount significance in shaping the nature and direction of political and social orientations. After all, when confronted with new 'givens', including such new givens as the imposition of a colonial order, groups and individuals determine their actions and attitudes on the basis of considerations as to what these new facts imply or 'offer', weighing them against alternative options and strategies, rather than purely on the basis of any innate cultural traits or other particularistic conditions. Attempts to formulate generalizations without primary regard for such specific contexts – colonial, national or otherwise – led to misconceived undertakings. Researchers searched for correlations between certain 'traditional' characteristics and political orientations to 'change' and then assumed that these patterns would be repeated in other societies of the same general order.

A second reservation that was attached to notions of traditional societies as somehow self-contained integrated units, concerned the implicit de-emphasis, or actual oversight, of conflict or potential socio-political cleavages within the groups themselves. That problem, of course, has had profound roots, and implications, in the social sciences more generally. Initially, however, a holistic perspective was probably even more salient in anthropology than elsewhere, if only because one of its principal objectives was to try and understand the functioning and integration of (pre-)colonial societies, and thus the mechanisms which made them tick. Thus the 'classical' generation of anthropologists, of Malinowski and Radcliff-Brown, in their studies actually employed analogies to biological organisms, where all parts supposedly make some meaningful contribution towards the maintenance of the whole. Such integrative and essentially 'harmonious' notions, however, did not easily permit a focus on opposed interests and orientations within a society; for some time, indeed, this has hampered the development of such foci.

Today, such biological analogies no longer command wholesale acceptance, but some effect of this orientation still appears present nonetheless. Notions of functional integration evidently remain potent ideas, whose reconciliation with the existence of internal conflict inevitably causes a certain amount of strain. A lack of focus on opposed interests and orientations within societies implies, however, that some of the most basic factors concerned stand a chance of being missed out. Patterns of conflicting interests and orientations are of primary significance to understand not only why certain groups might more (or less) readily comply with the dictates of central authorities than others, but also how the unit 'as a whole' continues to function. Again, therefore, this implies a need for caution in moving from individual experiences to generalizations about adjustment or resistance to change, as was the case in 'classical' works such as that of Fortes and Evans-Pritchard on African political systems (1940).

A great deal was made in this connection of the distinction between the so-called centralized societies and 'stateless' societies which historically existed in Africa. Societies with state structures had explicit offices to perform political functions, whereas in stateless societies these functions were dispersed through the system. From the moment this distinction was made, it became elaborated and amended by others, largely because it was felt that the original dichotomy was too rigid. In particular, Southall added 'segmentary states' as another distinct type (Southall, 1956). Nonetheless, the state-stateless society dichotomy continued to have considerable appeal to many scholars and asserted itself as a useful aid in evaluating adjustment to modern bureaucratic procedures. A central question that was asked in this regard was whether new administrative arrangements could be introduced more conveniently into traditional states or into stateless societies. This dilemma was illustrated, for example, in an early debate between Fallers and Apthorpe. Starting off from his work among the Basoga, reported in *Bantu Bureaucracy*, Fallers developed the general hypothesis that 'societies with hierarchical, centralized political systems incorporate the western type of civil service structure with less strain and instability than do societies having other types of political system – e.g. segmentary ones' (Fallers, 1956:242). This hypothesis was in turn related to a notion of presumed structural tension between hereditary and appointive criteria for recruitment to office, which had been advanced with reference to various parts of the interlacustrine area of East Africa by Audrey Richards (Richards, 1959:348). The assumption was that wherever this tension occurred, the development of modern bureaucracy would more readily find support in the traditional appointive principle, which in turn it would strengthen.

Apthorpe and his colleagues, on the other hand, arrived at exactly the opposite position. Based on their work in Southern Africa, their position was that 'it is in societies which are *not* hierarchically centralized that western ideas of bureaucracy can be more readily adopted' (Apthorpe, 1960:131). Their general argument to support this hypothesis was that

> [as] authority itself is diffused in these (non-centralized, politically acephalus) societies...there is a wider possibility for a number of people to accept new ideas. In more centralized societies, authority tends to repose in one or very few hands and so the introduction of modern bureaucracy is liable to be obstructed or made more difficult, according to the type of person who occupies that position.

Thus, a general conclusion put forward was that 'lack of centralization in an indigenous political structure appears to be less of an impediment to its reception of modern bureaucracy than lack of achieved status ideas and their correlate, an open form of social mobility' (Apthorpe, 1960:132). Nonetheless, it was also argued that, 'any imposed system of authority might operate more successfully if it is kept completely separate from the indigenous one' (Apthorpe, 1959:120, 203).

Faced with such diametrically opposed viewpoints, the casual onlooker might well have felt at a loss when trying to determine who was right and who was wrong. However, this might itself not have been the most relevant thing to do. For each of these positions, whatever their merits for the specific societies that were studied, was based on a premise that one could validly *generalize* from there about the adaptive capacity of similar kinds of traditional political structures. This, however, implied a procedure by which certain salient characteristics (for example: centralized, non-centralized) were turned into typological abstractions and then assigned a – deceptive – predictive value. What remained obscure was that such characteristics (like 'state' or 'stateless'), while evidently part (and no small part) of a total situation, were still no more than part of it. Hierarchical structures elsewhere and under different circumstances than those studied by Fallers, such as Ashanti or Bunyoro, proved capable of considerable resistance to the imposition of new political and administrative forms. Nor have all non-hierarchical structures necessarily been 'adaptive' (or 'non-adaptive' for that matter) in terms of new bureaucratic requirements, as for example the Masai or the Somali cases have exemplified. So much of it all had rather to do with plain interests, power positions, and individual or collective strategies for survival or gain, whether in 'state' or in 'stateless' systems, or in contexts dichotomized in other ways. The assumption that one could generalize about particular predilections of particular types of 'traditional' political systems appeared to be rather short-sighted.

Nonetheless, perhaps there was one difference after all, namely that once a centralized system (for example, a traditional state) had become incorporated into a larger political context, it might well prove itself more effective in mobilizing support and power in order to get its due share of resources, recognition, and so on, than previously non-centralized societies might be able to do. This could simply be the case because a state system, per definition, might have an organizational apparatus more or less ready for purposes of communication and mobilization, which could be used either for resistance (Bunyoro) or collaboration (Buganda) as the case might be. It would require further comparative analysis to see whether such a hypothesis could be sustained, however.

Significantly, in regard to some generalizations, such as those cited above, considerable attention was given, in the actual case studies, to specific conditions or factors that would go a long way to explain certain processes, features, or tendencies. In subsequent hypotheses, however, these features would be linked to the structural type as such, and no longer, not even in part, to these particular conditions. From the arguments put forward by Fallers, for instance, the readiness with which modern bureaucracy was received by at least part of the traditional élite of Busoga, – that is those who could be identified with a 'state' structure – would seem to be quite explicable in the light of the advantages which the new framework offered them by way of personal advancement or in the local competition for power, rather than in terms of some inherently accommodative trait of centralized structures. Thus only proper regard for the entire situational context, and for all the factors and forces involved, could have helped to develop sounder generalizations.

Today, of course, these issues have become largely theoretical, as examples of 'state' or 'stateless' societies being confronted with modern bureaucracy (read: colonial rule) hardly exist any longer. The above discussions refer to a period when some of these confrontations and adjustments were still taking place, striking as it may seem how recent this was. However, the matter is of continued interest in more than one sense. First, questions about the way in which 'traditional' structures did or did not condition responses to colonial intervention are still raised in the reinterpretation of the history of various regions. In fact, a new wave of historical research has been focusing on such 'early contact' situations, often arriving at significant reassessments of earlier anthropological work. Also, next to generalizations based on state-stateless distinctions, in other speculations about orientations towards change in 'traditional' African societies the same sort of point has often been made, and the same effect attributed to other structural factors of these societies – kinship structures, production relationships, or military traditions, for example. This indeed comprises a related discussion on predispositions to change, to which I will now turn.

'Cultural values'

A good deal of literature concerned with social change and social development, particularly in so-called non-Western situations, has commented on the presumed effect of *cultural values* on popular attitudes and social behaviour. In this *mer à boire* citations necessarily have a random quality. A paradoxical problem, however, is that the concept of values and the references made to it have been frequently elusive and yet at the same time definite. Whatever is considered to constitute the central values of a community has often been accorded the stature of sanctity and axiomatic finality; once an analysis has struck social or cultural values, further explication of social behaviour would often be considered unnecessary, perhaps because social or cultural values, popularly accepted as respectable, ought not to be questioned. This did not, of course, deter people from arguing that the value systems of certain societies are not very conducive to development, or even to suggest that they ought to be altered. Examples of that have also been many, though they very often led to the view that, if the values of a society are against a particular innovation, there is little more to be said about the roots of resistance, thus leaving unexplored the possibility that these 'values' themselves might be variable with contextual conditions.

The prominence accorded to values as a key to understanding social change and adaptation is an old one. Margaret Mead gave voice to it when she stated that:

> a change in any one part of the culture will be accompanied by changes in other parts, and . . . only by relating any planned detail of change to the central values of the culture is it possible to provide for the repercussions which will occur in other aspects of life (Mead, 1953:10).

Similar notions were frequently articulated by other scholars. Whatever was meant by values, the implication was that if innovations were not brought to correspond with them, difficulties and conflict might arise. Furthermore, that the elements of any value system were so interconnected that contact at any point would transmit tremors through the whole equilibrium. Finally, that if one wanted to assess receptivity to change, the critical factors would lie within the 'target unit', rather than within a wider frame of variables.

Rather imprecisely, the term 'values' has sometimes been used alternatively, or even interchangeably, to denote social norms and 'what is valued', interests. Further explanation of the term is often omitted, presumably on the ground that it would be 'understood' what values are. Such a consensus, however, is not really so certain. Either application of the term conveys matters of key significance in all societies. People are commonly aware of established norms of conduct ('values'), even if they do not always abide by them, and in all societies people seem to pursue what they 'value'. Obviously, then, there is an element of ambiguity here, and it would not be difficult to indicate areas in which values in these two senses differ or indeed conflict. More important though is that both what is 'valued' and 'values' as codes of behaviour would be articulated within whatever happens to be the context for social interaction. Thus, as long as the pre-colonial or 'traditional' society could be seen as the terminal unit, it was that which per definition constituted the context of 'traditional' values (of either sort). Once external, colonial and post-colonial frames of action and reference were superimposed, however, norms for conduct as well as valued interests would inevitably change. This by no means implies movement towards congruence. New political contexts, such as those created by colonial structures or by contemporary development strategies, might precisely cause various groups to come up against them, as has been true in many instances. To be sure, the resistance which any such new structures might encounter may at times have every appearance of an articulation or even a strengthening of 'traditional' value patterns, of either the 'norms' or the 'interest' variety. Even then, however, it would be necessary to view these patterns essentially in relation to the new context, which evidently has been prompting their assertion, rather than as being solely or intrinsically derived from pre-existing characteristics and conditions.

Not unlike theories of receptivity to planned change that concentrate on elements of traditional political structure, interpretations focused on cultural values often also had a strong element of abstraction and generalization, even though the analyses on which they were based might themselves have been situationally quite specific. Two opposite cases, included in an early but influential volume on *Continuity and Change in African Cultures*, edited by Bascom and Herskovits (1962), illustrate the point. The first is an account of 'Pakot Resistance to Change', in which Harold Schneider attributes great explanatory significance to the working of the Pakot value system in blocking the introduction of administrative and other socio-political innovations into this society. 'Initially' he writes:

> one is tempted to attribute the Nilotic conservatism purely to the fact that they possess the cattle complex, which has been defined as an intense devotion to cattle and a permeation of this value into all other aspects of culture.

Following this, however, he adds that this by itself was not sufficient to explain the 'conservatism of the Nilotics'. As other people also had the so-called 'cattle complex' and nonetheless proved quite adaptive to change, Schneider finally advanced a kind of compromise formulation, namely that 'the cattle complex...seems important when combined with an essentially pastoral way of life' (Schneider, 1962:165–6). The problem with this formulation, however, is that it introduces a set of conditions which only with the greatest difficulty could be identified in terms of just values, culture, or other such elusive categories. Just as other modes of existence, pastoralism surely involves pronounced social values, and besides may well itself be highly valued as a way of life. But pastoralism also continuously demands that delicate choices be made within a very narrow range of alternatives and difficult conditions. The survival of pastoral communities has often depended on whether or not these choices could be kept open; thus it is not without logic that innovations which would appear to constrain rather than to extend the scope of possible alternatives (as administrative measures so often do), would not so readily find acceptance.

Besides, the so-called 'cattle-complex' of people in Eastern Africa, surely one of the most celebrated examples of attributed cultural values in Africa, also proved less axiomatic than it had first been assumed to be. Among other things it was challenged on the basis of trade statistics. The economist Mark Karp, for example, in 1960 already showed a correlation between the price level at the international meat market and the readiness of pastoral people to sell their cattle. As large herds must be maintained to increase the chances of survival during possible future droughts, it was found that only when market prices are sufficiently high can cash obtained for cattle be a substitute insurance against climatic dangers (Karp, 1960:38–78). Rather than 'values' or 'culture' *per se*, therefore, it is people's assessments of their total situational context and the choices this offers which will determine their 'receptivity to change'. 'Cultural values', in terms of which resistance or accommodation may be argued or interpreted, are themselves likely to be derived from this context. The Chapters in Part 3 of this volume, on *Land, Pastoralism and the State in Eastern Africa*, comprise various illustrations of how survival and livelihood strategies compel pastoralists into particular reactions *vis-à-vis* institutional interventions.

A second example of theorizing on the basis of assumed cultural predispositions comes from Simon Ottenberg, in a companion article on 'Ibo Receptivity to Change' in the Bascom and Herskovits collection. In more or less similar vein as Schneider had done for the Pakot, Ottenberg suggested that special cultural characteristics could account for the strong degree not of resistance but of receptivity to change that was found in Ibo society: 'Certain elements in Ibo culture...play an important role in culture change' (Ottenberg, 1962:141). However, the actual factors then noted in support of this thesis show strong if not exclusive weight given to quite particular conditions, such as could only be subsumed under a heading 'culture' if this concept were to be accepted as a catch-all phrase, freely interchangeable with terms like 'territory' or 'society' and itself lacking any specific meaning. Considerable emphasis, for instance, was put in the analysis on the high population density in Ibo society, which tended to encourage social and physical mobility and adaptability to new situations as people were constantly forced to search for new possibilities of livelihood. In his analysis, Ottenberg also discussed what he termed 'the situation of culture change' and the 'culture contact situation', explaining that this situation had the effect of widening the range of choices available to members of Ibo society (Ottenberg, 1962:137, 139). That notion would not as such need to give rise to problems, though today it might no longer be cast in these terms; the trouble was rather that, once all conditioning factors had been explored, the end result was attributed to 'Ibo culture' and not to the socio-economic or political conditions determining that particular situation.

One final irony, though, is that if it has once been said, authoritatively, of a particular people that they are 'enterprising', 'innovative', 'change-oriented', and so forth, or alternatively 'conservative', 'tradition-oriented' or 'resistant to change', then chances are that such an image will henceforth prove hard to redress. It is not difficult to find examples of such representations. Stereotypes are highly resistant to change.

Conclusion

While the prospects of social development of African communities have often been interpreted in terms of particular cultural or structural characteristics, the question that might be raised is whether this vital area of interest has not overly suffered from a degree of mystification. An intricacy of concepts often needed, or needs, to be navigated before what appear to be plainly objective factors might be reached. *Prima facie*, it would seem very easy to lose one's way in this maze or, alternatively, it might be avoided altogether for fear of complexity. When it is argued, for instance, that 'since each culture has its own value interpretations and its own value hierarchy, specific information is necessary for the interpretation of each innovation' (Albert, 1960:70), the non-anthropologist might well refrain from treading on such delicate ground. Yet if he entered it, he might find that people's behaviour and orientations make perfect sense in terms of the alternatives that appear open (or foreclosed) to them, and hence it is puzzling and unnecessary to present these choices as inherently derived from intrinsic 'traditional' cultural characteristics.

The point is that over and above the possible implications of any 'internal' traditional features, social orientations and action are primarily explicable by the appraisals that individuals and groups make, and must make, of their own scope for action and of the intentions and strength of other actors with which they interact. Socio-political dispositions, in other words, will be largely derived from the perspective that people have on the strength of their own resources and of other contingencies in their arena of engagement. This may apply 'horizontally' in regard to the orientations and actions of social actors towards allies and competitors, and 'vertically' in regard to hierarchical power structures. This is not to argue that values and structures have no relevance at all for the understanding of political behaviour. The search for finite explanations of social and political change, however, incurs the danger that elegant and highly abstract interpretations will be made at the risk of missing out the obvious, namely quite concrete, individual or collective strategies and the primary relevance of the parameters within which these are pursued. Recognizing this enables one to reintroduce values and structures, in as far as appropriate, but as elements in a wider context and not as final determinants of choices made or to be made.

There are two caveats, however. One is cognitive and is merely to note the truism that orientations towards other actors will be relevant only if or to the extent that people are aware of each other's existence. For example, during colonization and the specific establishment of power and authority structures it entailed, various African communities for some time are likely to have remained unaware of the full implications of their incorporation into a new political structure. Today, similar kinds of discrepancies in cognitive interactions may play a role in the way different social or regional groups perceive processes of European incorporation. Obviously, then, a wider political context will have little or no bearing on social orientations until such time as it might assert itself more forcibly, though this itself infers very little about the nature of subsequent orientations.

A second reservation may appear to involve a more complex argument, but essentially amounts to restating the simple truth that social actors are likely to pursue what they 'value'. This can be explored at the level of action as well as at that of orientations. If social and political behaviour is more than just random opportunism, preference will be given to certain objectives over others. Thus, choice indeed has a subjective, if not a 'cultural' element. Therefore, though a primary significance of context and possibilities for alternative action should be emphasized, this should not be interpreted as rigidly deterministic. However, that in turn does not imply that one should turn full circle to traditional value systems as a key to motivation. The simple fact remains that choices are made on the basis of alternative actions open at a given time, not on those which were obtained at earlier points. Perhaps the caveat which a one-time Governor of Uganda issued in 1939 still retains its relevance today:

> Experience shows that officers are sometimes led by historical and anthropological research into an impractical and anachronistic regard for old forms and ideas, and endeavour to revive things which the changing conditions of to-day have rendered obsolete. (Uganda Protectorate, 1939:13).

That message no doubt had its own purposes and perspective. Still, one of its implications seemed to be to underscore that no predictive value can or should be derived from particular types of traditional political structure or values *per se*. In the final analysis, 'receptivity' to political change is primarily a function of the nature and objectives of political goals and strategies, and of popular assessments of their implications, rather than of the particular characteristics, cultural or traditional-structural, of recipient or 'target' groups.

Finally, though, it should be recognized that the preoccupations underlying many receptivity debates in fact have had less to do with 'culture', 'norms and values', or 'traditional structures' *per se*, but are in essence pre-occupied with the strategies and fortunes of incorporation and (colonial or post-colonial) state formation. The underlying concern is with 'obstacles' to incorporation strategies, which may be perceived or presented in cultural terms. The actual terms of these debates are continuously subject to further evolution. More recently, for example, they have largely come to be focused on state or project structures and participation. As noted in Chapter 3, there are also significant parallels to current debates in terms of 'good governance': here again, the focus and onus is implicitly placed on the 'internal' quality and characteristics of the management of public affairs, rather than on the aims and interests of the broader institutional frameworks which use 'good governance' as a measure by which to judge its performance. By and large, though, questions about autonomy versus incorporation remain key issues in any such interactive contexts.

The case study presented in Chapter 5 illustrates the potential redundancy or obsolescence which may become the fate of institutions that are incorporated into wider political frameworks, thus adding an imput to the debate about the (ir)relevance of 'traditional structures' in terms of 'receptivity to change'. At the same time, it offers us an additional perspective on notions of institutionalization. Institutionalization may invite, and in the end become exemplified by, ceremonial adornment. But to what extent is this a reversible proposition and can 'neo-traditional' ceremonialization be viewed as an index of institutionalization?

5

Institutionalization and Institutional Decline: The Neo-Traditionalization of Ankole Kingship

Introduction

'One man's death is another man's bread.' The dialectic implicit in this Dutch saying seems perfectly relevant to studies of societal development and change, particularly in connection with perspectives on institutional evolution. Indeed, long-term processes of socio-political transformation may best be viewed in terms of opposites, whether tendencies, directions or forces – first, because only then will it be possible to distinguish between different kinds of processes at play and second, because all too often the eclipse of one pattern of transformation has been related to, or caused by, the emergence of another.

It is the residue of such dialectical processes over time that we can see and are inclined to view and interpret in terms of long-term institutional transformation. What we may no longer see is a whole range of formations (and abortive transformations) that have fallen into decline and oblivion – though from an evolutionary point of view they are surely equally important. While they have clearly not 'evolved', they seem important in at least two ways: for their contribution, even if indirectly, to the formation of the 'residue' and for the questions they raise as to why it was that they themselves did not 'evolve' further. Should the causes of their eclipse be sought in some intrinsic destiny toward involution and eventual self-liquidation, or did they find their development thwarted due to confrontation with opposite forces of transformation? Or can yet other possible explanations be advanced for their collapse and disappearance? Besides, there is the plain but preliminary question as to how one can recognize instances of institutional decline in the first place.

It is illusory to expect firm (or even soft) answers to most of these queries, yet, for a better grasp of questions about long-term institutional change, it seems useful to pay attention to such contrasted tendencies wherever feasible. This chapter is concerned with some such 'opposite' tendencies, namely, with symptoms of institutional decline and the difficulty of interpreting them. Its focus and key example will be the neo-traditionalization of Ankole kingship, an institution that was much adorned but little adored before its termination in republican-minded Uganda in 1967. The case raises more general questions about the varied kinds of relationships between symbolic exaltation and patterns of institutionalization and institutional decline. More often than not, it will be argued, an inverse correlation may be found between processes of ceremonialization and institutionalization.

A propos institutionalization

Institutionalization as we have seen has been a favourite theme of many discussions of bureaucracy and political sociology; if public bodies are to function effectively, or at all, it is often assumed, they should be institutionalized. To become institutionalized, it is argued, political structures or administrative organizations must be accepted and legitimized in terms of the norms and values of the society concerned. Exactly how the chemistry of such 'norms and values' might work out is not entirely clear, but there seems to be widespread agreement that once institutionalization is achieved, a smooth routine of political and administrative practices should evolve.

Concern with institutions has also been shown from another angle, that is, within those branches of anthropology and adjacent fields for which traditional authority was a focal point. Here, too, the key to the functioning – and understanding – of institutions has frequently been held to lie within complex configurations of social values, belief systems and cultural norms, or in other, even more mystical, properties. Again, if the norms and values appear supportive of an institution, social legitimation and institutional continuity – the hallmarks of institutionalization – would be expected to obtain.

Of these two themes, the one evidently begins where the other ends. While one is primarily directed toward an understanding of inherited institutions, the other's orientation is rather more innovative, focused on future institutions. Nonetheless, they share at least two major premises. One is the postulate of the need for, or movement toward, socio-cultural congruence of institutions with their environment. The other, an in-built norm, is institutional longevity. The sum total of these qualities is *institutional legitimation*.

It follows that a certain premium is attached to the continued functioning of public institutions. Indeed, as was seen in Chapter 2, institutionalization in this sense has at times been equated with 'political development,' one of the highest awards of modernization theory. But it also follows that questions would inevitably be raised, and concern expressed, if institutional continuities were ruptured – through overthrow, abolition, or any other intervention.

Here, then, is something of a dilemma. Normatively, institutions are expected to last, though they often fail to do so. Instead, in a world full of conflict and change, numerous situations show institutional rupture rather than continuity, or disjointedness rather than congruence. Should all such situations be regarded as problematic?

To reverse Montesquieu and to assert that institutions that break down suffer the fate they deserve would appear prima facie to be just as gross a generalization as saying that all institutions should be maintained or should maintain themselves. Instead, it seems important to reconsider the normative implications of scholarly themes that converge in a concern with institutionalization and institutional maintenance; at the same time, it is evident that these issues cannot be adequately addressed without prior regard to the context in which the institutions operate.

In brief, the concern with the institutionalization thesis is basically threefold. First, it is a priori 'forward'-looking and, moreover, tends to be rather normative about this, making it difficult to relate it to possible patterns of decline. Second, there often appears to be a greater preoccupation with the maintenance and survival of institutions than with their functions – or the lack of them – as the case may be. Third, at yet another level, patterns of ceremonialization are at times (mis)taken for institutionalization, while in fact some such instances should more accurately be viewed as camouflaging processes of institutional decline. In turn, again, this throws up the question of how institutionalization should be distinguished from, and/or related to, institutional decline.

These issues are unlikely to lose their relevance within any foreseeable future. But stripped of their normative connotation, they may also be presented in an alternative way. Take the case of a centrally placed institution that has lost its essential purpose. It cannot simply fall into oblivion or wither away. Like the fall of the dilapidated roof of a house, its collapse might be obstructed by the walls and beams that remain standing. As an alternative to oblivion, however, an institution may be exalted into higher spheres and become not a ruin but a monument. Either solution implies a removal from the functioning core of the system. Thus, even if a political institution is increasingly decorated with gilt and glitter, its actual functions may, nevertheless, be subject to decay. And when most references to an institution begin to be concerned with its pomp and circumstance and no longer with any effective or affective role it might have had, then it is not unreasonable to suspect that it may have lost the essence of its former role and position. The question this gives rise to is why (and when) is it felt to be important to strengthen the ceremonial aspects of an institution. Closer consideration of one specific example, namely, the neo-traditionalization of Ankole kingship, may be instructive in this regard. From the records of the former Ankole District in Western Uganda, the impression emerges that the tendencies of ceremonialization and institutional decline described above became gradually more manifest during the last decades of the Ankole kingship, the *Obugabe*; i.e. from roughly the 1930s until the mid-1960s.

The ceremonialization of kingship

Ankole was one of four kingdoms incorporated within the colonial framework of Uganda, a status continued in the post-colonial era until 1967 when kingship was constitutionally abolished under the first Obote regime (Doornbos, 1975). The most important, populous and powerful of these kingdoms was Buganda, while during and after colonial rule the status and recognition of the other three, Ankole, Bunyoro and Toro, were heavily dependent on the kind of government policies that were pursued with respect to Buganda: when Buganda was accorded federal status in the constitutional package negotiated for independence in 1962, a watered-down version of 'semi-federalism' was devised for the other kingdoms. When Buganda was abolished as a kingdom following a confrontation with the Obote regime in 1966, the other three were similarly abrogated. And when Buganda monarchists in the early 1990s successfully pressed the Museveni government to allow the restoration of their monarchy, the path towards reinstallation of kingship was cleared again for the other three cases by the government's 'unbanning' order. In the Ankole case, however, restoration was not to be followed through.

The Ankole District, as established by the British at the turn of the century, constituted an amalgamation of various adjacent areas with the pre-colonial Nkore kingdom that made the latter more than twice as large in size, and also far more populous. The word *Ankole* was in fact derived from *Nkore*, whose *Omugabe* (King) was nominally placed at the head of the new and enlarged district. Ankole's kingship, however, had its roots in an ethnically segmented social structure in which a numerically small élite stratum of Bahima, originally of pastoralist derivation, were placed over a large majority of Banyankore or 'Bairu' peasant cultivators. Within the pre-colonial Nkore context the pastoralist and Bahima element had been much more predominant, but in the new Ankole District the vast majority (of 90 per cent or more) consisted of Banyankore peasantry. To many of them the notion of kingship was novel.

During the early decades of the century it seemed evident that the kingship fitted rather uncomfortably within the colonial command structure. Repeated role conflicts and ambiguities constituted a recurrent theme in the colonial records (Doornbos, 1975). After the mid-1930s, however, attention became focused increasingly on the ceremonial aspects of kingship. The effect if not the intention of this was that the Ankole monarchy became quite lavishly adorned, while at the same time the king's effective role was drastically reduced.

This dressing-up of the monarchy was done in symbolic, as well as more literal, fashion. There was, for example, the question of the state chair. This matter was first raised in 1934, when the District Commissioner of Ankole called his superiors' attention to the fact that the Omugabe did not have a throne. He suggested that the Governor of Uganda might wish to show his appreciation of the interest then being taken by the Omugabe in the affairs of Ankole through the presentation of a state chair. The Governor, however, considered this too rash an action. As the Chief Secretary communicated to the Provincial Commissioner:

> The Governor has learned with satisfaction that the Mugabe is now showing greater interest in public affairs, and the Mugabe may be informed to this effect if you so desire. His Excellency considers, however, that the question of conferring further distinction on the Mugabe should be postponed for a year, by which time it should be possible to form an opinion as to whether the present improvement is likely to be lasting (letter from Chief Secretary, Uganda Protectorate to Provincial Commissioner Western Province, 20th December 1936).

As it turned out, the opinion formed after this trial period did not seem to warrant the immediate conferment of a throne. And, in fact, as much as ten years passed before further steps were taken in the matter. It was then that the *Enganzi* (Chief minister) approached the District Commissioner again, requesting that 'the Protectorate Government would kindly provide a Coronation Chair' (letter from the Enganzi to the District Commissioner, Ankole, 9th November 1944). The new District Commissioner seemed somewhat at a loss when faced with this request. The Omugabe's demeanour was not so much the problem now, but as he knew a throne to be an integral part of the emblems of royalty, the District Commissioner wondered: 'Are there any symbolic decorations which you want to incorporate in the chair? Please let me know soon' (letter from the District Commissioner to the Enganzi, 12th January 1945). The reply was not without interest for an understanding of the sources of royal symbolism in Ankole. The Enganzi, while forwarding a sketch of *Bagyendanwa*, the royal drum, submitted: 'As you know this better than I do, I request you to incorporate some decoration in the chair you may deem suitable' (letter from the Enganzi to District Commissioner of Ankole, 24th January 1945).

This exchange of communications by itself was not of great significance and hardly constituted proof that the Omugabeship was being modelled after European style. But similar searches for symbolism occurred in regard to other royal attributes, seeming to affirm the tendency. In 1944, for instance, the Enganzi requested 'that the Government may grant us a crown for the Omugabe to wear on the Coronation Day' (letter from the Enganzi to the District Commissioner, Ankole, 9th November 1944). Apparently taken a little aback by this request, the District Commissioner responded: 'Will you please let me know what was the custom in the past when a new Omugabe was crowned? The Crown is such a symbol of the Omugabeship that I feel it should be locally made' (letter from the District Commissioner, Ankole to the Enganzi, 18th November, 1944). Again, he was soon put in the picture on the tradition of crowns, although the answer may have been somewhat unexpected. For the District Commissioner reported to the Provincial Commissioner that 'It . . . appears that in the past the Omugabe never had a crown and it is a new idea that he should wear one on his Coronation Day' (letter from the District Commissioner, Ankole, to the Provincial Commissioner, Western Province, 12th December 1944). Provided with this information, the Provincial Commissioner concluded that the request could not really be based on tradition. He informed the District Commissioner that:

> The use of the term 'Coronation' is inappropriate and should be avoided; similarly, if possible, the term 'crown' or reference to 'kingship'. The native term for the ceremony, if it can be distinguished from the Accession ceremony – and also for the head-dress – should be invariably used . . . I agree that if it is considered by the Banyankore that the Mugabe should wear a special head-dress on ceremonial occasions, one should be made locally. Similar head-dresses in Bunyoro are made mainly of cowrie shells; that of the Mukama of Toro was

made for him by his Mother, chiefly of parrot's feathers (letter from the Provincial Commissioner, Western Province, to the District Commissioner, Ankole, 18th December 1944).

Now, the Provincial Commissioner had been correct in surmising that a coronation and all it would involve was a novelty for Ankole. As Morris points out 'the word *engure* (which is really a head-band) is borrowed from Luganda and the idea of a "coronation" is a European importation' (Morris, 1964:82). But it seems possible that the Provincial Commissioner's reluctance to use such terms as 'crown', 'coronation' and 'kingship' stemmed not from their lack of traditional referents but was based primarily on a premise that too much exaltation should be avoided. Judging from the tone of the instruction, there seemed to be some fear that a too explicit recognition of 'royalty' might elicit identifications and sentiments that could prove harmful to regular administration. If and in so far as that fear existed, however, it was overly pessimistic. Interest in and demands for neo-traditionalization continued to come from local quarters but were largely restricted to members of the Bahima establishment of Ankole, the élite stratum closely involved with the institutions of kingship, who, because of their vantage point in the administration, were able to note what standards developed elsewhere in the country. Royal *bon ton* in Uganda, in fact, largely evolved on such a comparative basis and, in a district like Ankole, neither tradition nor popular opinion necessarily had much to do with it.

The determination to oppose anything but 'genuine' tradition did not persist. Before long the door was opened for symbolic innovations of many kinds, virtually inaugurating a *regalia galore*. A full-fledged coronation ceremony, for example, was held in 1945 on the occasion of the accession of Omugabe Gasyonga. Some of the colour of that ceremony is indicated by the enlistment of the services of Mr. Georgiadis in Alexandria. Mr. Georgiadis was asked to provide a suitable 'Ceremonial Robe embroidered in gilded silver threads' for the Omugabe (letter from the Acting Resident, Buganda, to Chief Secretary, Uganda Protectorate, 9th August 1945). A climax in the ceremony was the 'crowning' of the Omugabe, performed by Bishop Stuart of Uganda. Nearly twenty years later, a resolution was submitted that the place where the Omugabe had been crowned should be 'preserved and kept as a monument to remember the day in future'. The argument then was that the kingdoms of Buganda and Toro had 'examples of such places of royal significance', while moreover, 'such places could boost tourist trade' (News Release, Department of Information, Uganda Government, 11th July 1964).

In later years, the anniversary of the Omugabe's accession became an important annual event in Ankole, being rationalized at one time by the Enganzi in the following terms:

In the past years, the birthday or accession ceremonies of our late Omugabe, like those of his contemporaries, were not observed as it was impossible to know their exact dates. With the new generation, however, it has been possible to know the dates of these events and consequently in Buganda, Bunyoro and Toro these ceremonies are held every year by new rulers who succeeded their predecessors. Our new Omugabe has just succeeded to the Ankole throne and so it is our great desire that he should not be the exception (letter from the Enganzi and Chiefs to Provincial Commissioner, 12th June 1967).

Thus, each year on 26th September, elaborate festivities were staged in Mbarara to celebrate the Omugabe's coronation anniversary. They had little to do with Ankole tradition, but they served to suggest status and dignity through the display of pomp and protocol, which was their characteristic feature. The programme for these occasions ran from church services to sundowners and included standard items such as a march by schoolchildren, the inspection of a guard of honour (not mounted by any Ankole constabulary but by the Uganda police), the release of prisoners, speechmaking and football matches. Not of least interest was the detailed care that went into establishing the order of precedence in which visiting dignitaries would take part in the proceedings.

The tendency to make Ankole royalty more royal also entailed the redesignation of many contingent elements in the system. Early on, various quasi-traditional titles of chiefs had been introduced under the auspices of Ankole's monarchical status. Among the titles that had thus gained currency were those of the county, or saza, chiefs and of senior officials: Omuramuzi (Chief judge), Omubiki (treasurer), Kihimba (administrative secretary) and Omujasi (head of Ankole askaris). Once again, many of these styles happened to be borrowed from Buganda, but while proposals were made from time to time to 'ankole-ize' them, Ankole tradition proved to offer insufficient equivalents to make this operational. What is more, the titles of the county chiefs (Kahima, Kitunzi, Kangaho, Pokimo, Kaigo, Mukwenda, Sekibobo, Katambera, Kashwiju and Mugyema) each had a specific meaning in the Buganda context, though not in Ankole.

Styles were also reconsidered for the circles most intimately associated with the Omugabe. Western models of royal family patterns seemed reflected in questions concerning the proper nomenclature for the

Omugabe's official wife and children. In the past, Roscoe asserts, 'it was quite evident that there never was a queen' (1923:34). In 1945, however, the Eishengyero (District Council) debated whether the Omugabe's wife should be called Omwigarire or just Omugabe's wife and a decision was reached in favour of the former (Eishengyero, minute 13, July 1945). The English equivalent was accepted to be 'Queen.' Similarly, the Omugabe's children became known as princes and princesses and the family's composition thus came to resemble that of a standard royal house.

Inevitably, perhaps, other questions arose about proper royal standing. Their significance lay not so much in their contents or in the way they were resolved, but rather in the fact that they were raised at all. A few examples may illustrate the point. In 1952, the Eishengyero was asked to discuss the desirability of acquiring a 'special dress' for the Omwigarire, a matter that did not prove difficult to decide. As one member said, 'she had a good dress which she had put on at Coronation Day and that could serve' – an argument with which the council concurred (Eishengyero, minute 47, June 1952). A year later, similar questions were raised and similarly resolved in respect to the Omugabe's children. Again, the Eishengyero did not see grounds to assume responsibility for their style of dress on public occasions (Eishengyero, minute 90, 8th July 1953). Meanwhile, however, considerable care was given to a rather different matter, the memory of kings, for the sake of which the Ankole government agreed to build a mausoleum.

The monarchy was embellished in yet other ways as well. Most of them were trivial, but together they created a pattern and image. The Omugabe's residence, for instance, came to be known as *Mugaba* (palace), as distinguished from the more humble traditional term *ekyikari* (enclosure). A sizable two-storey building, the palace showed little regal inspiration, traditional or modern, in its interior decoration. Also, a royal standard was designed for the Omugabe, 'set on yellow cloth with his Coat of Arms, drums in white and a lion in brown, against a black background' (*Uganda Argus*, Kampala, 16th March 1964). In 1954, the words 'Omugabe – Ishe – Nyina – Bagyendanwa' (Omugabe – Father – Mother – Bagyendanwa) were inserted into all official stamps and seals of the Ankole government (Eishengyero, minute 18, 21th April 1954). And in 1959, the picture of the Omugabe and the royal drum appeared on opposite sides of a medal, to be awarded to individuals who had distinguished themselves in his service (Eishengyero, minute 47, 9th October 1959). Again, there was the Eishengyero's resolution to display the Omugabe's photograph in all official buildings in Ankole and its subsequent ruling, as of 1956, that the picture of the Omwigarire should also be shown in the Eishengyero Hall (Eishengyero, minute 42, June 1952 and minutes of the Eishengyero of 17th–23rd January 1956). In the same year, there was also concern that the Omugabe's platform in the Eishengyero Hall was not of adequate beauty and standard. A decision was reached in favour of such improvements as would 'show both tribal and Western fashions' (Eishengyero, minute 27, 1956). Clearly, the pursuit of regalia led in many directions.

Only in a few cases did the search for decorum involve an attempt to preserve or to revive traditional cultural attributes. One such example concerned the customary greeting due to the Omugabe. The district records more than once reaffirm that this should be given in the traditionally proper way, 'Osingyire Nyakusinga'; while 'Obukama Nyakusinga' was to be used for bidding farewell (Eishengyero, minute 31, 18th October 1948 and Ankole Government, 1964). The motive for reiterating these forms, as stated, was that they had been falling into disregard.

The best example of successful preservation, however, remained Bagyendanwa, the royal drum. This was kept in a specially built house, which was maintained out of Ankole government funds. The drum had a permanent keeper, an old lady of the Bakururu clan, whose duties included seeing that the fire was kept burning, as this should never go out. A striking degree of personification was maintained in respect to Bagyendanwa: the drum had its own land and herd of cattle and was referred to as an individual. Bagyendanwa was flanked to the right by his 'wife' and to the left by his 'Enganzi.' Nevertheless, no matter how admirably it was done, this preservation essentially amounted to the upkeep of an antiquity. Apart from the keeper of Bagyendanwa, virtually no one in Ankole believed that the drum's disappearance would really cause the end of the world. Irreverently, radical Bairu members of Ankole society regarded the whole thing as nothing more than a piece of wood.

Symbolic exaltation and institutional relevance or decline: four configurations

In the light of the tendencies described above, the question might well be raised whether the Ankole monarchy had not become a redundant institution whose discontinuation made little particular difference to the socio-political framework and policy processes of Ankole. It should be stressed that the tendencies described represented the principal attention that was publicly devoted to the kingship. If we raise the question of redundancy it will be evident that the argument must hinge largely, though not necessarily exclusively, on the accuracy of the lukewarm reactions by the people of Ankole that were evidenced in the terminal years of the monarchy. This must be the case because, with regard to institutions that are basically expected to command popular allegiances (such as religious institutions and other symbolic structures), a key test of institutional 'redundancy' should lie in the nature of the orientations exhibited toward them by their presumed 'clienteles.' Lack of power *per se* would not necessarily be a criterion of such redundancy. Clearly, as long as an institution has an impact, no matter how this may be evaluated, it cannot quite be described as 'redundant.' Power and influence may be viewed or experienced in either positive or negative terms, but to talk of institutional redundancy will make sense only if such influence is lacking in either way. Rather, therefore, it might be suggested that an institution is redundant if it no longer serves an essential purpose within its socio-political context; in other words, if its presence or absence makes no difference to the overall social and political process (cf. Landau, 1971).

In the case of symbolic institutions such as the Ankole monarchy – and it is evident that hardly any other role could have been claimed for the Omugabe in its terminal years – their relative relevance or redundancy might thus be seen as an expression of the extent to which members of the society concerned are knowledgeable of, identify with, or instead are indifferent towards these institutions, or perhaps might openly reject their role or existence. In this sense, then, institutional redundancy comes in as a variant and a measure of assessment of institutional decline. It does not essentially matter in this respect that normally there will be only few issues on which an entire society may share the same views. 'Complete' redundancy in this sense, in fact, is an abstraction that in reality will occur only in exceptional cases; institutional redundancy in terms of popular allegiance, in other words, means neither more, nor less, than that this quality seems present in some predominant measure. In 1967, indications were that this was the case with the Ankole kingship. For present purposes, I shall assume it to have been so.

Still, this leaves unexplored further questions connected with the ways in which patterns of neo-traditionalization, as manifested in increasing ceremonialization or other forms of symbolic exaltation, may relate to issues of institutional relevance and decline. It should be noted that the case presented here says nothing about the specific *causes* of institutional decline suffered by the Ankole kingship, nor about the conditions or chances of adaptation or obsolescence of institutions whose continuity is at stake. Such questions require separate discussion and analysis, focused on the particular transformation of an institution's social and political contexts and the extent to which these affect its long-term prospects of survival (Doornbos, 1978). Our present interest is much more limited, namely, under what conditions is it justified to point to neo-traditionalization as a potential index of institutional decline? In other words, to what extent is it possible to generalize about this connection, and what does the Ankole case indicate in this regard?

The Ankole example seems relatively straightforward and in a sense simpler than many others because the ceremonialization of its kingship was paralleled by growing popular indifference and, in the end, by quite lukewarm reactions to the monarchy's abolition. Whether symbolic exaltation equals institutional decline and redundancy is yet another matter, however. Several examples from recent decades raise questions about that; for example, the cases of Emperor Bokassa and of Field Marshal-cum-President Idi Amin. Each of these figures, in his heyday and in his own way, indulged in many novel forms of ceremony and symbolic exaltation, often with an inventiveness and a taste for the grandiose that would have made Ankole's Omugabe seem extremely modest by contrast. Whatever else could be observed about them, however, they did not exactly appear to be 'in decline' when they were at the centre of things. Or were they? What they had was power, not allegiance; whatever allegiance they might have had was clearly dwindling. This distinction is potentially important and should be explored further.

Meanwhile, there are other possible reservations to the equation of symbolic exaltation and institutional decline. One is derived from the *Nkore* context, Ankole's direct precursor as a political unit, where it was evident that the Omugabe was invested with some kind of above-average qualities (Doornbos, 1980). What is more, it seemed that adherence to the myth of his omnipotence was in some way 'functional' in terms of maintaining the political cohesiveness of the society. In the absence by and large of an administrative apparatus that could enforce collective decisions, this was in fact virtually the only antidote to centrifugal forces. Paradoxically, though, the 'functionality' or 'relevance' of symbolic exaltation for maintaining an institutional context seems to denote rather the reverse of symbolic exaltation as an index of institutional decline. Once again, therefore, there is reason to question whether these opposites can be reconciled.

Some further reservations are implied in a very different form of precedent. Is it not institutionalization *par excellence*, one might argue, if, in regard to a particular office, careful attention is paid persistently to subtleties of decorum, protocol and public image? If one takes two celebrated examples – those of the Vatican and of British royalty until some years ago – it is difficult to see how they could have maintained their special image and position except through continuous and meticulous care of symbols and symbolism – coupled, to be sure, with a good intuitive insight into what the public's eye demands. Prima facie, it would seem difficult to argue that these examples represented institutional decline rather than institutionalization. In recent years that logic has been less self-evident in the case of the British monarchy, though the wide-ranging public discussion and the pledges made to 'modernize' the royal house in the wake of the death of Princess Diana seemed to reaffirm recognition of these crucial linkages.

In sum, therefore, four distinct positions suggest themselves regarding the relationship between manifestations of symbolic exaltation and questions of institutional relevance and decline. The first, exemplified by colonial Ankole, amounts to quasi-traditional ceremonialization paralleling and, in fact, camouflaging institutional decline and loss of effective power. Second, there are the cases of Bokassa and others, which exhibited grandiose ceremonialization combined with the exercise of excessive coercive power. Third comes the example of pre-colonial Nkore, which seemed to have exaltation as a sort of substitute for central power; and fourth, we have neo-traditionalization as an index of institutionalization.

The first and second of these, though at extreme ends from each other in terms of the central ruler's effective powers, are perhaps less contradictory than they might appear at first sight. In the final analysis, both try to make up for, or cover up, what is essentially the same sort of predicament – namely, an acute lack of popular support and allegiance. These two situations have that in common, notwithstanding the fact that in one the ruler exercises absolute power, while in the other he is absolutely powerless. Together they re-emphasize that form and expression in lieu of substance is an old phenomenon indeed, predating even its baroque versions and certainly constituting a recurrent feature in the contemporary context.

But how does this position relate to the third connection between power and symbolism, that is, the situation where symbolic exaltation almost seems to take the place of central power? Part of the answer must be that this cannot really be a matter of substitutes. Although the pre-colonial Nkore system lacked a central state apparatus, nonetheless, it had a definite collective power basis in the form of the senior chiefs in command of physical forces. In part, it probably was the case that this collective body politic needed to find (symbolic) ways in which to present itself and be recognized. Moreover, the symbolism that had developed around the Omugabe may have functioned internally as a mechanism to ensure stability and as an antidote to mutual rivalry within the collectivity. Although quite different, therefore, from the mock symbolism characteristic of the earlier examples, given the quite different structural background, this distinction hardly seems to obviate the need for a priori scepticism in regard to manifestations of ceremonial exaltation. Rather, it would seem that the kind of symbolic imagery through which the collective body politic of Nkore sought to assert a common political identity may have been closer to certain examples of 'institutionalized' symbolism, such as that of the Vatican, identified above as a fourth distinct configuration. Notwithstanding their vast differences of scale and elaborateness, and their differentiation of functions, the two latter cases had in common that the incumbents of central roles performed essentially symbolic functions. To followers and outsiders alike, they suggest a supreme level of unity and power associated with these roles, although on closer inspection this impression may not reflect quite accurately the level and diversity of actual power divisions. In fact, an inverse correlation is again suggested, namely, the greater the ceremonialization of a particular role, possibly the weaker the actual 'command' powers of its incumbents. Is it not the case, for example, that, like the Omugabe of Nkore, the papal incumbents of the Vatican – with its worldly presence reduced to an absolute minimum – basically have no way to exert power except by calling on certain supra-human and metaphysical values or qualities? Both the Pope and the Omugabe, incidentally, have been viewed as direct earthly representatives of God and Ruhanga respectively.

But to consider these inverse relationships between symbolism and actual power is by no means to deny that spiritual or ideological influence may emanate from a particular office, role, or institution. In some instances, including the two just mentioned, such influence may, in fact, be extremely pervasive and therefore powerful. It is even conceivable that this non-physical (but so highly visible) 'power' will constitute a key antidote to centrifugal forces, ensuring the continued cohesiveness of the political or religious community concerned. That again was found to hold true for the Omugabe of Nkore (Doornbos, 1975), and it has been equally applicable to the Vatican.

The particular kind and quality of influence that may radiate from a symbolic office (however weak it might otherwise be) has evidently caught the attention of many political figures and aspiring leaders who hope to cultivate rapport and obtain support from the populace. It is evident that this symbolic power cannot work unless there is indeed such a sense of popularity, allegiance and legitimacy to begin with. Examples of its working *do* no doubt occur, though they are definitely fewer than they are claimed to be. In fact, it is quite probably because such examples are known to have occurred and are conceivable in the first place that mock symbolism such as that identified among the first and second types above can occur at all, offering form in lieu of substance. For this reason, too, and especially in the case of new ceremonial, chances are that Ankole kingship will prove to belong to the surrogate, rather than to the genuine, variety.

Thus we have a double inversion: of 'high' symbolism and weak actual powers; and of 'mock' symbolism and lack of popular allegiance. In reality, to be sure, these inverse correlations may well occur in some fused form. In particular, the dividing line between examples of high symbolic exaltation and mock ceremonial is one along which variations and mutations are likely to be found in day-to-day reality. Movement through time is equally conceivable along this line. The Nkore-Ankole case is an example of such movement; increasingly, it has shifted from the first to the second kind of inversion, in other words, from an intrinsically symbolic role into its caricature. As it happened, the change remained relatively minor in terms of actual power: at both ends of the line, the Omugabe's powers *vis-à-vis* the other forces within the political context of Nkore and Ankole, respectively, were quite limited.

Finally, while such distinctions and contrasts may be traced at many levels, in diverse contexts and in different historical epochs, thus adding a certain universal quality to the phenomena as analytical problems, it is interesting to note that they were also identified in this way in times long past. Thus, Gibbon, in *The Decline and Fall of the Roman Empire*, contrasted the exaltation and actual powers of the German and Roman emperors, respectively, in a way that is still perfectly relevant to our present concerns: 'If we annihilate the interval of time and space between Augustus and Charles, strong and striking will be the contrast between the two Caesars; the Bohemian, who concealed his weaknesses under the mask of ostentation, and the Roman who disguised his strength under the semblance of modesty' (Gibbon, 1789:312). Again, *plus ça change, plus c'est la même chose*.

Postscript (1998)

Political developments in Buganda in the early 1990s led to an unexpected revisit of the kingship issue in the former Ankole area. Ankole as such no longer exists as an administrative unit, having been substituted by the new districts of Mbarara and Bushenyi in 1976 and additionally by Ntungamo in the early 1990s. But as monarchical restoration in Buganda, which took effect from 1993, had necessitated an abstract general ruling 'unbanning' all previously existing kingships in Uganda – provided that 'the people so wish' – the other ex-kingdom areas were suddenly faced with the question as to whether or not to initiate steps towards reinstatement of their traditional rulers. Bunyoro and Toro eventually did so, though not without having to negotiate some hurdles: a succession struggle between different claimants in Bunyoro which had to be arbitrated by the Uganda High Court, and reluctant acceptance on the part of the proponents of the Toro court that its jurisdiction would no longer include the new districts of Kasese and Bundibugyo that had gained their separation from Toro.

With respect to the Ankole kingship, a small royalist body did indeed make moves towards restoration, and in November 1993 actually organized a ceremony to 'crown' Prince Barigye as the 22nd Omugabe of Ankole. The coronation ceremony had been publicized as the last funeral rites for the late Omugabe of Ankole, Gasyonga II, so as to keep the initiative a secret until it would be a fait accompli. On the question of restoration, Prince Barigye and his supporters, organized in the Nkore Cultural Trust, were of the opinion that it concerned a purely non-political, cultural institution, and therefore did not require any further popular endorsement or government approval. Pro-restoration advocates argued that kingship was and is of the essence of Ankole culture, and that its restoration therefore was a *sine qua non*, culturally speaking.

Nonetheless, the official 'unbanning' order had specified 'if the people so wish' and the District Councils of Mbarara and Bushenyi had already passed resolutions that they 'did not wish' any such monarchical restoration. Similarly, a second organization that had emerged in defence of Ankole culture in recent years, the Banyankore Cultural Foundation, argued that there is no one-to-one relation between kingship and culture, citing the example of French culture that kept thriving even though the monarchy was terminated, and emphasizing that the same held true for Banyankore culture (Doornbos and Mwesigye, 1995). It should not have been too surprising, therefore, that no sooner did the Museveni government learn of Prince Barigye's coronation as Omugabe than it declared it null and void. Seemingly a non-political, cultural institution, its restoration in a context where a very large majority had little affinity with it, and where it might have come to serve as an untimely reminder of previous ethnic inequality, potentially introduced a highly sensitive political issue that the government felt was better deflated instantly.

Was there a kind of institutional relevance, even if in the negative, to Ankole's kingship after all? One plausible retort with respect to the Ankole example could be that if an institution considered irrelevant is pushed beyond a particular point, it becomes politically relevant again. Whether that is or was the case with the Ankole monarchy may be doubted, however, even if in times to come the idea of revival might be reasserted again. The key fact is that the requisite social basis for the monarchy's restoration just does not seem to exist.

What is most telling about this recent episode, meanwhile, is the fact that for the possible restoration of an institution that in essence is a symbolic one, and thus in principle belonging to the public domain and the public eye, one has thought it opportune to opt for a secretive, in fact a clandestine coronation ceremony, away from popular scrutiny. The contradiction this implies in terms of what this kind of institution is about is enormous, and in final analysis tragically self-defeating.

Part 3

Land, Pastoralism and the State in Eastern Africa: Institutional Interventions

6

Land Tenure, State Intervention and Political Conflict in South West Uganda

Introduction

Among the institutional interventions that have impinged upon socio-economic relations in Africa, those connected with new land tenure arrangements have been among the most pervasive. In design and implementation, institutionalization of land tenure policies has often had major political and social aims and consequences, and thus deserves more detailed analysis within the present context.

Discussions of land tenure arrangements and policies in Africa have often been hampered by the desire to make generalized statements and the practice of restricting the perspective to that of one particular concern at a time. Debates have thus often centred on questions such as whether 'in general' one kind of system, such as individual freehold, is preferable to others, usually some form of communal tenure. And evaluations of such questions are often undertaken with only one set of implications in mind, most frequently agricultural growth alone.

Many such debates have been, and will continue to be, inconclusive and the reasons should not be difficult to see. Usually against the proposition that one form of tenure is 'good' for agricultural development other cases can be cited where it is not good, or not so good. For other or even for the same kind of arrangements the argument can often be reversed, that is, the contention that a policy is not suitable, 'generally', may be countered by an example of where it appears to be relevant. Such confusion appears to result not primarily from complexity of land tenure but from simplicity of thought. *General* pro and con debates are erroneously based on an assumption that alternative land tenure systems are *intrinsically* good or bad and that they can thus be evaluated irrespective of specific situational contexts stand strategies of rural development.

Significantly, this kind of argument seems to be related to, and pre-suppose, a particular view of African realities as far as land tenure is concerned. It is not uncommon to come across propositions which say, with greater or lesser explicitness, that this or that system is 'suitable for Africa'. Can one conceive of any such points being made about Europe? Evidently not; conditions would most probably be found too complex and diversified to allow such generalizations to be made, and the likely retort is that it will largely depend on the specifics of a particular situation. Then why is the point made in regard to Africa? If this is taken one step further we may note that 'suitable for Africa' postulates usually find their corollary in an accompanying statement that African land tenure is based on 'communal ownership'. In actual fact, however, African realities too are far more complex and diverse than that they would justify any such generalized description. For long already, it has been recognized that the term 'communal tenure' is exceedingly obscure and confusing (Brock, 1968). Rather than representing any reflection of reality, therefore, one is led to suspect that the postulation of generally similar conditions, supposedly true for much of Africa, is but a logical requisite for claims of general applicability of particular policy proposals, whether for freehold tenure or any other arrangement.

Restriction of the analysis to only one set of implications, usually production, accelerates the ease with which generalizations are made, for the simple reason that it ignores other effects. For example, if no increase or decrease in production is demonstrated following some land reform innovation, then all too easily the instrument on the books may be regarded as simply irrelevant. This disregards other effects, especially social and political implications, which in some cases may be momentous and which might possibly even prevent reaching any more specifically production-orientated objectives. (To be sure, policies *may* well remain dead letters but even that, it should be understood, depends on context). Such approaches not only amount to oversimplification of analysis, they also have potential policy-*making* implications. While broad generalizations about 'the system in Africa' can be seen to have an effect on the kind of policies being suggested, concentration on one set of effects (and disregard for others) can lead to an essentially *experimental* attitude towards policy-formulation. Preoccupation with agricultural growth alone may preclude awareness that policies which agriculturally remain irrelevant can produce social side-effects which, once created, may become extremely hard to undo.

These initial remarks are just to suggest that a variety of variables as they pertain to specific conditions must be taken into account both in evaluating and in anticipating policy effects. More concretely, it implies a need to (1) *increase* the range of analytical dimensions to be considered (thus, the political and social as well as the economic effects, to use these inadequate terms); and (2) *decrease* the level of generality of analyses or, in other words, to concentrate rather on the specific conditions of particular situations. The first of these requirements points up the necessity to explore policy repercussions in terms of, among other things, potential group conflict, relative advantages and disadvantages and long-term social differentiation effects. The second requirement means that these effects must be explored as they may arise in whatever particular regional or local context in which the policies concerned are being applied.

It is only on such a basis that one can begin to meaningfully undertake comparative analysis of policy impacts and hope to arrive at more generalized propositions. One may then well find that similar policies have different effects in different situations, depending on the way in which different variables relate to one another in each case. Also, if a simple heuristic distinction between economic and social effects is made, then to the extent that land policies *have* effect they may be found to be either (1) economically productive and socially counter-productive or detrimental; (2) economically non-productive and socially 'productive', that is, just or equitable; (3) economically unproductive and also socially counter-productive; or (4) economically and socially productive. Of course this is no more than a crude rule of thumb and not the least important qualification that must be added is a further need to be alerted to a very possible divergence between political and social objectives and/or effects. Particularly, criteria of political expediency and social equity may be found to be at variance in the formulation or implementation of land tenure policies.

Again, one will further want to see how different situational factors are interrelated and impinge upon one another. Quite conceivably, for example, a policy aiming at agricultural growth may turn into a political issue which, for that very reason, prevents the objective from being reached. In another situation that same policy might well have some discernible effect on growth; or not, if the instrument itself is of questionable efficacy. Similarly, a policy which is initiated primarily for reasons of political gain may have negative effects agriculturally and eventually, perhaps, will turn out to be politically counter-productive. It is thus plain that a variety of factors must be carefully considered before any relevant assessments of land tenure policies can be made. Equally plain is that policy makers need to be clear about exactly what objectives they have in mind.

Two caveats must finally be added to these introductory points. One is that saying that much depends on specific contexts and conditions is *not* the same as saying it all depends on traditional systems, practices of land use, allocation and so on. As already noted in Chapter 4 in more general terms, demands may well be mediated by cultural factors but what usually emerges in response to externally initiated programmes are plain interests which can hardly be explained by reference to traditional values or structures alone. What we can note here, though, is that basic to any assessment of policy responses – and thus effects – must be an examination of the relative opportunities offered and perceived in the instruments concerned. It is thus quite conceivable that new policy propositions will elicit entirely novel and differentiated individual and collective reactions and interests.

The other point is implicit throughout the above, but still worth stating. It is that when reiterating the need to consider the political implications of land tenure policies over and beyond their immediate agricultural ramifications, this is not to say that policies may or may not have political implications. In an important sense there are *always* political implications; at times, however, they are more explicit, visible or problematic than at others. Shortage of words may induce usage of the term 'political' in a more restricted and specific sense, but that is by no means to imply that an absence of immediate political issues surrounding the introduction of a land tenure programme absolves us from the need to anticipate its likely effects on political relationships in the longer run.

Land tenure and political dynamics in Ankole

This chapter will discuss two examples of how land tenure questions have come to be related to political conflict. The data are derived from the former Ankole District in the Western Region of Uganda (now subdivided into Mbarara, Bushenyi and Ntungamo Districts), more specifically from the centrally located Shema County within the district. The cases, concerned with *mailo* land grants and the introduction of individual freehold titles respectively, are examples of two different ways in which land tenure policies have cut into social networks. In both situations the effects of land policies on social and political relationships over and beyond their immediate economic and land use implications became matters of major conflict and concern.

Before detailing how issues have arisen in connection with these policies, some brief background to Ankole society and to land use in the district will be necessary. Ankole came under British rule at the turn of the century, its formal incorporation into Uganda being based on the Ankole Agreement of 1901 between the British and the Omugabe and principal chiefs of Ankole. In 1975 the district comprised close to a million inhabitants, most of whom were indigenous to the area. Two socio-political divisions of concern to the land issues to be discussed are (1) the historical ethnic division between Bairu and Bahima; and (2) a religious cleavage between Protestants and Catholics. Over and above its ethnic base, the Bairu-Bahima division was based on social status – the Bairu majority, about 90 percent of the population, for long enjoying fewer political and economic rights than the Bahima minority, about 5 percent – and on different occupational pursuits – Bairu being primarily agriculturalists, the Bahima primarily cattle-keepers. The religious cleavage resulted from the vagaries of missionary penetration and, with the exception of a small Muslim minority, had split the population of Ankole into roughly 50 percent Protestants and 50 percent Catholics, with virtually all converted Bahima identifying as Protestants and Bairu Catholics being in slightly larger numbers than Bairu Protestants. For many years the resulting ethnic-religious cleavage has been basic to the complexities of political conflict and coalitions in Ankole. Major issues arose out of differential access to resources which each of the three groups (Bahima, Protestant Bairu and Catholic Bairu) could expect from the common pool. Bahima privileges were initially sustained and strengthened by the British and for many years Bairu political pressure was therefore directed at challenging the ethnic inequality in the allocation of resources during colonial times. In a (Bahima and British) Protestant-dominated framework, Protestant Bairu nonetheless stood a better chance of obtaining political rewards such as jobs, scholarships and government assistance than did Catholic Bairu. As a result, Protestant Bairu had an earlier and somewhat larger share in economic welfare than the Catholics, as evidenced for instance in a lead in cash-crop cultivation and educational performance by the Protestants. Protest against Bahima hegemony, however, did also largely emanate from Protestant and not from Catholic Bairu circles, the reasons for which lay partly in the fact that educationally and economically Protestant Bairu felt more strongly that they were entitled to political benefits equal to those of the Bahima. Catholic Bairu felt left out by the entire Protestant camp (Bahima and Bairu) and finally saw a greater threat in the political ascendancy of Protestant Bairu than in the declining Bahima overrule. When in the 1950s party politics made its entry in Ankole, Catholic Bairu thus joined the Bahima in the Democratic Party to contest the Protestant Bairu, while the latter all moved into the Uganda People's Congress (Doornbos, 1970).

The general picture of land use and acquisition in Ankole during the first half of this century and beyond could either be called simple or complex, depending on how one looks at it and what one would look for (see Map 1). Access to land was relatively unproblematic for most people during most of the time. Pre-1900 there were mainly two ways in which individuals could get access to a piece of land: by inheritance or by opening up a new plot (Stenning, 1958). The latter involved the need for consent of the local people and chief, which does not seem to have been particularly difficult to obtain. In recent decades, there have been three main ways of getting access to land. Again inheritance and opening up new land (though the latter possibility has been rapidly coming to a close) and in addition purchase, either of land held under customary tenure or freehold. Land is nowadays purchased either for cultivation or for purposes of investment, speculation and prestige. The latter rationale has become increasingly popular in recent times. One of the things 'to do' for members of the Banyankore élite or aspirants to it is to buy a piece of land in the vicinity of Mbarara, Bushenyi and other urban centres. In other areas land is also acquired and often involves quite sizeable portions, with examples of stretches of up to several square miles. Among other things, this trend has suggested a shift from investment in cattle as the traditional embodiment of wealth to one in land. A different arrangement, which has been the object of similar kinds of economic and political pressure, is the *Ankole Ranching Scheme*, which will be discussed in Chapter 7 of this volume.

If for both the pre-1900 period and the recent past the picture of access to land was relatively straightforward, it is more difficult to ascertain the basis and mechanisms of ownership (as opposed to acquisition). Though these questions are not the main concern of this chapter, some brief discussion will be useful. Puzzles about 'ownership' appear to be partly due to complexity of arrangements, to confusion in terminology, and to interests aroused in ownership. These three sources have been reinforcing each other in no small degree. Complexity of 'ownership' is suggested by the fact that at least at four different intervals, in 1906, 1926, 1961 and 1965, official enquiries were conducted to clarify the system of land tenure in Ankole. Without going into details, one may further note that in either period a variety of different kinds of rights were exercised in land in Ankole, thus suggesting a degree of 'real' complexity. Pre-1900, for instance, it was clear that a peasant who cultivated a piece of land had certain rights in it, his clan members or neighbours had other rights, the local chief had a further say, while the Omugabe was seen as the notional 'owner' of all land. Obviously, none of this meant ownership in any strictly legal Western sense of the term, though failure to recognize this has not been conducive to clarity. In recent times, again, ownership questions have yielded diversified answers, though of different kinds, including notions of customary tenure, individual freehold, *mailo* freehold (until recently official and private), leasehold, and simply government land. Without detailing these forms here, it should be noted that the exact status of any particular piece of land has not always been immediately clear by reference to any of these descriptive terms; cryptically 'ownership' may well at times clash with 'ownership' (Apthorpe, 1968).

More pertinent is the fact that complexity and confusion have spiralled following new interests. This is not a novel phenomenon, but it has been basic to the kind of land issues which developed in Ankole. In part, the pursuit of interests has been made possible by exploiting the area of terminological confusion with regard to land rights. Already in 1907, an Acting Collector in Ankole reported:

> It is not even easy to tell what were in fact the old-time customs, and what are the changes in these. For in most cases one finds that the stories of witnesses have a way of coinciding with their interests. The Kabakka [king] and those who follow his lead bring forward the view that the Kabakka had absolute and unqualified ownership of all Ankole and all the property in it. Certain of the chiefs lay stress on the idea of a system resembling the Feudal. The peasants are of course for the most part inarticulate, in so far at any rate as the Government Official is concerned, but from what has been said by the Revds. Father Le Tehic and W. E. Owen, from certain remarks let fall by chiefs, and from what has been told me by a few of themselves, I think that they may be credited with considering that they possess something in the nature of ownership of the lands they occupy (letter from the Acting Collector, Mbarara Collectorate to the Sub-Commissioner, Western Province, 8th April 1907).

These observations hardly need further comment. They illustrate how different kinds of 'rights', traditionally exercised at various levels and each of a different order and specificity, can be advanced to support a particular position by translation into the term 'ownership'. The strategy did not easily subside; even at the time of issuing the first new freehold titles, in the late 1950s, opposition to the scheme was in part based on the contention that all land belonged to the Omugabe and thus could not be 'alienated'.

While noting some of the complexities in regard to the status of land in Ankole, it must be reiterated that well into this century matters of land use and acquisition were relatively unproblematic for most people, notwithstanding the fact that there has been a good deal of litigation about where fences are drawn up and related kinds of questions. (Enclosure in recent times occurred not only on freehold land but increasingly also on customarily held land, which strictly speaking belongs to the government). To be sure, the exhaustion of possibilities of opening up new land and the foreseeable shortage of land leading to the emergence of a landless category are likely to make these questions highly problematic. The point is that the issues to be discussed here have long tended to be atypical for the whole of the Ankole region, though that does not lessen the importance of the effects of policy measures which they exemplify.

Further complexities aside, one significant difference immediately suggested by a pre-1900 and post-independence comparison is the commercialization of land as a factor of production. No matter what mechanisms were used or what was the legal basis of acquired plots (*mailo*, freehold, customary tenure or even leasehold), increasing frequency of sales and rents indicate the basic fact that land had acquired a new economic value, expressed in monetary terms. That fact would require its own explanation, for the general process of which one would need to turn to an examination of how capitalism pervaded this rural part of Africa. Although certain policies (*mailo*, individual freehold) undoubtedly added to this trend or provided an alternative route towards commercialization, this does not necessarily mean that they were the most important single factor in this process. Nonetheless, stating that is already throwing up one implication for land policies. While often one argument advanced in favour of introducing individual freehold tenure has held that it will better enable farmers to make investments, cultivate the land as they see fit and engage in cash-crop cultivation, much of the Ankole region provided another example of how even relatively capital-intensive cash-crop production (coffee and tea especially) could be undertaken without there being any prior 'security' of tenure of the kind provided by a freehold land title (Brock, 1968). That fact in turn suggests the possibility that if new economically-based interests can be seen to be aroused in land following policy innovations, such interests may not primarily be for cultivation purposes but rather in land as a commodity, hence arising from extra-agricultural objectives.

The Shema context

Other interests than agricultural ones were of no small importance to the questions of *mailo* land and individual freehold land titles in Ankole.

Shema county, in which these issues prompted most attention and controversy, in several ways represented a microcosm of Ankole society. Somewhat ambiguously, this very fact had a great deal to say, first, about why the two schemes were located there in the first place (the freehold issue played in Shema only, the *mailo* question was not restricted to Shema but had a greater impact there than in other counties); and, second, about why the schemes – even if they were also introduced elsewhere – should have provoked dispute particularly in Shema. (There is also a third connection, in that the freehold issue was probably enhanced by the fact that *mailo* was present in Shema, and vice versa.)

One characteristic of Shema was the presence of Bairu and Bahima in roughly similar proportions to their distribution in the Ankole district as a whole. While in contrast Nyabushozi county to the east, for example, traditionally had a predominantly Bahima population, or Buhweju to the north an almost exclusively Bairu population, in Shema the large majority of people were Bairu and a small minority, estimated to be around 5 percent, Bahima. Thus, any Ankole-wide Bairu-Bahima cleavages stood a greater chance of being physically and visibly manifested here. By the same token, Shema inevitably was one of the areas where two different ways of land use, for cultivation and for pasturage, would coexist and potentially clash. It needs re-emphasizing that Bairu had acquired increasing numbers of cattle throughout this century; nonetheless, as long as Bahima had their primary interest in cattle, and Bairu in cultivation, these contrasting (pre-)occupations could not but enter into their respective assessments of access and rights to land.

These and other questions tended to be further emphasized because of the fact that Shema was one of the most densely populated areas of the Ankole district. New land was and is virtually non-available in Shema and pressure on or about land would accordingly be more intense. As we will see, it was also the density of population in Shema which first brought some of the major *mailo* estates there (because of the 'availability' of tenants, inevitably Bairu; the *mailo* estates here have been mainly if not exclusively Bahima-owned). Later that density was one of the reasons for the land title scheme, since it was believed that this kind of programme would be the next logical step in a situation where land was becoming scarce and expensive.

It must also be noted that Shema's relatively central geographic position had made it 'first' in a variety of respects: first in major school expansion, first in the impetus to cash-crop cultivation, thus first too in the spread and creation of new interests, new skills and to an extent new wealth. In part it also accounted for why the two land schemes became an issue in Shema. Protest against a newly institutionalized inequality, as the *mailo* system was experienced, was likely to become more intense in an area that became otherwise highly exposed to new influences. Furthermore, the land titles which were coveted by those farmers who were very much products of these transformations, were resented by those that had a less active, or less profitable part in that process.

Shema county also reflected the religious divisions within Ankole as a whole. While some areas such as Bunyaruguru were solidly Roman Catholic and others more predominantly Protestant, Shema was one of the counties where Protestant and Catholic missionaries for long competed in proselytizing efforts. Both Protestants and Catholics were strongly represented in Shema, though in more than one way Protestants have had a certain edge over the Catholics. To readers unfamiliar with the Ankole area, linking religion to economic welfare may well sound like reintroducing Weber's Protestant Ethic as an explanatory variable. While that is not intended here, and while statistical data are lacking, the common observation that there have been more 'better-offs' among the Protestants than among Catholics still needs to be related. Nor is this surprising, for, as suggested earlier, in a society where government had been very strongly Protestant based and biased it stands to reason to expect Protestants to have had better chances educationally, economically and occupationally.

Thus, if we juxtapose and relate these various factors we can see that in Shema, in an even more pronounced way than in Ankole as a whole, ethnic and religious cleavages were compounded and were being reinforced by economic and political differences. A Protestant Bairu challenge to Bahima preponderance in Ankole had special relevance, and roots, in the Shema situation. Catholic Bairu misgivings about Protestant Bairu ascendancy had an immediate origin in, and bearing upon, socio-political relationships within Shema. Density of population and differential economic change exacerbated these contrasting interests and orientations to a greater degree than in most other parts of Ankole. No wonder, then, that questions arising out of newly defined rights in land should have become particularly salient and controversial here.

The mailo scheme

The *mailo* issue was simple in origin, complex in consequence. This term is derived from neighbouring Buganda and refers to square 'miles' which the British also issued there, though in even greater numbers. Its background was basically political. In Ankole the British 'gave' away square miles to members of the *élite* who in 1901 signed the Ankole Agreement and thus sanctioned and facilitated British entry. At the original allocation the Omugabe received 50 square miles, the Enganzi 16 miles, while the ten most senior chiefs were given 10 miles each. With one possible exception, all these beneficiaries were Bahima. Mailo estates were further granted to churches, while later (notably between 1921 and 1924) additional allocations were made partly to reward newly recruited chiefs who replaced some of the original *mailo* allottees who had been removed from office, partly to some of the World War I veterans, and partly to some incumbent chiefs who were successful in pressing for more. Each of these allocations were of private freehold land which could be alienated; in addition the Omugabe and chiefs received official *mailo* land, that is, specified distributions of square miles as lifetime estates or as long as their holders remained in office.

Technically these alienations were made possible because the British had in the same Ankole Agreement declared all land in Ankole to be Crown land. Another technical provision, however, was not followed up. It was that, according to the terms of the Agreement, the *mailo* grants ought to be demarcated in 'waste and uncultivated' land. Instead the allottees were allowed to carve out their grants in populated areas and their interests were almost immediately focused on some of the most densely populated parts of the district. Shema county was one of these and even in the immediate vicinity of the location where later the first freehold titles would be issued some 8.5 miles of *mailo* land were consolidated. Not until a very late stage, too late to make any alterations, were questions asked about the deviation from the principle that only waste and uncultivated land could be considered for demarcations. Meanwhile, stipulations that were introduced on the books about the amount of rent and other privileges derivable from the *mailo* estates suggested that this shift met with definite official approval.

It is illustrative to note how *interests* were induced by the policy of *mailo* grants. Early on already some transfers took place from less to more heavily populated areas, indicating an appreciation of the capitalized value of the new estates. The interpretations of the 'traditional' system that we noted were offered by the Omugabe and chiefs of Ankole may also be seen in this connection. These interpretations provided rationalizations and claims for benefits in the new system on the basis of a very narrow translation of 'rights', and only one kind of rights, that existed in the old. The inducement of interests was further evidenced by an appetite for more. Instead of appeasing the Ankole *élite* through the special privileges bestowed upon them, the policy came to be understood as one that contained the possibility of being extended and thus created an interest group that was disgruntled because pleas for more were not readily accepted. Misunderstandings further complicated the situation and prolonged haggling evidently was the result. For instance, in 1923, according to a statement of the Enganzi, 'the chief dissatisfaction over the land settlement is over the 800 miles [*sic*] which was promised to the Ankole Chiefs ... and which have not yet been granted' (letter from District Commisioner, Ankole, to the Provincial Commissioner, Western Province, March 10th, 1923).

Piecemeal adjustments were nonetheless made from time to time and possibly stimulated escalation of demands. In the same statement quoted above, the Enganzi continued to say that as for himself, 'I was not grumbling as my miles were increased to 30'. District reports and minutes of *baraza* meetings with the Ankole chiefs throughout the 1920s and 1930s (the period in which this reporting became more complete and elaborate than it had been in previous years) almost invariably contained a standard item on *mailo* issues. Some examples illustrate this recurrence; they also indicate some of the complexities of administration – and some apparent inconsistencies – that arose following the introduction of the *mailo* system:

1922: The Land Officer who was able to attend for a few minutes informed the Baraza that their Mailos could not be marked out by Surveyors till next year. He reminded them that no land could be transferred or sold until final Certificates had been received, and that no work could be done at present on any land other than Agreement mailos.

Shamba Evictions: This always has caused ill feelings and tends to emigration. Owners cannot turn people off their land unless they refuse to pay rent. The people must be made to feel that their homes are permanent. P.C. gives a public warning that such evictions must stop, as the government is strongly opposed to them, and will if necessary take action by Legislation.

Ntende (brewing): Is illegitimate and further is cause of increasing drunkenness. On private mailos government will not interfere. But on Official mailos it is expressly forbidden; this also applies to Lukiko Estates.

1923, January. Land: (1) All claims that have been passed must be marked out at once. Those that have not been passed may be heard in the Saza Courts, and if undisputed will be recommended forthwith by D.C. If disputed, they will be forwarded for D.C.'s decision. (2) No claims for private mailos which include cultivated land not belonging to claimant, will be entertained. (3) Chiefs should check the extent of Mission plots. In the majority of cases they have much more than they are entitled to.

Rents: P.C. cannot agree to Lukiko's proposal that hut tax should not be reduced. It must in future be Rps.2, instead of Rps.3. Until further notice rent will only be collected from private and official mailos and in every case a receipt will be given and Registers kept.

Extra land: P.C. cannot agree to the extra private mailos asked for.

Shambas for Banyiginya (Babito): Reference yesterday's petition for land for Babito, Mukwende requests Gombolola chiefs to be included. P.C. says no. If a man who had done really good work retires he may get a grant of Lukiko Butaka for life which was the reason for the Lukiko Butaka. Out of a very large salary and large number of private mailos the Omugabe has, he should make provision for the great majority of his relations.

1924: Mailos: Certain lists of miles still outstanding ... Informed the Lukiko that the Provincial Commissioner will be coming in August to finish the Mailos and that if the men entitled to Mailos don't send their lists they will have to mark them on waste-land [*sic*].

Markets on Chief's Private Mailos: Pokino asks if Mailo Owner can get some part of market dues in these cases. Told him not on any account. Rather than that the markets must be moved to Official land.

1926: There would be nobody turned out of his shamba if he cultivated outside a private mailo unless that shamba were wanted for public purposes; then compensation would be paid to the shamba owner. That had been provided for by the Land Rules given out by the District Commissioner.

Mutuba II Kashali asked what was to happen to the coffee planted on a chief's official land on that chief's transfer elsewhere. The P.C. replied that coffee need not necessarily be planted on their official land. It could be planted on their chief's land and they could leave somebody in charge of it . . . The Muwali asked if in mailos the chiefs should include shambas of others. The P.C. replied that land was given for the use of the church and the growing of teachers' food and was not to be used for collecting rent.

1930: The Katikiro enquired about the position of Native Landowners under the new arrangements whereby Poll Tax and Busulu are paid on one ticket. The Provincial Commissioner repeated the assurance of H.E. The Governor that these Landowners would not lose financially; and reminded the Chiefs that money was available for refund when the Landowners applied for it. He trusted they would do so with greater promptness in future.

1934: 3 Saza chiefs to be given a mile: Yihimba said that we recommended 3 Saza chiefs, Rubuga and the son of lgumira to be given a mile each. But D.C. answered that I will have to answer you in future.

These various entries not only suggest how *mailo* land over the years continued to attract the attention of the Ankole chiefly *élite*, but also that all sorts of arrangements in regard to demarcation, registration, transfer, rent collection and other obligations and privileges became necessary following the initiation of the policy. In effect the instrument of colonial development that the chiefs were designed to be itself came to command a very central share of time, energies and resources. Not surprisingly, perhaps, in his farewell address a departing District Commissioner thus told the chiefs: 'When you are in your barazas, you prefer discussing about chieftainship, about your salaries, your cattle and so on; but you discuss nothing regarding the peasants' (Baraza held on December 18th 1929, D.C.'s Baraza Book, Ankole).

In the give and take of *mailo* land it was the peasants who received the short end of the stick. *Mailo* land for a long time entitled their owners to rent, labour and tribute from the peasants living within the estates. Besides, the Bairu tenants often found difficulty in upholding their property rights on their crops and belongings, faced restrictions imposed by their landlords on the improvement of their houses and gardens, and for long lacked any security of tenure and could be evicted at the whim of the *mailo* owner. These burdens and constraints were felt even more strongly because peasants who happened to live just outside the *mailo* estates could develop their land without restriction and interference. From time to time new regulations were introduced that were intended to strengthen the position of the tenant, mainly by restricting his obligations to his landlord to rent only and by putting checks on the landlord's right of eviction. A variety of these new rules were codified in the Ankole Landlord and Tenant Law of 1937. While this constituted an improvement on the books, it did not alter the basic dependency relationship nor the contrast to non-*mailo* peasants. It should be realized that it first required a good deal of evidence of the exercise of powers by the landlords before ameliorative legislation was undertaken and that it further required a fair amount of time before the implications of the new rules would be appreciated by both landlords and tenants.

As it happened, the Ankole Landlord and Tenant Law was not published until 1957, which did not seem conducive to creating this clarity (Uganda Protectorate, 1957). That it was not, can be gathered from the fact that the recommendations of a commission appointed in 1965 by the Ankole government to enquire into the question of *mailo* lands again included the need for abolition of tenants' tribute and labour, the prohibition of arbitrary evictions and the requirement of proper compensation for the tenants' property. The list of tenant grievances with the *mailo* system has been long and includes such varied items as the demand to vote for the landlord's party, the destruction of their crops due to the landlord's cattle running through their fields (at times, it is claimed, on purpose), the extra rent demanded from shopkeepers operating on the *mailo*, and the landlords' practice of settling disputes in their own 'courts', in addition to the basic issues of rent, tribute, labour, property restrictions, evictions and compensations. Over and above individual inconveniences and hardships, the *mailo* system had adverse economic and political consequences for the district as a whole. Economically the system's negative effects have been beyond question. Restrictions of many kinds prevented tenants from making lasting improvements to their plots and from reinvesting towards increased production. Involving some 20,000 tenants at the beginning of the 1970s, this category would have been able to contribute more fully to the district's development if they had not been incorporated into the *mailo* system.

Politically the system gave rise to a sense of insecurity and grievance which tended to be shared by people who themselves were not immediately affected. Coupled with the ethnic subordination of which it was both a result and a condition, the *mailo* system operated as a major factor in sustaining the basic divisions and moving forces of Ankole politics. Protests were picked up and reiterated over the years in the Protestant Bairu camp as additional grounds for their grievances against the Bahima. The 1965 enquiry was essentially a product of this sentiment, but one reason why it did not lead to major changes was the make-up of political divisions within the district's leadership at the time. This leadership did not wish to openly identify itself with the causes of any ethnic or religious section of the population and it consequently adopted a willy-nilly attitude both to the enquiry and to the recommendations (Ankole Government, 1965a, 1965b).

The Ankole *mailo* system thus turned out to be one of those issues whose negative aspects have been outstanding but which are nonetheless extremely hard to undo. Its anomalies were many and stood out even more sharply due to general advancements in the areas in which *mailo* estates were located, particularly in Shema. It was nonetheless continued, partly because of the fact that *mailo* land had been irrevocably issued as private freehold property (and part of which had been alienated by the original owners or their inheritors and has continued to change hands since then) and because general applicability of statutes forbade repealing those which happened to govern the Ankole *mailo* system. Political and social conditions militated against change in addition to these legal constraints. Without going into details, it must be noted that the balance of powers in Ankole district politics at the time, first between Bahima and Catholic Bairu on the one hand and Protestant Bairu on the other, then shifting to a more subtle but no less profound cleavage that also involved a division among the Protestant Bairu, prevented consensus from emerging on issues in which historically one ethnic group, or a section of it, had been the losing party.

Socially this position was reinforced by a variety of conditions which might have worked out differently in another constellation. One of those pertains to the question why mailo tenants did not move out to new land where they would not face interference by landlords. Some no doubt have done so. The many others who did not, however, clearly belonged to the category whose limited resources would make such a move extremely difficult to undertake. Not only did they generally have a weaker economic base than other people in the area, but the prospect of receiving none or at best a very minimal compensation for their property was not particularly conducive to their migration. Another factor that for long perpetuated the dependency relations inherent in the *mailo* system was the fact that, contrary to what happened to the much larger *mailo* grants issued in Buganda, for a long time *mailo* land in Ankole was rarely sold.

A good part of the *mailo* land is still in the hands of the original owners or their successors. Generally exchange only became more frequent since the 1960s and, incidentally, the fact that some leading members of each of Ankole's ethnic and religious political groups since then had acquired pieces of *mailo* land did not help to get the issue clearly defined. Of particular significance remained the fact that by and large the Bahima élite who acquired the *mailo* estates for long did not sell them and neither felt induced to turn them into agriculturally productive propositions. In part they lacked these inducements because their major concern was commonly with livestock. Livestock itself required a certain freedom of movement, which was to an extent guaranteed by the rights in *mailo* land. In addition, and perhaps more basically, the *mailo* arrangement was a convenient and strategic way of ensuring a domain within which ethnic inequality, and the prestige derivable from it, could be maintained. With the spread of new occupational roles which are no longer based on a syndrome of relationships that involves cattle-ownership on the one hand and landlord-tenant roles on the other, the *mailo* system has tended to lose this function. Until that process is completed, however, the *mailo* system is safeguarded by a combination of legal and political obstacles; and it is conceivable that in the end only increased transactions and fragmentation will finally obliterate the arrangement. If nothing else, the case may illustrate that land policies at times face greater problems in undoing or correcting previous measures than in innovating new ones.

The individual land titles scheme

The land title scheme was a second externally initiated policy applied to Ankole. Following increased attention for matters of land tenure during the terminal colonial period and more specifically on the basis of the 1955 East African Royal Commission Report, the Uganda government undertook the encouragement of individual freehold ownership with the declared objective of promoting economic development (Uganda Protectorate, 1955). The policy was discussed with all district councils but met with little enthusiasm or understanding (Uganda Protectorate, Government Printer, 1962:41). There was some interest only in Kigezi, Ankole and Bugisu and consequently pilot schemes were launched in these three districts. In Ankole the scheme was sited in the densely populated Kagango and Shuku sub-counties of Shema county.

The scheme was rationalized in terms familiar for policies of individualization. A freehold title would help establish clear property rights, boundaries and fences, provide the security of tenure that would permit the making of improvements on land conducive towards further commercialization, facilitate sales and loans, and prevent transmission of infectious cattle disease. To this end a system of adjudication and certification was established which involved a procedure that seemed more characterized by concern for constraints and precautions than for complexity. Among other things, it called for the application of the adjudication rules by official notice to a particular district, followed by the declaration by the District Commissioner of a parish to be an adjudication area, then the election of an adjudication committee composed of between fifteen and twenty-five adult male taxpayers of the area, the surveying of the land by air photography and the erection of beacons to be photographed, the application by any occupant of land to be registered as a freehold proprietor, the issuance of an official adjudication notice to be publicly displayed for thirty days, a meeting of the adjudication committee to which representations can be made and objections raised, the preparation by the committee of a certificate giving all details of the land concerned for use by the District Commissioner, the public display of this certificate for another thirty days and reference of the case to the court if anyone wished to appeal against the proposed issuance of title, the signing of the certificate by the D.C. and again its subsequent public display giving the name of the recognized owner, the application by the owner for a freehold title, and the issuance of such title after his payment of the fees (Uganda Protectorate, 1962:9–1).

A beginning was made with implementation of the scheme in 1958, but it soon became the subject of political controversy. Action was suspended between the end of 1958 to 1959 pending an appeal to the High Court that the scheme's legality was unfounded (the Ankole district council had had no quorum when giving it its approval; but that, the court ruled, was immaterial since its approval was not called for), then resumed for the period that the Uganda People's Congress formed the Ankole government, suspended again from early 1962 till September 1963, during the Democratic Party's tenure as the Ankole government, and resumed from 1963 onwards after the UPC had come back into office. Thereafter it became increasingly clear that the mechanics of the scheme required more administration and manpower than was available, so that an estimated backlog of many man-years in surveying piled up; as a result, implementation on the basis of available resources was given low priority while a search for new procedures and even new tenure arrangements was undertaken. In the end the land title scheme, even for purely technical reasons, thus became one more project that simply lingered on, with at most a few thousand titles granted and paid for, having far from reached (or moving to) the level of fulfilment first envisaged in the mid-fifties, but, as it had already been started, it was a project that was difficult to either remove or improve upon.

Whether any agricultural improvement followed in those cases where land titles were obtained is doubtful. Brock suggests that the Uganda pilot schemes, including that of Ankole, led to no discernible increase in economic activity and that as far as sales are concerned plots held in customary tenure continued to be bought and sold without the benefit of surveys, registers or titles (Brock, 1968:11–12). Perhaps one may wish to reserve final judgement on this, if a longer experience with land titles would be required on which to base such an assessment. When doing that, one should be particularly interested to see whether in fact any of the new titles have been used as securities against loans, the one purpose for which it could be claimed that they provide a new element. However, such evaluations are in any case difficult to make because the farmers that applied for titles generally appear to have been those who already were in a stronger economic position than others.

While technical complexities and constraints and also the economic results of a project like the Ankole land title scheme themselves deserve attention, they must not be seen in isolation from the potential social and political ramifications of the project. The latter have been of particular importance in determining attitudes towards the scheme and even in retrospect it is useful to consider these implications and see what social effects the project, if unhampered by technical constraints, might have had. The simplest way of doing this is to relate the project's objectives to the broad interests of the various socio-political groups in the area and to try and see whether there was any logic to the antagonism that followed its introduction. One possible distinction to be kept in mind here is between arguments advanced and the reasons for advancing them; they may be, but are not necessarily the same.

Reasons in favour of the scheme given at the 1961 enquiry and reported by the commissioner included:

1 The concept of freehold land is not a new thing, many notables having held freehold since the 1901 Agreement.
2 The scheme has been voluntary and no one who does not wish to have a title need apply for one. Conversely, if anyone wishes to have a title, he should not be prevented.
3 A freehold title gives the owner a sense of real ownership, and he will take care of what is his.
4 With proper boundaries and a registered title, a man [*sic*] will no longer be plagued by petty boundary disputes, and the courts will be spared much work.

5 With a title, a man can obtain a loan from a bank to help him improve his land.
6 Improved land will benefit the cultivator, the rancher, the mixed farmers, the trader and Ankole as a whole.
7 With a title, a man will be able to fence his land (according to his needs), and thus stop the spread of cattle disease which is the result of 'free for all' grazing.
8 With a title, a man will be able to rest his land without fear of its being spoilt by the indiscriminate grazing of neighbours (Uganda Protectorate, 1962:171).

Reasons against the scheme listed in the report were:

1 All the land in Ankole belongs to the Omugabe, and it should be distributed by him through his Eishengyero. The land titles policy should not interfere with existing rights to land under native custom, and should not interfere with places of common benefit such as pasture, wells, places for the gathering of firewood, thatching material or clay. It should be administered by a body in which people have confidence.
2 The existing policy was introduced by underhand means, the Protectorate Government siding 'in a mysterious alliance' with a few well-to-do people in order to force it on the poor. It was introduced through a court of law 'whose decision is still understood only by lawyers'.
3 The introduction of the policy was accompanied by insults to the Omugabe, and by the arbitrary violation of human rights and the arbitrary taking away of human liberty, never recommended by the World Bank Mission, the Royal Commission on Land in East Africa or the Munster Report 'under which the Protectorate Government is taking refuge'.
4 ...appeals to the District African Court included cases of people who had tried to defend their property rights against the chiefs. Because of the expense and delays in the appeal procedure, many cases went unheard.
5 It was understood when the Shema scheme was introduced that only a man's property would be dealt with. In fact other people's land was taken and added to that of an applicant for title.
6 Areas of pasture, sources of firewood and building materials were taken into adjudicated areas.

7   As a result of such detestable consequences, the scheme is very unpopular, as is instanced by the small number of applicants for titles. Since 1959 about 26 people have obtained final certificates: only about 30 have paid survey fees, and applications for land titles number 800 in the pilot scheme and 1,200 outside it.

8   The question of land titles should be decided by the London Conference, and the Protectorate Government must be undermining that Conference by implementing a policy before the results are known.

9   The chiefs take advantage of the scheme to snatch land for themselves and their friends.

10   Communal grazing areas are taken by chiefs and given to cultivators. Cattle owners are therefore squeezed out.

11   Chiefs compelled many people to apply for title.

12   People were not given sufficient time to study the scheme before it was put into operation.

13   The survey fees were too high: only the rich could afford them.

14   That the titles scheme is a device to enable Europeans to take the land.

15   That the muluka chief should not be chairman of the adjudication committee (Uganda Protectorate, 1962:11–13).

Most of these views need little further comment. Some are concrete and represent straightforward pros and cons. Others are evidently rationalizations (for example, the Omugabe argument), attempts to refer the issue into a dead alley (the London Conference point) or justifications on other than the scheme's own merits (the 1901 analogy). However, none of these reduce the sense of controversy which surrounded the issue, some of the basic motivations for which may not have been expressed, or expressible. Also, the commissioner looked into actual grievances submitted, and in his report dismissed most or all of them, but that did not necessarily mean that fears or suspicions of future implications were allayed.

Of the three main socio-political groups in Ankole, the Protestant Bairu stood clearly in favour of the scheme, whereas the Bahima and the Catholic Bairu opposed it. One simple reason for the latter's opposition may have been that the former group was in favour, following a pattern that was not infrequently manifested in Ankole local politics; nonetheless, that factor was by no means a sole and sufficient condition. Reasons why precisely the Protestant Bairu could be expected to be in favour involved the fact that they comprised most of the advanced commercial farmers in the area, those who were more likely to be interested in the improvement, sales, loans and boundaries arguments for the scheme – whether or not in the end these possibilities would make much difference. If these were rationalistic grounds, they were strengthened by others which derived from the historic relationships between social groups in Ankole, particularly the Bairu–Bahima contacts. For one thing the land title scheme was perceived as one that would remove any final area of insecurity about tenure and in fact make any title holder as secure about his land as the *mailo* owners. Besides, to become in a sense like a *mailo* owner promised no small amount of satisfaction, if only as a way of asserting equality of status to those who had long been regarded as an overprivileged group. This motivation, though hardly ever explicit, was of considerable significance in Protestant Bairu quarters. Finally, population density in the area probably made the project seem more desirable there than in other places as long as the right to enclose land was associated with freehold tenure. More concretely, it would help to keep off cattle from land under cultivation, which was experienced as a nuisance. Added to this, perhaps, was also a chance to be of some nuisance to the cattle people. It was speculated with keen interest that if most of the land came under freehold and were fenced, it would almost certainly mean the migration of Bahima pastoralists away from the area.

To the Bahima the scheme was objectionable for precisely opposite reasons. Cattle required freedom to move and it was felt that if the land was to be increasingly enclosed this movement might become seriously impaired. This would especially be the case if enclosures, as was likely, were to include the sections of land to which a farmer could lay a customarily recognized claim but which he would not normally, or continuously, have under active cultivation. Rights to trespass such sections with cattle have been conventionally accorded, but would be jeopardized by the development of freehold enclosures. Bahima themselves would find difficulty claiming freehold titles for large enough stretches of land to engage in cattle husbandry. Ultimately the possibility of forced migration from the area thus loomed as a prospect. Specifically for the pilot areas, these possibilities were not always of immediate concern; but if the scheme was successful here, it would be extended and pose a much greater challenge elsewhere. Hence there was considerable Bahima concern about the principle being adopted. In addition to restriction of movement itself, two more limitations suggested themselves. One was that Bahima were likely to be excluded from defining the rules of the game governing access to land with the adoption of freehold arrangements, thus terminating a role which they had been able to play, implicitly at least, on the basis of the (convenient) fiction that all land belonged to the Omugabe. Loss of control was matched by a prospect of loss of prestige. To lose control was itself to lose prestige, while also the prestige of *mailo* ownership would be likely to suffer through the introduction of free-hold of 'equal' status. Finally, the latter would point up the anomalies of the *mailo* system in even sharper form since it would show *mailo* tenants, again, as the losing party. For Bahima, with or without *mailo,* there was no conceivable advantage in the scheme but instead potential drawbacks at various levels.

Catholic Bairu opposed the scheme partly because of their alliance with the Bahima. Also, if they were against it because the Protestants were for it, that was based on more than considerations of party rivalry *per se.* In Ankole as elsewhere politics had frequently, and never entirely unjustifiably, been seen as a winner-takes-all game; in other words, as a competition entitling the incumbent party at least to first access to available benefits. As they had for long been out of the official establishment, there was a fear among Catholic Bairu that they might lose out at boundary demarcations and that they would not be sufficiently well-placed to carry through cases which were more than normally complicated. Besides, since there were fewer advanced or better-off farmers among them than among the Protestants, there was a correspondingly more limited interest on the part of Catholics in land titles as a means to secure loans, to make claims for final boundary demarcations and arrange enclosures, and so on. Neither for practical reasons nor prestige did these benefits have much appeal to them. Neither were they as much motivated as the Protestant Bairu to challenge the *mailo* system, or the Bahima, by opting for land titles. Finally, in the light of these reservations, the expenditure in fees may often not have seemed worthwhile. For up to two acres the total fees were Shs. 50, up to ten acres Shs. 90, and so on, which hardly constituted negligible expenditure for peasants who did not belong to the economically most successful category.

Evidently, then, the scheme aroused considerable discussion and controversy. The fact that it was voluntary, and thus only for farmers who wished to apply for a land title, did not reduce objections because in the long run the programme could lead to the emergence of a group of property owners versus a group of 'non-property' owners. Again, for Bahima it was not a matter of their own interest in the new land titles but rather of the scheme affecting them by implication.

One does not even need to favour one reaction above another to see at least that a project which provokes such conflicting interests does not provide a particularly stable basis for rural social development. These reactions it appears could for the larger part have been anticipated because there were clearly divergent interests involved. Failure to do this has led to an experimental attitude to the social and political dimensions of the scheme, viewing these as of lesser concern or consequence than the primary objective of agricultural growth. Besides, whether the growth objective has, will be, or would have been reached is extremely doubtful. The experiment has nonetheless created a project which, like the *mailo* scheme, revealed an inadequate fit with local social and political interests (not to speak of customary arrangements). While it is difficult to show its economic utility, it was far from an irrelevant factor in the local society because it created a taste in land as a commodity, had potentially harmful implications for social relationships and finally, once started, was hard to undo.

By way of conclusion, from an unexpected source

> On the land problem in Ankole, [President Amin] urged those land owners who bought a lot of land in the past not to evict their tenants at very short notice. To ask, he said, someone who has been living on your land for 20 or 60 years to leave at short notice is not human. How would you feel, he asked, if you were the one asked to leave? (*Uganda News*, 1972, No. 4220).

Postscript (1998)

Just three years after President Idi Amin of Uganda had articulated his concern for poor tenant farmers facing the prospect of eviction, his government introduced new and drastic land legislation (1975). The effect of this was to obliterate in one stroke all or most of the remaining constraints to an unprecedented acceleration of land grabbing and privatization of land property by economically powerful groups in Ankole and elsewhere in Uganda. In his statement quoted above Amin conceivably had still been anticipating new land conflicts to be emerging, rather than just calling for past issues to be resolved. Whatever his (re)thinking, while the 1975 Land Reform Decree ruled that ' ... no holder of a customary tenure shall be terminated in his holding except under terms imposed by the [land] commission, including the payment of compensation and approval by the Minister having regard to the zoning scheme...' (art. 3), in subsequent practice this appears to have been about the least adhered to clause in the Decree. By declaring all land to be state property (which was not exactly novel), but also allowing interested parties to put in claims for freehold titles even over land occupied by peasants under customary tenure, it triggered off a massive wave of land appropriation and privatization by the wealthy or relatively wealthy sections, with grave consequences for poor and vulnerable tenant farmers. From all accounts it transpires that protective legal provisions had little meaning or effect, and that the thirst for individualization of land holdings led to forced eviction of peasants in many instances. As happened elsewhere under similar circumstances, peasants thus driven off their land were forced to move towards marginal and vulnerable lands, or to encroach into forests and other reserves, invariably augmenting environmental pressures and ecological crisis (Platteau, 1996:39–49).

This whole new wave and transformation was to have lasting and irrevocable effects, both in terms of sharpening social differentiation and of ecological crisis. In the context of the Ankole region, it also cast a new perspective on the earlier interventions in land tenure and land utilization practices (see Map 2). Essentially, peasant farmers lost the basic security that had been inherent in continued customary tenure, and instead found themselves at the mercy of the state and/or of new landowners. Thus there was at once a striking resemblance to the colonial *mailo* landlord-tenant arrangements, even though under the 1975 decree *mailo* holdings as such were abolished as a separate category of land tenure. There was also an unmistakable link to the earlier experimental individual land title scheme, albeit with the difference that all legal provisions that at that time had been devised to ensure proper procedure and theoretically equitable treatment appeared to be reduced to virtually zero. Instead, what may have first appeared as an experimentation with debatable pros and cons in terms of its appropriateness towards longer-term social transformations now rather took the form of an uncompromising assertion and consolidation of command by new dominant economic strata. That these are not necessarily rural strata is illustrated by not a few virtual mansions built in rural areas by individuals who accumulated their power and wealth in government, politics, army careers or private business, the latter especially the risky but lucrative illegal trade during the chaotic years of Idi Amin and Obote II. Hence this movement towards privatization of land had less to do with interests to obtain security for productive loans, but more with interests in protective and 'inflation-free' security for newly acquired wealth.

By the same token, this evident crystallization of processes of social differentiation also sheds a new light on the kind of political engagements and interest conflicts of earlier periods, especially that around the experimental introduction of individual freehold up until the early 1960s. What could then still be seen, and handled, as an issue on which representative members of different segments of the population, differentiated along lines of ethnicity cum religion (Bairu/Bahima, Protestants/Roman Catholics), could each articulate a position of their own and with its own historical logic, would subsequently transform itself into a broad dividing line which differentiated between winners and losers without much regard for religion or ethnicity. Poor Bahima pastoralists lost out as much – or even more – as poor Bairu peasants, and in the latter's case their particular Christian denomination did not help to avert or reduce social and economic hardship. The new dominant strata in what formerly constituted Ankole have become more 'ecumenical' as well, comprising as they do powerful Bahima strata as well as important numbers of individuals of Bairu descent, though probably the latter still preponderantly Protestant. But the dividing line that matters has definitely shifted into a different one altogether, that is one in which access to and control over land has come to be of vital importance.

7
Ranching and Scheming: A Case Study of the Ankole Ranching Scheme

with Michael F. Lofchie

In the analysis of development projects, even while there may be recognition of the complexity of factors that intervene at various stages of the planning processes through which they are given shape, it is only in relatively few instances that these are adequately documented. Again, as a result, many discussions of these problems tend to be conducted at a non-empirical, 'general' level, leaving room for a considerable amount of speculative thought. The present study traces some of the major conditions and considerations which were operative in a concrete case, that is, the planning process of a single development project. Actions at different levels of policy making have been analysed as to their effect on some of the most critical aspects of the project's institutionalization. It was found that several of the recurrent problems encountered in development planning were strikingly exemplified in this case:

1   The difficulty of carrying out effective government planning in situations where central government authority is weakened by the presence of countervailing local élites.
2   The possibility that development strategies, conceived of and initiated as forces of egalitarian social transformation, may, in the process of being implemented, lead to exactly opposite consequences.
3   The highly political nature of 'administrative' decision making, minimizing the role and effect of technical criteria in these processes.
4   The operation of certain guiding norms of foreign policy, in this case American, in opposition to one another, which makes it possible that the principle of non-interference in the domestic affairs of another country may nullify the principle that aid ought to serve equity-oriented social and political objectives as well as the objective of economic growth.

The Ankole Ranching Scheme was a project assisted by the United States Agency for International Development (USAID) and undertaken by the government of Uganda to promote commercial cattle ranching in southwestern Uganda. Officially the scheme was known as the 'Ankole/ Masaka Ranching Scheme' as it was projected to extend over a large plains area which overlapped both Ankole District and the adjacent Masaka District of Buganda. Since most work was concentrated in the Ankole area, the scheme was commonly referred to as the 'Ankole Ranching Scheme'. The declared objective of the scheme was to construct more than one hundred cattle ranches, of several thousand acres each, and to place them in the hands of competent ranchers who would be able to undertake large-scale beef production on an economically viable basis. The highly complex scheme involved a wide range of activities such as tsetse fly eradication projects, the construction of roads, bridges, and valley tanks, perimeter fencing, pasture research, and the creation of an experimental cattle breeding station adjacent to the ranch area proper. As such, the ranching scheme went through several phases – from initial planning to the selection of ranchers – and involved a host of governmental decisions about a wide range of economic, technical and, due to US financial involvement, foreign policy matters. By 1968, while the scheme had not yet been completed, the first forty of an anticipated 125 ranches had been allocated.

The ranching scheme was expected to have a dramatic effect on the economic development of Ankole. It also had a great potential for exacerbating or modifying social tensions that existed there. Exactly how the scheme's impact would be felt depended very much upon the institutional arrangements that would determine the distribution of social benefits. The present case study is primarily concerned with the most important of these arrangements, the criteria for the recruitment of ranchers. These criteria, more than any other administrative feature of the project, would determine which individuals and strata would benefit from the vast outlay of funds, from the long period of government planning, and from a considerable investment of expertise.

The selection of ranchers was also one of the most important economic aspects of the ranching scheme, for the success of the entire project was viewed to depend upon the capability, commitment, and responsiveness to novel methods of the individual ranchers. Since the basic concept of the scheme was that each ranch would have to be large enough to achieve a high degree of productivity, individuals selected as ranchers would almost automatically be thrust into a position of major economic prominence in the society. If the first group of ranchers was unable to meet exacting standards of performance, their failure would not only compromise the expenditure of over \$4,000,000 (at 1960 values) but was expected to have serious repercussions for Uganda's economic development.

The determination of criteria for the selection of ranchers became a matter of intense controversy both within Uganda and between the government of Uganda and USAID. Underlying this controversy was the possibility that highly placed politicians and administrators or other political influentials, attracted by the material benefits of ranch ownership, would use their position to gain possession of the ranches. This possibility, it was feared, could jeopardize the economic goals of the scheme and lead to serious political consequences. For it would be in direct contradiction to the original concept of the scheme, namely, that ranches were to be awarded only to resident owners on the basis of proven ranching ability in order that the project might serve as a model of social change. Though rarely articulated directly, fear of political exploitation precipitated a lengthy and heated dialogue over whether ranchers would be expected to reside on their ranches or whether the principle of absentee ownership would be accommodated in the scheme. The final outcome of the controversy was that residence would not be required and that individuals who were selected as ranchers would be allowed to place managers in charge of their ranches. As a result, of the first forty ranches allocated, it became possible for at least fifteen to be awarded, on an absentee basis, to members of a political élite.

The distinctive and possibly unique feature of the political élite that was able to exploit the Ankole Ranching Scheme was its local character. It is not an uncommon phenomenon in developing countries for government projects, especially those that involve heavy investment of foreign capital, to fall into the hands of influential politicians. Usually, however, the individuals who are able to benefit in these situations exercise power and influence at the national level. Often, regardless of the ethnic composition of areas where such projects are located, those who profit represent different ethnic groups, ones which are nationally dominant. This was not so in the case of the Ankole scheme. While the political élite that gained control of the majority of the ranches allocated on an absentee basis included two cabinet ministers and several members of the Uganda parliament and central government administrators, it was predominantly composed of individuals whose political basis was within the Ankole area. Even those who occupied formal positions at the national level were members of Ankole society and had risen to national prominence by virtue of their ability to exercise influence within Ankole. The vast majority of the members of the Ankole political élite who had been given ranches and who began to manage them as absentee owners were members of the ethnically differentiated Bahima élite. In addition, all but a few of the remaining twenty-five ranches were acquired by other prominent Bahima. As discussed in previous chapters, the former district of Ankole had historically been composed of two ethnic groups, the Bahima and the Bairu. The former, constituting about 5 percent of the population, were traditionally the dominant political element. The Bahima had always been engaged in cattle herding and, until the early part of this century, had exclusive ownership of all cattle. This formed an important buttress to the political status of the Bahima élite stratum. The Bairu, the overwhelming majority of the population, had primarily been cultivators.

Although the Bahima were the traditional cattle keepers of Ankole, Bahima identity was not presumptive evidence of superior cattle-keeping ability. Despite the fact that Bairu had been permitted to acquire cattle only since 1907, by the middle of the century they already possessed more than the Bahima. As early as 1938 an official government report observed that 'the Bairu seem to have certain advantages over Abahima as stock-keepers' (W. L. S. Mackintosh, 1938:26). During the 1960s and 1970s, the Bairu had been gradually absorbed into the political élite of Ankole. In spite of Bairu upward mobility, however, the Bahima for long retained a disproportionate amount of political influence and until today remain an important element of the Ankole political élite. Because of past discrimination, many Bairu still have a sense of resentment against the Bahima. Indeed, one of the most conspicuous features of Ankole politics over the years has been a continuing tension between the two groups. Bahima preponderance in the initial distribution of ranches added to a Bairu sense of unequal treatment and thus accentuated the tension between the two groups. Consequently, the pattern of rancher selection not only threatened the economic viability of the ranching scheme, but also made it a source of political irritation in Ankole.

The objective of this case study is to explore the conditions that permitted a locally based élite to take advantage of a largely foreign financed project whose implementation was the responsibility of the central government of Uganda. Broadly speaking, four separate conditions can be distinguished. These are: (1) the special political climate of Uganda which, in the early post-independence period, was characterized by a generally tolerant attitude toward local élites and considerable flexibility in accommodating their interests; (2) an ineffectual planning apparatus at the national level which was unable to govern the specifics of plan implementation; (3) the particular problems and attitudes of American foreign policy in central and eastern Africa; and (4) the ability of the Ankole élite to exercise influence at the national level, together with an absence of effective opposition within Ankole. Although the politics of the Ankole Ranching Scheme should not be construed as being necessarily typical of the pattern of decision making in Uganda at the time, the case study may help illuminate a set of factors which can be expected to influence decision making in a wider context.

The Ankole Ranching Scheme had its origin in the long-standing efforts of the Uganda government to eradicate the tsetse fly (*Glossina morsitans*) from southwestern Uganda. As early as 1908, the fly had begun to cross the Kagera River, part of the boundary between Uganda and Tanganyika, and moved steadily northward into an area of Ankole where cattle raising was the traditional occupation of a significant sector of the local population. Throughout the early decades of the century, there was a substantial migration of cattle raisers out of the infected areas. Large numbers of Bahima moved into other parts of Ankole but many migrated into Buganda and some Ankole cattle herders went as far as Lango and Teso districts in central and eastern Uganda. The problem of tsetse infestation became especially acute during the 1940s and 1950s, when further encroachments of the fly led to an increasing incidence of trypanosomiasis (sleeping sickness) among the remaining cattle of Nyabushozi county of Ankole. By the end of this period, an area of nearly 2,000 square miles of open grassland had become affected.

Danger that the entire cattle industry of the area would be wiped out necessitated emergency eradication measures by the Uganda government. In 1959, after other approaches had proven ineffective, the government decided to evacuate all the remaining cattle, by coercion if necessary, and also to kill off the game species in the area in order to remove the carriers of tsetse. These measures, combined with large-scale bush clearance to destroy the habitat of the fly, finally proved successful in halting and even pushing back the tsetse infestation. Effective tsetse control proved so costly, however, that it posed a difficult dilemma for the Uganda government. To abandon or even cut back on fly eradication would leave the cleared area open for reinfestation, invalidating all previous efforts, and would place an additional 400 square miles in jeopardy (Loan Application to USAID by the Government of Uganda, 1964). To continue the tsetse elimination programme while allowing a reoccupation of the area by traditional Bahima cattle herders, it was thought might pose a crippling financial burden and would, in the long run, be grossly ineffectual. Traditional Bahima pastoral practices were expected to invite renewed spread of the fly over the entire area.

A third approach to the problem, favoured by veterinary officers of the Uganda government and supported by the visiting World Bank Mission to Uganda of 1961 (International Bank for Reconstruction and Development, 1961) was to create a settled commercial cattle-ranching operation in the area. It was argued that this would not only justify the economic costs of continued eradication programmes but could be organized in such a way that it would, in itself, constitute an impediment to the movement of the fly. An additional advantage of stabilized commercial ranching was seen to lie in its potential as a model of modern practices and a stimulus of cultural and social transformation. If the largely semi-nomadic Bahima pastoralists of Ankole could be induced to adapt their traditional livelihood strategies and to adopt new methods of animal husbandry, it was expected that they would become more fully absorbed into the commercial sector of the Ugandan economy and would be encouraged to take advantage of educational and other opportunities for social advancement.

In order to explore the feasibility of stable ranching, a Land Use Investigational Unit was set up in Nyabushozi county in 1957. This unit, which occupied 30 square miles, created approximately half a dozen ranches in order to conduct experiments on such problems as pasture improvement, land rehabilitation, and optimum cattle density per acre. These ranches were the prototypes of the ranches on the Ankole scheme and were eventually incorporated into the scheme.

A major impetus to the creation of commercial cattle ranching in Ankole came in the early 1960s, when USAID, which had been giving support to the bush-clearing operations, became interested in the broader idea of large-scale ranching and beef production in southwestern Uganda. In order to assess the prospects of such an industry, USAID sponsored an American research team which spent several months, during early 1963, conducting an intensive on-the-spot investigation of the ecological, economic, and social conditions in the plains area of Ankole. This team produced a comprehensive analysis entitled *The USAID Livestock Survey Team Report* (1963), which was commonly referred to as the 'Gregory Report,' after its team leader, Dr. E. Gregory of the University of Nebraska. It strongly endorsed the principle that cattle ranching could become a major source of wealth for Uganda and an important vehicle of socio-economic transformation in the Ankole area. The technical recommendations contained in the Gregory Report became, in large measure, the basis of the Ankole Ranching Scheme.

Among the various factors enumerated by the Gregory Report as preconditions for the success of commercial cattle ranching, the form of ranch tenure was singled out as being of central importance. In a lengthy analysis, the report stressed the necessity of adopting some type of individual tenure which would ensure that the owner-operator actually reside on his ranch. The basic argument was that in order to provide the maximum incentive for efficiency and productivity, the economic rewards of ranch operation must accrue to the person having responsibility for day-to-day management. In opposing any form of absentee ownership, the report commented that 'the family which must rely solely upon a ranch for its existence and financial progress is much more apt to bend every effort towards its successful operation than if their interests are divided between the operation of the ranch and other activities' (Gregory Report:4). A second reason for compelling the ranchers to reside on the ranch was that this would assure effective communication between veterinary experts attached to the project and the ranchers. Such communication was essential if improved techniques of animal husbandry emanating from the adjoining experimental breeding station were to be put into practice on the ranches. Only if this were accomplished would the broader educational purposes of the scheme be facilitated. Effective diffusion of modern cattle-raising methods throughout the Ankole area required that the Ankole Ranching Scheme itself function as a conspicuous model of successful innovation and adaptation.

While the Gregory Report tended to place primary stress on the economic and educational factors as grounds for advocating individual tenure and on-the-site residence, a final and perhaps more persuasive argument lay in the historically known social consequences of the institution of absentee landlordism, namely, the tendency towards a growing economic cleavage between different strata in the society. The Gregory Report warned that:

> caution needs to be exercised ... by both Central and District Governments in order to prevent the concentration of land ownership in the hands of a small number of owners. *Concentration of ownership, particularly in the hands of absentee owners, too often has resulted in a peasant type agriculture in which land owners have little interest in anything except 'mining' both human and land resources* [authors' emphasis]. In the interests of a strong and viable economy in Uganda, every effort should be made to avoid development in this direction (Gregory Report:127).

Thus absentee ownership or control would not only present a major obstacle to accomplishing the communication and educational purposes of the plan, thereby preventing it from functioning as a model of social change, but would inevitably intensify the social and economic cleavages in Ankole society. An important theme in the Gregory Report was that a successful commercial ranching scheme, of the type envisaged, could only come about as the result of a slow, balanced development in a number of areas such as breeding experimentation and rancher training. The Gregory team had recognized that there was not a sufficient number of adequately trained people to man the ranches. They argued that, since the first group of ranchers would have to play a crucial role if fundamental social transformation of the area was to be achieved, it was essential not to rush the scheme ahead until a competent cadre of ranchers had been formed. The team's report also recommended that a substantial enlargement of the experimental cattle breeding farm should precede any major construction work on the ranches. Following these suggestions, USAID agreed to finance the expansion of the breeding farm and thus became further involved in livestock development in the Ankole area.

There was a discernible contrast between the viewpoint of the Gregory team – that the establishment of cattle ranching should be a gradual matter – and the keen expressions of interest in more rapid progress which emerged from certain local quarters. The most conspicuous of these local persons were officials of the Ankole kingdom government, veterinary officers working in the field of livestock development in Ankole, and high-ranking administrators in the Ministry of Animal Husbandry, Game and Fisheries. The Gregory team indicated some concern at the desire of local leaders in Ankole to move rapidly ahead with the project and warned that such an attitude was not compatible with effective, long-range development (Gregory Report:10). Implicit in their caution was an anxiety that if Ankole notables, who perceived the scheme merely as an opportunity for immediate economic gain, were to obtain control, the opportunity for using the ranches as a vehicle for recruiting and training individuals who could function as a nucleus of socio-economic development, would be lost. Indeed, as a means of ensuring adequate rancher responsiveness to the broader objectives of the project, the Gregory team went so far as to spell out an elaborate set of special requirements for operators, which placed particular emphasis on an appropriate attitude and commitment, a sufficient level of education, and demonstrable management potential. To be able to delay the scheme long enough to develop a competent cadre would have required a central government sufficiently strong to resist local élite pressure.

Local and ministerial pressure for quick action on the ranching scheme also presented a contrast with the more routine approach taken by government planning officials. The Ministry of Animal Husbandry, in which the Ankole élite had strong representation, had forwarded first drafts of an application for USAID assistance for the project to the Ministry of Economic Affairs (which then performed the function of plan evaluation) towards the middle of 1963. Officials in Animal Industry expressed the urgent hope that the Uganda government would take action quickly enough so that Washington could approve the loan as early as July of that same year. The planning machinery was simply not equipped, however, to act on such short notice. Serious consideration of the loan request was not begun until early 1964.

At this time it became quite clear that there was a marked discrepancy between the manner in which the Ministry of Animal Husbandry conceived of the ranching scheme and certain of the original ideas contained in the Gregory Report. In particular, there was basic divergence over the question of land tenure. In a draft of the loan application prepared by the Ministry of Animal Husbandry in December 1963, the anticipated mode of ranch tenure was described as follows: 'The ranches would . . . be offered on lease to farmers selected as candidates of sufficient capacity, business acumen, educational background and integrity or some satisfactory combination of these requirements, *or, to individuals, Co-operatives or similar bodies who would undertake to put in a Manager of the same calibre* (authors' emphasis). Another difference between the loan application and the Gregory Report was that the loan request did not include provision for a marketing co-operative for the ranchers. This indicates that among the Ugandans concerned to promote the ranching scheme, absentee ownership had become an accepted principle rather than an exception. For co-operative arrangements are feasible only when those on the spot have authority to make important decisions about the day-to-day economics of ranch operation. Even in the daily routine of plan reviewing, these departures from the original formulation of the ranching scheme caused raised eyebrows among members of the government's planning staff, who felt that the innovations were sufficiently questionable to refer the loan application back to the Ministry of Animal Husbandry for specific explanation. However, when a rewritten version of the loan application, with no significant changes in the approach to ranch tenure, was submitted again to planning officials, it was accepted without further ado. On the basis of the new version, the Uganda Planning Commission (a select cabinet committee with special representation from parastatal bodies), which had supreme statutory authority over all governmental development programmes, agreed to make a formal request to USAID for financial assistance. The official loan application of the government of Uganda (dated May 1964), which included a request for $1,830,000 out of a total projected scheme cost of over $4,000,000, was thus quite explicit in accepting the principle of absentee ownership. In a section entitled 'Economic and Technical Soundness Analysis,' paragraph 48 read: 'Most ranches will be run by resident owner-managers, though some may be run by managers on behalf of co-operatives, companies, or individual absentee-owners.'

The inclusion of the principle of absentee ownership in the official loan application was a concrete demonstration of the relative weakness of the planning staff in the Uganda government. Despite the fact that the departures from the Gregory Report might lessen the appeal of the project to USAID, the Ministry of Animal Husbandry and its Veterinary Department had been successful in pressing for their version of the scheme against the better judgement of the planning officials. The Ministry of Planning and Community Development, which had succeeded the Ministry of Economic Affairs in carrying out project evaluation, was unable to make any significant impact on these aspects of the loan request.

The Ministry of Planning was weakened by the fact that it did not possess final authority to approve or disapprove foreign aid requests. This power rested solely with the Uganda Planning Commission which, as essentially a cabinet committee and, therefore, a political rather than a technical body, did not necessarily base its decisions on purely economic considerations (which could have been the case had the commission been composed of politically neutral technical experts). The ineffectuality of the Ministry of Planning was also a result of a combination of other factors, the most important of which was that it did not possess administrative mechanisms of its own, such as budgetary powers, for exercising effective control over other governmental ministries. In addition, it was weakened by shortage of staff, lack of independent access to critical information, and chronic organizational changes.

Exactly why officers of the Veterinary Department in charge of implementing the scheme should have been so anxious to press for quick acceptance of their particular version of the project is a complex question. One possible factor was a belief that unless some rapid results could be shown, the Uganda government might lose interest in supporting livestock development in the Ankole area. There was also a fear that the cattle herders who had migrated due to the incursion of tsetse fly would attempt to move back into the cleared area and resume their traditional method of grazing with the attendant dangers of reinfestation and economic stagnation. Only if ranches were established, it was felt, could the gains made through eradication programmes be preserved. A third factor was that the scheme had long since begun to arouse considerable interest among part of the local population and there was already some pressure to adopt a format which would leave the matter of ranch tenure flexible and open to alternative arrangements. The local veterinary officers had begun to identify with Ankole, possessed close social contacts with leaders of the community, and were highly responsive to these leaders' sentiments and interests. Moreover, their intimate association with the early development of the idea of a ranching scheme had created a sense of personal stake in its successful fulfilment and this may also, to some extent, have led to a willingness to accommodate local preferences in order to be able to produce visible results.

The tendency for field officers to become personally absorbed in such a syndrome of local conditions is a widely observed phenomenon of administrative behaviour. The critical difference in the case of the Ankole Ranching Scheme was that there was during this period no countervailing pressure on the local officials from the central office of the ministry to adhere closely to a predetermined set of rules. Indeed, perhaps partly because some key officials in the ministry were themselves an integral part of the local interest group, one of the unique features of the ranching scheme was the extent of the discretion and autonomy left to the field staff in the entire development of the project. This could never have occurred in a country where the political process did not exhibit a high degree of regional pluralism. In Uganda there was then a marked tradition of pragmatic adaptation by the central government to local demands and pressures.

After several months of co-operation with the Uganda government in ironing out various technical and statistical details, USAID/Kampala forwarded the loan application to USAID/Washington for its decision in August in 1964. Included with the loan request were some of the remarks of Dr. A. J. Howarth, one of the members of the Gregory team, who had been asked by USAID/Kampala to comment on the Uganda government's proposals. Dr. Howarth called attention to the fact that the loan application did not give serious consideration to the question of who, in the last analysis, would be helped most by the project:

> In discussing the benefits to be derived from this ranching scheme very little is said regarding its most far-reaching benefit. This is the educational and demonstrational aspects of a stabilized ranching

project as compared to traditional nomadic raising. When the project is successful, it will be an example to Africans in Uganda and elsewhere in Africa. The final impact of this ranching scheme would not be measured on the benefits to 700 square miles of land in Ankole/ Masaka but to untold thousands of square miles in Africa (USAID/ Kampala).

The specific paragraphs of the loan application criticized by Dr. Howarth (nos. 43 and 165) referred to the creation of a cadre of experienced ranchers and to the impact of the scheme on the general standard of living of the people of the area. The brunt of his argument was that, as judged by its written proposals, the Uganda government was giving only token consideration to these matters. Concern over the *human factor*, first articulated by Dr. Howarth, became the heart of the entire controversy over the ranching scheme between the United States and Uganda. As of autumn 1964, USAID/Washington had not acted on the ranching scheme. There was evidence that it had become reluctant to proceed with the project until several questions, especially that of social benefits, were satisfactorily clarified. USAID officials had become acutely sensitive to criticism of projects that served to entrench local élites. Persistent requests were made that Uganda 'describe procedures and criteria in selection of ranchers and allocation of ranches to successful applicants.'

The tone of USAID's position indicated a growing suspicion that the issue of rancher selection was more than an abstract consideration and that there was an active lobby in Ankole eager to capitalize on any flexibility in the criteria of eligibility for ranch ownership. Washington's tendency to take a critical position, in turn, aroused the sensitivity of officials in the Ministry of Animal Husbandry, who became impatient at what they viewed as 'America's dilatory tactics.' Official contacts between the two countries were accompanied by mounting tension as the problem was treated in a more and more unequivocal manner. Toward the end of 1964, the issue of ranch tenure became the all-absorbing focus of attention in the negotiations between USAID and the government of Uganda over the ranching scheme. From being, at an earlier point, one among a host of administrative, technical, and economic details which seemed to require last-minute tidying up, it now loomed as a major political issue which forced all other considerations into the background.

The growing estrangement of the two governments over this matter generated strong expressions of indignation among Uganda officials. They claimed that the United States' desire to have a voice in the policy of ranch allocation was an unwarranted interference in the exclusive right of the Uganda government to implement its development programmes as it saw fit, and amounted to nothing less than an accusation of bad faith on Uganda's part. There was a noticeable closing of ranks among the government branches connected with the scheme and the view that the country's integrity was involved became readily accepted. A few radical politicians soon found this issue a convenient one for expounding anti-American views. Sentiments of righteous indignation, whether genuine or contrived, had become so much a feature of the political climate that the officials concerned could afford nothing less than complete triumph. By the end of November 1964, some went so far as to declare that if Uganda's stature as a sovereign nation were to be properly upheld, it must either insist on complete acceptance of its terms or withdraw its application from USAID. This suited the narrow interests of the Ankole élite more than those of the society as a whole since this élite was basically indifferent to the ranching scheme unless its members were to obtain ranches.

A tactical error by USAID enabled this group to turn the confrontation to their own advantage. The Director of USAID/Kampala, prophetically aware that political interests were ready to exploit the ranching scheme, became impatient at the interminable haggling in the abstract. On 2nd December 1964 he addressed an outspoken letter to the permanent secretary of the Ministry of Animal Husbandry, in which he sought to make it clear once and for all that USAID viewed the principle of absentee ownership as a thinly veiled subterfuge by which a pressure group of political influentials wanted to acquire ranches. The critical passage of his letter read:

> We wish to reiterate our reservation and deep concern over the procedures for the selection of ranchers for the Ankole Ranching Scheme and the problem of absentee-landlords. I think that it is unlikely that the United States A.I.D. would be able to participate in a project that allows people of political influence in your government to secure any of the ranches in the Ankole Ranching Scheme which the U.S. is asked to help finance. We believe in the original concepts of the project in which the U.S. was requested assistance [*sic*] specifically for cattle producers in Uganda ... The second problem of absentee landlords is also of concern to U.S.A.I.D. since this would tend to subvert the real purpose of the scheme wherein bona fide cattle producers would be the benefactors [*sic*] of this project and who would eventually spearhead the development of the livestock industry in Uganda (USAID/Kampala).

The author of this letter was determined to prevent the US government/USAID from being drawn into supporting the economic enrichment of an established political élite. The tragic irony was that, precisely because of his attempt to elicit a more egalitarian approach on the part of the Uganda government, the director of USAID/Kampala inadvertently supplied fuel to the charges that the United States was interfering with the internal affairs of a developing country. His letter furnished Ugandan spokesmen with the ideal opportunity to present their government as the offended party.

The nature of the reactions among government circles to the USAID letter was quite significant. Instead of denying that the principle of absentee ownership would lead to political influentials gaining ranches, the Ministry of Animal Husbandry made the observation that participation by the local influentials would enhance the prospects of the ranching scheme. In a statement remarkable for its candour and insight into the élite pattern of Ankole society, one high official observed that 'it is quite impracticable to exclude people with some standing in Ankole, as so many of them are closely connected or related to someone or other wielding good influence.' The same spokesman, offering a sort of 'opinion leader' theory, took the position that 'if local leaders, political or otherwise, are excluded, other local farmers may become suspicious of the Scheme as they may not understand the reason for their leaders not taking part in it.' He further asserted that 'experience elsewhere has shown that absentee landlords may be very suitable ranchers, provided that they have a suitable manager.'

None of these views, however, took into account the argument at the basis of the Gregory recommendations – that unless the owners resided on their ranches, the educational and developmental objectives of the scheme could not be achieved. For the scheme would not produce any visible or dramatic changes in the lives of ranchers whose basic involvement was other occupational pursuits. This is the basic reason to doubt the validity of an opinion leader theory based on popular allegiance to established traditional leadership as a justification of absentee ownership. The purpose of the scheme was not simply to gain local acceptance in a traditional context, but to employ a modernizing cadre of ranchers as opinion leaders to induce a fundamental transformation in the socio-economic culture of the Ankole area.

At the next scheduled meeting of the Uganda Planning Commission, in December 1964, the Ministry of Animal Husbandry recommended that the government of Uganda withdraw its loan application from USAID. It offered three principal reasons for urging this course of action. Most importantly, it considered USAID's position to constitute interference in Uganda's internal affairs and took the view that 'it is vital that internal operations be unfettered by unreasonable terms and conditions imposed by donor countries.' Secondly, the ministry argued, USAID's charge that the Uganda government had departed from the original concept of the ranching scheme was ill-founded since the 'original' loan application, submitted in May 1964, had explicitly provided for the possibility of absentee ownership. This argument was somewhat paradoxical since the original formulation of the scheme had, in fact, been contained in the Gregory Report and not in the loan request which, precisely because of its innovations, was being questioned by USAID. Lastly, ministry officials felt that it was unlikely that USAID would change its position and they concluded that it was therefore pointless to continue negotiations. The Uganda Planning Commission accepted these views. It decided to withdraw the application from USAID and to go ahead with the project on the basis of Uganda's own financial resources, meanwhile seeking alternative sources of foreign assistance. On 17th December 1964 the Uganda government officially informed USAID that the application had been withdrawn.

Shortly after the withdrawal had been effected, Uganda took the position that the wording of the USAID letter of 2nd December was so offensive that it constituted more than simply an unacceptable condition of economic assistance and was a major breach of diplomatic etiquette. It was decided that the minister of state for Foreign Affairs should raise the issue with the American embassy. This was done, and in response the US ambassador to Uganda sent an official apology for the incident on 9th January 1965.

In his apology he stated that the letter signed by the director of USAID/Kampala did not reflect the policy of the American government. He also took pains to point out that any innuendoes contained in the letter were made without the knowledge or authority of American officials either in Washington or the embassy. The American apology was followed by a series of *ad hoc* meetings between the US ambassador and his chargé d'affaires and representatives of the Uganda government, particularly the ministers of Foreign Affairs and Animal Husbandry and the prime minister of Uganda. The purpose of these meetings, which were held during the remainder of January and in early February, was to explore whether the Ugandans could be persuaded to reconsider their decision to withdraw the loan application. Some Uganda officials left these meetings with a clear impression that if they should decide to resubmit the loan request, there would be no need for further negotiation and that the application would be given immediate favourable attention on the terms proposed by the Uganda government. As the Minister of Animal Husbandry put it, 'the only final procedure will be the signing for the loan by the Uganda Government and offering the money in the normal channels.'

The US embassy's effort to persuade the Ugandans to proceed with the project revealed a significant difference in approach between the State Department and USAID. Whereas USAID had viewed the ranching scheme in developmental terms as a stimulus of economic growth and social change, and was largely concerned with organizational safeguards, the State Department was primarily motivated by diplomatic considerations and saw the scheme as an aspect of American-Ugandan relations. Once the issue had been raised to the diplomatic level, the State Department placed strong pressure on USAID to relax its restrictions on ranch ownership in the interest of broader international objectives.

The American State Department is generally anxious to keep the support of developing countries and this is a strong incentive for its diplomatic personnel to strive for cordial relations. This concern alone would probably have been sufficient reason for the American ambassador to Uganda to seek to smooth over the Ankole Ranching Scheme crisis. Ordinarily, since the reputation and career of high-ranking diplomats often depend heavily upon their ability to maintain an untroubled atmosphere, American ambassadors are frequently motivated to reduce friction by considerations other than the merits of a situation. In early 1965 the American ambassador to Uganda was under increased pressure, for American relations with Uganda had already begun to suffer considerably due to the Congo crisis and to United States support for the Tshombe regime. It had been reported that the Tshombe forces, using American aircraft, had bombed two Ugandan villages in February of that year and this had aroused considerable anti-American feeling as well as suspicion of America's objectives in central and eastern Africa. This situation coincided exactly with the critical moment in the controversy over the ranching scheme. Consequently, the State Department was especially determined to prove the goodwill of the American government and to show that the United States had no desire to interfere in Uganda's internal affairs.

The intention of the American authorities to conciliate the Uganda government and to have the loan application reactivated was also the product of several additional factors. USAID had already become deeply involved in paving the way for the ranching scheme, for example in supporting bush clearing and tsetse-eradication projects as well as the experimental cattle breeding station, and there was a natural desire to show results after several years of effort and expenditure. Budgetary considerations were equally important. US officials in Kampala had already persuaded Washington to set aside funds for the ranching scheme and feared that if these funds were unused, subsequent requests for appropriations might not be granted. This became such a compelling consideration that at one point in the discussion over resumption of the loan, the acting director of USAID/Kampala, the official who had replaced the writer of the controversial letter, offered Uganda an outright capital assistance grant, to be spent on any project of Uganda's own choosing, which was equivalent to the sum budgeted for the ranching scheme. Moreover, several previous offers of American assistance, including aid for police housing and Peace Corps projects, had been declined by the Uganda government. Ultimately this proved to be an incentive on both sides to reconsider the ranching scheme loan. Underlying this entire controversy was the legacy of America's failure to finance the Aswan Dam and the fact that this had helped to strengthen the ties between Egypt and the Soviet Union. USAID and the Department of State were both anxious to help finance the ranching scheme if only to prevent this sort of situation from arising.

One noteworthy feature of the American government's response to the ranching scheme controversy was its ability to present a single policy to the Uganda government. This could in large measure be attributed to the fact that, when the crisis occurred, the State Department was able to assert its exclusive authority to represent American policy. This enabled it to submerge USAID's position and, thereby, to conceal any differences between the diplomatic and technical assistance perspectives toward the scheme. Thus, a façade of unity was created which gave the impression that the US was willing to accommodate Uganda's political sensitivities, especially regarding ranch tenure.

The appearance of unity on the part of the American government was in stark contrast to the disarray on the Ugandan side during the first few months of 1965. Each sector of the Uganda government involved with the scheme took a different position. Lack of experience in handling this sort of situation resulted in confusion over exactly who had authority to decide whether and on what basis aid negotiations with the United States should be resumed. There was also a failure of communication within the Uganda administration; the various branches of the government were essentially uninformed as to each other's viewpoints and activities with respect to the loan application. The Ministry of Foreign Affairs, viewing the conflict in diplomatic terms, felt that its discussions with the American ambassador had cleared the ground for a resumption of negotiations and asked the Ministry of Animal Husbandry to reopen discussions with USAID. The Ministry of Animal Husbandry took the view that the American government had already agreed to finance the project on Uganda's terms and that therefore further discussions were not called for. The Uganda Planning Commission took the position that it had decided to withdraw the loan application from USAID and that there was no need to reconsider this decision. It stated that it would be prepared to allow the Americans to finance another project but not the Ankole scheme.

Once these positions had been taken, each government branch developed a vested interest in its own viewpoint. The Ministry of Foreign Affairs, for example, believed that it had undertaken a diplomatic commitment to the American embassy and argued that it would be 'diplomatically bad' not to resume negotiations. To this, the Ministry of Animal Husbandry responded that further negotiations would result in little more than 'delaying tactics' by the American government and now asserted that it would be preferable to finance the scheme from Uganda's own resources. The prime minister of Uganda, Milton Obote, whose view corresponded roughly with that of the Ministry of Foreign Affairs, had meanwhile acted on his own authority and agreed with the US ambassador to allow USAID to finance the scheme. Finally, the Uganda Planning Commission, which had been unaware of the discussions with the American embassy, was forced to seek clarification of its position as the sole body empowered to approve development loans and, in early April, asked the prime minister whether it was expected to reconsider its previous decision.

The prime minister decided, at that point, to use his influence to resolve the deadlock. He was concerned that the ranching scheme should move more rapidly toward implementation since it had already been announced several times in parliament and had received considerable press coverage. In his opinion, the preliminary work done by USAID entitled it to some consideration and the Uganda government should not be precipitate in dismissing the contribution American assistance had already made to the development of the Ankole scheme. Moreover, he noted, the Uganda Planning Commission's decision to withdraw the loan application was prompted less by a sense of offence at the USAID letter than by reluctance to accept the restrictions USAID was imposing on ranch tenure. Since the American government had apologized for the letter, the Uganda government should, in his view, take the wider political and diplomatic repercussions of its decision into account and resume discussions with USAID.

Obote's perspective on this issue was strongly influenced by evidence he had received confirming the USAID allegation that absentee ownership would lead to political influentials acquiring ranches. An official Rancher Selection Board, appointed by the Ministry of Animal Husbandry (which was proceeding with the ranching scheme on its own), had held its second meeting on 1st April 1965, and had allocated the first twenty-eight Ankole ranches. A substantial number of these ranches had been awarded to people of high political status. Concerned with the fact that this was damaging Uganda's image, the prime minister called a special meeting of Ugandan officials to settle the ranching scheme controversy. At this meeting, which was held on 3rd May 1965, it was decided that subsequent allocation of ranches should be handled by a subcommittee of the Uganda Planning Commission and that the loan application should be resubmitted to USAID. Significantly, the Uganda Planning Commission was not asked to confirm this decision. On 18th May USAID/Kampala was informed that the Ugandan government wished its loan application to be revived.

This was by no means the end of a confused situation as regard the status of the loan application. Somewhat belatedly, the Uganda government had also begun to make internal adjustments in its personnel and transferred several of the officials who had been most deeply involved in the conflict. The new officials, however, did not immediately become familiar with the background of the project or the details of the controversy and this led them to make some erroneous assumptions about the previous contact between USAID and the Uganda government. A member of the Ministry of Foreign Affairs, for example, stated that USAID had wished to interfere unduly in the details of how the money was to be spent and to participate directly in the selection of ranchers. And a Ministry of Planning spokesman asserted that the original breakdown was caused by USAID's desire to influence the appointment of the director of the ranching scheme. The basic cause of confusion, however, was that most of the Ugandan officials were unclear as to exactly what concrete changes the American embassy had brought about in USAID's policy toward the ranching scheme.

The essential misunderstanding, from May until August 1965, was that the Ministries of Animal Husbandry and of Planning believed that the loan application would be approved immediately, whereas USAID/Kampala felt that the entire situation had merely reverted to what it was before the 2nd December 1964 letter. When USAID asked to be informed about the composition of the Rancher Selection Board, the Ministry of Planning responded that the American embassy had already agreed to regard this as a matter of Uganda's internal affairs and to approve the loan without delays for information of this kind. There was also a rather minor misunderstanding over whether Uganda would be allowed to apply for funds to finance the entire ranching scheme or whether the project would have to be financed in separate stages.

These misunderstandings were, in fact, highly anticlimactic. By the autumn of 1965, it was clear that USAID had no alternative but to accept absentee ownership. Once the American embassy had intervened in the principal dispute, it became diplomatically impossible for USAID either to take a strong position on the question of ranch tenure or to refuse to finance the ranching scheme. The diplomatic factor constituted an enormous and visible pressure on USAID to proceed with the scheme on terms acceptable to Uganda. Moreover, it was necessary to rationalize the distribution of the first twenty-eight ranches, many of which were already awarded on an absentee basis. Indeed, the pressure on USAID was so great that it led to a curiously harmonious working relationship between American experts and Uganda government personnel. The Ugandans, probably recognizing that a victory on ranch tenure was imminent, agreed to supply technical and organizational information, to frame procedures for the Rancher Selection Board which met with USAID approval, and to co-operate with USAID in preparing an acceptable version of the loan application. During the final stages of discussion, the two groups of officials worked closely together to formulate the detailed regulations governing ranch tenure. Thus, paradoxically, USAID was placed in the position of having to assist Uganda to draft precisely the sort of ranch tenure arrangement to which USAID had previously raised such strong objections.

USAID's efforts to help the Ugandans prepare an acceptable formula for ranch tenure led to a rather ironic exchange of correspondence. In a letter to the acting secretary of Planning, dated 30th August 1965, the acting director of USAID/Kampala forwarded a paper entitled 'Rancher Selection' which, he said, 'was prepared by Uganda Government technical personnel with some assistance from USAID technicians.' Suggesting that this document would satisfy Washington's requirements, the acting director of USAID/Kampala wrote that 'this paper, if transmitted to us officially, would provide the information required' on 'procedures and criteria for selection of ranchers.' The critical passage in the paper read:

> In general terms the ranches will be offered on conditional lease for two years to individuals selected on the basis of business acument

[*sic*], educational background, integrity, experience and financial capacity or some satisfactory combination of these criterion [*sic*], or to individuals, cooperative societies or companies who would employ a Manager of similar calibre.

The following day, the acting secretary of Planning responded that:

As regards the procedures and criteria for selection of ranchers, the proposals contained in your paper headed 'Rancher Selection' have been *approved* [authors' emphasis] by the Minister of Animal Husbandry Game and Fisheries, and as such, are acceptable to the Government subject of course to correction being made of two words contained in the first paragraph, i.e., 'acumen' in place of 'acument' and 'criteria' instead of 'criterion'.

Agreement on this formulation of ranch tenure removed the major obstacle to completing the actual loan agreement.

The last remaining snag concerned those of the twenty-eight ranches already allocated which had been given to political influentials. USAID/Washington was extremely reluctant for American funds to be used to finance 'men of top political influence' and wanted assurance that this would not occur. After consultations with Uganda officials, USAID/Kampala cabled Washington, in early October, that the Uganda government had offered 'full assurance that USAID funds will not be used to finance ranches for any politically important people.' This assurance was impossible to fulfil. The Uganda government was in a position to take steps to minimize the amount of benefit enjoyed by political influentials, for example, by denying certain specified ranchers such facilities as credit arrangements. Since, however, the bulk of the expenditure was being used for the simultaneous physical preparation of the ranches, it would be quite impossible to distinguish the funds spent on one ranch from those spent on another. The inescapable conclusion is that Uganda's assurances and USAID/Kampala's confirmation of these assurances were largely for Washington's consumption. Thus, against the background of existing absentee ownership and the striking prominence of high-ranking politicians as ranchers, the critical wording of the official Loan Agreement, signed April 1966, had a sardonic quality:

Selection of Ranchers. Borrower warrants that during the life of this Agreement with respect to any ranches approved hereunder, it will maintain a system of rancher selection satisfactory to USAID (USAID/ Kampala, 1966).

Against this background, the assertion made in a paper on the scheme that 'the Ranching Selection Board has been particularly careful and unbiased, and has refused applications, even from prominent persons, if it has not thought them suitable' is most surprising (Bunting (ed.), 1970).

The final irony of the conclusion of the ranching scheme controversy was that the decision to allow manager-operated ranches came at precisely a moment when important voices in Uganda had begun to echo USAID's early fear that political influentials would exploit any flexibility in the criteria for eligibility of ranchers. After the prime minister of Uganda had voiced his dismay over the allocation of the first twenty-eight ranches, as early as May 1965, several other political leaders in the country started to take up his viewpoint. The director of the Uganda Planning Commission, for example, stated that the 'common man' had been neglected and should be given top priority. On 6th September the minister of Animal Husbandry went so far as to direct that 'in future, applications made only by Co-operative societies or similar associations will be allocated ranches'.

However, none of these concerns made any immediate impact on subsequent allocations of ranches. For adequate mechanisms whereby the central government could exercise effective control over its local personnel and ensure their full compliance with its directives had, at that time, not yet been established in Uganda. Moreover, by the autumn of 1965, the Uganda political system was in the shadow of an impending crisis and political leaders became more preoccupied with basic problems of stability and survival than with the details of development projects. Resentment within Ankole over ranch allocation had also been too late and ineffective to alter the distribution of ranches. Popular expressions of grievance had only begun to emerge after the announcement of the first allocation of ranches. Until that time, there had been very little effort to inform the people of Ankole about the ranching scheme and especially about such fundamental matters as eligibility, and how and when to apply. Moreover, there had been practically no attempt to bring about an awareness of the anticipated widespread social benefits which might accrue from the scheme.

Several distinctive structural features of Ankole politics also made it extremely difficult for local resentment to the ranching scheme to gain effective national political expression. Of the six Ankole members of parliament, four received ranches. Three of these were influential members of the Bahima élite and two were ministers in the Uganda government. These individuals were evidently unprepared to scrutinize the social equity of the scheme as it developed, or to act as spokesmen of discontent after the first allocation of ranches had been made. The two remaining Ankole MPs were not particularly influential figures and were, at the time, rather dependent upon the others. Indeed, it is remarkable that, of the national political leaders who spoke out in favour of a more equitable distribution of ranches, none came from Ankole. Nor did the Ankole district council become a voice for the dissension which had emerged, largely because the most influential leaders in Ankole were personally interested in the ranching scheme.

Perhaps the most important reason why local resentment of the scheme did not find adequate expression was that local leaders of both national political parties had an interest in the project. This meant that an issue which otherwise might have become an ideal subject of partisan conflict, remained outside the scope of party politics. It is, indeed, indicative of the absence of channels for the articulation of popular discontent, that the only group which organized an opposition to the inequities in the scheme were the Ankole students at what was then still Makerere University College. Discontent remained and the scheme persisted as a political irritant.

Postscript (1998)

Following the controversies surrounding its inception in the mid-1960s, in subsequent years the implementation and realities of the Ankole Ranching Scheme led to aggravating conflict and crisis. Rather than serving as a model for technological advancement and social change in the wider region as it was intended, it came to function as a nucleus from which waves of social dislocation were radiated over large areas of Uganda. The exclusive claims to control over and access to pasture lands by the ranch owners materialized into the privatization, fragmentation and fencing-in of large tracts of lands that hitherto had been devoted to common grazing by ordinary, that is, non-élite Bahima pastoralists. Thus the establishment of the ranches in effect led to displacement on a large scale of many pastoralists who were forced to seek refuge in other parts of Ankole, in Buganda and even in Lango and Teso. Over the years these displacements added to increased pressures on available land elsewhere, resulting in deepening environmental degradation and fierce conflicts over shrinking resources. Many of the new absentee-owned ranches, meanwhile, suffered from gross environmental mismanagement in the absence of traditional herdsmen possessing the necessary skills and technology for optimal utilization of pastoral resources, such as grazing and water. Thus in 1990 government officers came to identify sixty-two ranches owned by political and military figures in different ranching areas as 'total failures' in terms of their management (*New Vision,* 26th January 1990, quoted in Kafureka Lawyer, 1993).

The displacement of common pastoralists from the ranching scheme and the mismanagement of the absentee-owned ranches combined with other factors to precipitate several waves of 'squatters' coming on to the scheme, culminating in a virtual squatter crisis in 1990 and beyond. Contextual factors external to the scheme included the rapid pace of land privatization and enclosures occurring also in many other parts of Uganda to which displaced pastoralists had been migrating, in turn forcing them to try and move back, as well as the politically disturbed and volatile situation that had come to characterize the 1970s and 1980s with the regimes of Idi Amin and Obote II. During this period the habitat of many pastoralists from Ankole in Buganda, especially in the infamous Luwero triangle, plus further north into Teso and Lango, had become increasingly susceptible to armed conflict at the hands of government soldiers *vis-à-vis* dissident forces, including those of the National Resistance Army that brought Yoweri Museveni to power in 1986. Not surprisingly, pastoralists were both among the major victims of these onslaughts but were also actively enlisted in the various guerilla struggles, each of them contributing to the waves of squatters back to the area of the Ankole Ranching Scheme. In addition, the eviction of pastoralists from the adjacent and recently declared Lake Mburo National Park (1983) added significantly to a stream of pastoralists 'settling' back on the ranching scheme.

Squatting and the increase of cattle numbers led to overgrazing, to soil erosion and the deterioration of soil fertility, and to the depletion and silting of scarce water resources (Kafureka Lawyer, 1993). Squatting took on different forms, 'legal' and 'illegal': 'illegal' squatters naturally faced stronger threats of eviction, partly depending on the particular political situation, while 'legal' squatters obtained rental contracts with the new ranch owners (or informally with their caretakers), though disputes often continued to occur over the terms of implementation or renegotiation.

The creation of new private assets which the allocation of ranches had come to signify increasingly led to corresponding economic behaviour on the part of both ranch owners and squatters. Many ranch owners became interested in the possibilities of 'mining' their new resources by maximally renting out land to squatters. Squatters on their part often sought to include as many relatives with their cattle as possible under the terms of the rental contracts they had concluded. Ranch owners and squatters thus developed parallel competitive interests in augmenting the numbers of pastoralists and livestock on the scheme's ranches, in turn adding in no small measure to the area's environmental degradation. Tragically as well as ironically, this pattern became accelerated rather than attenuated when in 1988 the new NRM Government set up a Ranches Restructuring Board charged with preparing plans for redistribution of a substantial number of the ranches among squatters. The influx of new – including some that had no previous involvement in pastoralism – squatters then increased dramatically because of expectations of redistribution of land to squatters as well as of compensation to ranch 'owners' (Kafureka Lawyer, 1993). Final solution of this crisis is still awaited, but may prove to be complicated due to the difficulty of devising equitable ways of defining and settling different kinds of claims, but also in the light of President Museveni's repeated public statements to the effect that nomadic pastoralism in his opinion is outdated and should be outlawed in Uganda. As will be discussed more extensively in Chapter 8, this represents a position which has become quite common among governments in Eastern Africa, with vast implications for the livelihood prospects of the population segments concerned.

8

State Policies and the Predicaments of Pastoralism in the Horn of Africa

with John Markakis

Introduction

East Africa is home to the largest remaining concentration of traditional livestock producers in the world. The countries of the region – Sudan, Somalia, Ethiopia, Kenya, Tanzania, Uganda – rank among the top ten in the world in terms of pastoralist population size. Pastoralists in this region occupy a variety of ecological niches, exhibit the full range of socio-economic modes of organization found in the pastoralist milieu and have diverse linkages and forms of interaction with neighbouring sedentary communities. Their interaction with the market and their relationship with the colonial and post-colonial state have also varied significantly. In short, the region offers sufficient variables for testing any hypothesis purporting to account for the declining fortunes of pastoralism in Africa generally.

Before the colonial intrusion, the people of East Africa maintained themselves mainly through cultivation and livestock production, with fishing, hunting and gathering as supplementary food-producing activities. Both cultivation and livestock production were subsistence orientated, little surplus was produced and trade played a minor role in the domestic economy. In most instances, pastoralists maintained a symbiotic relationship with sedentary neighbours, exchanging produce and services. By design, this economy was self-sufficient, though it lacked reserves to overcome crises caused by the vagaries of nature. This design was upset during the colonial period by the development of commodity production mainly for export, which withdrew land and labour from the subsistence sector without any compensating returns. The number of people involved in commodity production, marketing, service and administration multiplied rapidly. As a result, food production per capita declined steadily for a century, and today the East African states are net food importers.

Until very recently, the way out of this predicament was sought in attempts to imitate the experience of developed economies with a rapid intensification of cultivation through mechanization, irrigation, fertilization and all the aids of modern technology in large-scale schemes. The subsistence sector, where the majority of East Africa's cultivators are engaged, was ignored. To keep up with population increase, new land was brought under cultivation in this sector, often intruding into pastoralists' domain. Lately, the universal failure of this strategy and the, not unrelated, onset of famine in the region, have forced a partial reappraisal. As a result, the focus has shifted to boosting peasant production through a variety of inputs and incentives, though the main emphasis is still on production for export rather than local consumption.

Marginalization of pastoralists

No such reappraisal has taken place concerning traditional livestock production. In the accepted view, this sector of the traditional economy entered a period of uninterrupted decline under colonial rule. It was then that pastoralists were incorporated into states; a novel experience for most of them who had never been subject to state authority. They lost their freedom of movement, an imperative of traditional livestock production, when state and provincial borders, grazing zones, quarantine restrictions and other impediments were put in their way. Many also lost prized pastures in riverine regions to irrigated commercial cultivation, and other lands to the expansion of subsistence cultivation. Moreover, while their habitat shrunk, their herds expanded, thanks to newly introduced veterinary services. However, market take-off did not increase to compensate for the proliferation, because nothing was done to integrate pastoralism into the colonial economy. The result was overcrowding, overgrazing and ecological degradation, a process that is commonly claimed to have reached catastrophic proportions today.

The marginalization of pastoralism accelerated in the post-colonial era, when economic development followed the pattern laid out earlier. Encroachment into the pastoralist domain by commercial agriculture accelerated, while efforts by the independent states to limit pastoralist movement intensified. The degradation of the pastoralist habitat was hastened by recurrent drought, raising the spectre of desertification in many areas. Devastated by famine several times in the last two decades and unable to rebuild their herds, many pastoralists have been forced into what has been called 'sedentarisation through impoverishment'. This accords well with official policy in the East African states, whose governments regard 'settlement' as the only solution to the many problems posed by wandering herders. African officialdom inherited the prejudices of its colonial predecessors against the footloose herders and, regardless of the nature of the regime, the policies of the East African states towards their pastoralist subjects have had similar results. Little thought and no effort was expended in the post-colonial period to improve production in the traditional livestock sector, although efforts were made to persuade pastoralists to sell their animals in order to provide the urban and export markets with cheaply priced meat. The failure of these efforts has been blamed on the 'cattle complex', a notion which attributes pastoralist reluctance to part with their animals to psychological and cultural reasons overriding rational economic considerations. Consequently, no heed was paid to the subtle economic considerations that apply in the subsistence livestock-producing economy, nor, according to the accepted view, to obvious ones like unfair terms of trade with the modern sector.

Instead, a way was devised to provide the urban and export markets with low priced meat, while bypassing the traditional livestock producer. These are the ranching schemes, many of which purchase young animals from the pastoralists and proceed to fatten them in feedlots for the market. Supported by international capital, they represent the latest intrusion into the pastoralist domain. They are designed to use land and labour withdrawn from traditional production and to consign the costs and risks of reproduction to the latter, while depriving it of the profit realized from the sale of mature animals. This mode of articulation with the market entails the direct exploitation of pastoralism's remaining resources for the benefit of the urban sector.

The crisis of pastoralism has had serious political repercussions. Pastoralists proved the most difficult subjects of colonial rule, when they acquired a lasting reputation for rebelliousness. Today, living on the margin of post-colonial society, they remain alienated and prone to dissidence and lawlessness, contributing significantly to the political instability that afflicts East Africa in general. Every state in the region has faced challenges from this quarter, ranging from major civil wars that have occurred in Sudan, Ethiopia and Somalia, to regional uprisings in Kenya and Uganda. Pastoralists have made common cause with other social and ethnic groups to threaten the stability of regimes and the integrity of states in the region. Symbiotic patterns of interaction between pastoralist and sedentary communities have often broken down and conflict ensued. Another aspect of pastoralist malaise is the intensity of tribal warfare among the herders themselves, the indication of a desperate struggle for diminishing natural resources in the pastoralist habitat. Such warfare has afflicted regions in northern Uganda, southwestern Sudan, northern Somalia and northern Kenya, where, armed with modern weapons, pastoralists are wreaking havoc. State authority is only spasmodically exercised in these areas, often in highly arbitrary and violent forms that do nothing to reinforce its legitimacy.

Economic and political forces have combined to push pastoralism to the margin of society in East Africa. Should this trend continue, an ancient and unique way of life seems condemned to extinction. Aside from other considerations, this possibility raises basic questions concerning the continent's already declining capacity to feed its people. Pastoralists now hold a major portion of the animal population, which they maintain in arid regions unsuitable for cultivation. In normal times they feed themselves and are involved in regular exchange with their sedentary neighbours, in addition to their involvement in the market; a factor that varies from place to place and time to time. Indifference to their fate is premised on the assumption that the vast areas they roam in can be turned to better use, that is, made more productive, (1) through cultivation of irrigable areas; (2) through ranching schemes elsewhere. This assumption is unproven. In fact, the available evidence, including that on the experience of the Ankole Ranching Scheme reviewed in the preceding chapter, suggests that it appears quite ill-founded. Should the latter prove generally true, the demise of pastoralism is only likely to aggravate the problem of food production insufficiency in East Africa.

The situation sketched above is also the result of glaring contradictions between the requirements of traditional societies for survival on the one hand, and on the other, the state's need to assert its authority throughout its domain and to determine a strategy for development. Mobility, an imperative of traditional livestock production, nullifies the political and administrative controls upon which state authority rests. The material foundations of the state in East Africa rest on commercial cultivation, a sector upon which current strategies of development are also based. State revenues and economic development rely on continuous expansion of this sector. The insulation of vast areas of land and huge numbers of livestock within a self-sufficient pastoralist economy is an obstacle in its path. Traditional pastoralism, therefore, appears to violate fundamental political and economic imperatives, and pits the hapless herder against the bureaucrat and the entrepreneur. So unequal a contest can only end one way. The likely consequences of the extinction of pastoralism, however, will be to reduce food production, add to the size of the indigent and dependent population and, thereby, slow down overall development.

The inexorable logic that seems to determine this course of events holds that traditional pastoralism is incompatible with the state and the market in their modern forms. The history of the past one hundred years certainly supports it. However, until very recently, it was similarly held, on the evidence of the same historical experience, that subsistence agriculture was irrelevant to the requirements of development; consequently, it was ignored. This view has changed recently, and for very good reasons. What needs to be seriously considered now is whether there are flaws in the logic that condemns traditional pastoralism, and whether this unique way of life can survive with adaptation and continue to contribute to the welfare of the people that practise it and the economy in general.

In the light of the tendencies sketched above, it is essential to come to a proper assessment of the condition of pastoralism in East Africa at present. Since pastoralism undeniably is going through a serious crisis, it is essential to identify and analyse the causes of this malaise. As indicated above, causation is manifold and its roots can be traced to the early phase of the colonial era, which should be the historical starting point of longer-term analysis. The focus should be particularly on the relationship between pastoralism and the main forces that impinge upon it during the colonial and post-colonial period, namely those emanating from the market and the state, as well as the relationship between pastoralists and their sedentary neighbours. The accepted view of the pastoralist crisis cited above needs to be carefully examined, since it is not without its critics. The latter object to the blanket use of the term decline, citing numerous instances of human and animal population increase in pastoralist areas, of expanding commoditization in the pastoralist economy, improvement in the terms of trade and other contrary trends. They question the claim of overcrowding, overgrazing and desertification in the pastoralist habitat, pointing to areas denuded of human and animal population and covered by inedible scrub. In short, in this view, pastoralism in East Africa is experiencing, and adapting to, stresses and strains of the contemporary world. The outcome of this experience is by no means determined. The region of East Africa encompasses the full range of pastoralist modes of existence; from pure nomadism without cultivation and habitation, to transhumance combined with cultivation, fishing and gathering. The evolving relationship of the various groups with the market and the state is also diverse. Variety also characterizes pastoralist interaction with their settled neighbours. Such diversity needs to be carefully considered if one wants to derive meaningful conclusions concerning the reasons for the current crisis of pastoralism.

Another area for comparative analysis is the consequences of this phenomenon. Certainly, the most obvious of these is widespread pastoralist alienation from the states that claim them as their subjects, although it is not unusual for pastoralists to ally with the state, albeit opportunistically. While the political reaction of pastoralists in East Africa to the decline of their fortunes is not uniform, alienation has created a conducive climate for widespread lawlessness in the pastoralist milieu and to many instances of outright rebellion. More seriously, pastoralists have often made common cause with other social groups to challenge the state through powerful 'liberation' movements. At present, few pastoralist communities in East Africa are not involved in violent conflict. It is thus important to establish and better understand the connection between the crisis of pastoralism and endemic political conflict in this region.

In the remaining part of this chapter, we will consider the changing relationships between the pastoralists and the state in Somalia, with special attention to the shift of the social basis of power away from the pastoralist domain to that of the new urban-based ruling classes. Though this transformation has been particularly dramatic in the Somali case, providing an important backdrop to the crisis and collapse of the Somali state system, similar processes have been underlying the political marginalization of pastoralists in many other East African contexts.

Somali pastoralism and the state

The transformation of the basis of political power in Somalia prima facie appears paradoxical. How has it been possible that in one of the two countries in the world with a majority of pastoralists (Mongolia being the other one), pastoralists have gradually lost their pivotal position to become progressively peripheralized in what was to be 'their' state? Historically, pastoralists were politically dominant in most of the territory now comprised of Somalia and beyond. Political control was essential to them in safeguarding their grazing lands and to keep rivals at a distance. This pastoralist hegemony was pervasive, though it allowed for various kinds of accommodations with the agricultural communities living in the region.

Loss of political power by pastoralists is, as noted, by itself not uncommon in African countries. On the contrary, in many instances, population pressure and the demands for land by peasants have signified a gradual encroachment on available pasturage and a concomitant shrinking of pastoralist political domains. But in the Somali case, with its vast non-cultivable territories, this factor cannot provide an adequate explanation. Nor would it suffice to assess current state policies and settlement programmes *vis-à-vis* the pastoralists, illustrative as they are of prevailing market-oriented, incorporative designs and orientations. These policy approaches are themselves a signal that the focus of power has shifted, and that initiatives for interventions into the pastoral economy are now being taken outside its own domain.

How, then, has it been possible for this shift to take place? As we shall see, the roots of this transformation should be traced in the colonial era and in the development of new state structures and interventions. Basic to the transformations have been the growth of an urban-pastoral divide and various political interventions reflecting as well as inducing it, particularly the ascendancy of new urban-based ruling groups. While colonial rule had by and large left Somali pastoralists unaffected for a long time, towards the end of the colonial presence a hasty preparation for independence took place, which concentrated on the installation into positions of power of new urban-based bureaucratic cadres. Their ranks soon waxed and through a variety of political and juridical interventions and means they extended political control over the pastoralists.

Still, one should not conceive of such an emerging division as comprising undifferentiated social and economic categories on either side. On the urban side, a rapidly expanding bureaucratic class, the salariat, was no doubt of central importance. In addition, however, there was an increasingly significant category of traders, who had important historical antecedents in the main coastal towns. An increasing share of all trade, especially foreign, concerned livestock exported to Saudi Arabia and other Middle Eastern countries, which was to receive a major boost during the oil boom of the 1970s. This growing involvement in livestock trade related closely to processes of social differentiation occurring on the pastoralist side.

Generally in African studies, pastoralism has too often been regarded as a communal affair with undifferentiated interests to begin with (Herren, 1988). In Somalia, as commercialization of livestock proceeded, differentiation – and increasing competition for resources such as pasturage – between wealthier and poorer categories of pastoralists manifested itself (Samatar, 1989:6–7). In the course of this process some of the wealthier segments of the pastoralists themselves branched out into livestock trading, which usually involved establishing an urban basis and added to urban class formation. With urban-based merchant as well as bureaucratic classes eager to exploit the country's pastoral resources maintained by rank and file pastoralists, the Somali case in the end began to provide a plausible illustration of the urban bias thesis (Lipton, 1977), less debatable here than it had been with reference to other, especially Asian, countries.

During its brief prelude to independence, initial state formation politics in post-colonial Somalia, marking a crucial formative period in Somalia's political history, significantly influenced and shaped a tendency towards the political marginalization of Somali pastoralists. Political marginalization in this context may be understood as a process in which certain categories within a political framework, be it classes, ethnic minorities or occupational strata, are gradually losing access to and involvement in the making of decisions about their own affairs, instead becoming progressively subjected to decisions being made by other forces or centres of power and seeing their scope or autonomy of action increasingly being circumscribed by external restrictions. It does not strictly imply impoverishment, though a relative decline of resources, both productive and for sustenance, is a virtually inevitable implication. One does not necessarily need to choose sides therefore in the interesting debate between Jamal (1988) and Samatar (1989) on the correct reading of Somali statistics on income levels and the performance of the economy, to subscribe to the notion of a basic pattern of pastoralist marginalization having taken place in Somalia in recent decades.

In several respects the tendencies concerned constituted a familiar narrative which has often been encountered in accounts of state building strategies in African states. Policies and interventions which are ostensibly adopted in the name of creating unification and political homogeneity, in many instances need to be understood as the opposite; namely, as ever so many steps prompting the political marginalization of pastoralists, indirectly sowing the seeds of disunity and conflict. By the same token, the adoption of centralizing state institutions has often been at the cost of what potentially might have been an alternative route of institutional development, namely one in which non-state, 'civic' and decentralized institutions would be strengthened and might ensure a stronger say for pastoralists in their own affairs, movements and dealings with urban linkages.

When trying to understand the political dynamics that have been at play in the Somali context, it would be simplistic to presume that all the various measures restricting the scope of action and political involvement of the pastoralists have been part of some grand 'conspirational' design. Nonetheless, the overall pattern and direction of the interventions concerned have been no less unequivocal for that. Ultimately this may best be explained by reference to a prevailing ideological climate, in a Gramscian sense, which left no doubt that the point of gravity of political power in the new Somali state was increasingly located within the new urban-based political and bureaucratic élites. In this particular climate, which they helped shape as much as it was shaping them, members of this stratum almost self-evidently considered themselves licensed to redesign the modes of political involvement in the country at large. This redesigning was not influenced by any consideration or attempts to strengthen the kind of institutional arrangements which traditionally had enabled competitive clan groupings to reach compromises over questions of conflicting interests, such as access to grazing and water resources. Rather, it involved the extension of administrative command structures directed from Mogadishu. The dismantling of the *shir*, the traditional Somali council for the settlement of clan disputes, which conceivably might have (been) developed into a pertinent civic institution, is a case in point.

These tendencies are familiar also in an additional respect. In many parts of Africa, too, new bureaucratic ruling classes came into command while subordinating peasant populations. There are important parallels in the processes of marginalization of pastoralists and of African peasants. Both categories have tried to escape the squeeze – often successfully – either by resorting to informal and subsistence strategies of non-compliance or through similarly informal ways of laying claims on state resources. Peasants and pastoralists thus often have played similar parts in the same historical scenario.

Nonetheless, there is a difference, though only one of degree. Historically, African cultivators in many instances were not autonomous masters of their own decisions, but were subject to greater or lesser degrees to mechanisms of surplus appropriation by various overlords – not a few of whom with pastoral credentials. In the best of cases there was something of a healthy tension between state structures subsisting on and seeking to enlarge an agrarian surplus and peasant production. Pastoralists by and large are new to such experiences and usually still have various ways of avoiding or resisting them. The essential point to note is that in most instances the key to a mutually beneficial production relation between the state and pastoralists in the livestock sphere has yet to be found (Samatar, 1989:11).

Associated with the tendency towards establishing central control over pastoralist affairs in Somalia as elsewhere were several basic implications. Above all, interventions into the pastoral economy and society were increasingly dictated by a different interest: that of powerful urban-based groups, potentially conflicting with that of the majority of pastoralists themselves. As urban growth and class crystallization proceeded, pastoralism as practised by a majority of the Somali population came to be regarded not as a mode of existence with its own needs and demands but rather as an unpredictable nuisance or threat, which should be kept under control, or, at best, as a resource to be tapped and exploited in the 'national' interest. The keen interest of livestock officers in Somalia as in other African countries in the 1970s and 1980s to try and 'develop' the sector through settled ranching and other controllable devices flowed directly from this particular perception of pastoralism as a potential 'resource' towards increasing the country's GNP and foreign exchange earnings. However, as migratory pastoralism has considerable capacity to evade external control, for this resource to be captured and to be made more amenable towards meaningful exploitation beyond the present practice of tapping the 'traditional' livestock economy, various prior interventions would be required.

To be sure, when looking back at the 'preparation for independence' exercise in Somalia, to have attempted to further strengthen existing local or 'sectoral' institutions, or to have allowed their autonomous development, (thus strengthening the 'non-state' rather than the state sphere) might not only have gone against the perceived interests of the new emerging ruling classes. It would also have gone against the dominant mode of development thinking at the time as well as against the international agenda and directives as far as Somalia was concerned. During a brief ten year Italian Trusteeship programme (1950–60) not much more may have been possible than a hasty introduction of standard government institutions, on the assumption that this was what all independent states required and in the hope that it might work. The problem, whatever the merits of the standard package *per se*, was that Somalia was by no means a 'standard' country.

Somalia's numerically dominant pastoral society and economy gave the country some quite distinct and relatively unique social and political characteristics, for which any 'standard' institutional package would almost per definition be inadequate. Instead, Somalia's special features would have required a good deal of unorthodox and original thinking about what might be appropriate institutional solutions in a largely pastoral context. Above all, it would have required approaches which would have allowed a larger role to (a larger number of) the pastoralists themselves in developing the kind of institutions and the kind of codes and contractual arrangements considered most appropriate in the running of their own affairs. This is not necessarily to plead for a 'non-state' or 'anti-state' position. It is just to underscore that no matter how compelling the centralizing inclinations of post-colonial states and ruling classes, Somalia not excluded, working towards the construction of a different 'balance of power' between state and 'civil' institutions would have seemed highly desirable, and a priori not impossible.

When reconsidering Somalia's formative, early institution-building period, the question may be asked again as to how come, if the pastoralists represented a majority in the population and were politically dominant historically, that they lost this ultimate control and were not able to regain it with the departure of colonial powers? Beyond the ideological climate already alluded to, – though the pastoralists did not necessarily have to share this – three main factors, each of continuing relevance, seem to have been responsible. One was the specific form of midwifery practised by the departing colonial powers, which was hasty and standard. Second was the notorious lack of unity among the various Somali pastoral clans and sub-clans, which basically did not seem to have a way of acting as a collectivity or of jointly organizing themselves politically in opposition to the state. Ironically the latter factor did not prevent the state itself from posing as the champion and representative of all-Somali unity, no matter how far-fetched its claims in this respect were to become. Yet, after the complete collapse of the Somali state in 1992/3, that same incapacity to join forces militated against its resurrection (Doornbos and Markakis, 1994). But the third and related factor explaining the shift of power away from the pastoralist domain was, as noted, that of mechanisms of social and economic differentiation operating among as well as in relation to the pastoralists.

Though arguably more egalitarian than most sedentary societies, pastoralists in Somalia and elsewhere in Eastern Africa in recent decades were increasingly exposed to the dynamics of growing economic and social inequality. As part of this complex, possibilities of 'out' – movement into and liaison with the politically pivotal urban sphere were of key significance. Permanent or semi-permanent urban residence became socially attractive as well as politically compelling – for those who could afford it – on the theoretical ground that access to and involvement in the political centre would be important to the fortunes of pastoral clan members in the field. These factors in turn lent support to the gradual shift of the point of political gravity from the pastoral non-state to the state sphere and eventually contributed to the political marginalization of the majority of the pastoralists. Social differentiation became a powerful mechanism of incorporation and the consequent marginalization of pastoralists. But as the early 1990s would dramatically demonstrate, the unified state thus constructed was in effect extremely fragile and contained the seeds of its own fragmentation and collapse.

Part 4

Dairy Aid and Dairy Development in India: Institutions and Resource Strategies

9

Premises and Impacts of International Dairy Aid: Institutional Interest and the Politics of Evaluation

with Manoshi Mitra and Pieter van Stuijvenberg

Introduction

In the next two chapters, the focus is on institutional interventions in resource utilization patterns of a different kind and magnitude than were dealt with in the previous chapters. The concern here is with the premises and prospects of dairy development in India, and the institutional strategies that have been adopted towards these ends. The interest thus shifts to the pros and cons of quite different modes of livestock utilization than was the case in the Ankole Ranching Scheme discussed in Chapter 7, or are inherent in the pastoralist livelihood strategies in the Horn and Eastern Africa as discussed in Chapter 8. Nonetheless, a significant parallel, particularly with the Ankole Ranching Scheme, lies in the way in which issues of local resource management and competition have come to be linked up and transformed in the context of international aid programmes. In both instances the foreign aid connection gave rise to new expectations about alternative development routes, but in both cases, too, it prompted the emergence of novel and unprecedented institutional complexities, new choices about resource utilization priorities, and, last but not least, additional areas and levels of contestation.

The present chapter is essentially concerned with the *pivotal role of international dairy aid programmes in the globalization of production and distribution of dairy products*. The key example is the Indian dairy development programme 'Operation Flood', which has been assisted by the World Food Programme (WFP), the European Community (EC, now EU) and other donors. The chapter starts out with a reconsideration of the international dairy situation in the 1960s and the major policy intentions then associated with dairy aid. Following this, the next section examines the premises and impacts of the Operation Flood programme. The final section discusses the institutional implications of the incorporation into global market arrangements which the case exemplifies, and the vexed questions of evaluation which have arisen in this context. The next chapter (10) will continue the analysis of the Operation Flood programme and review its impacts in several key respects as well as the debates to which they have given rise up until the early 1990's.

International dairy aid programmes: origins and objectives

Research into food problems as well as into food policies within and *vis-à-vis* Third World countries has highlighted several recurrent facts, factors and actors. Food production as well as food products are increasingly subjected to global investment and marketing strategies. The chain of industrial processing and transporting stages between primary producers and final consumers is progressively being prolonged, causing final products to become increasingly cost and energy intensive while at the same time reducing the value added by agricultural producers to relatively marginal proportions. These trends are accompanied by increasing global (inter)dependence with respect to production and distribution of food commodities (cf. George, 1976; Lappé and Collins, 1977; Power and Holenstein, 1980; Garcia, 1984).

Few global transformations therefore have such profound implications for basic needs fulfilment as the processes by which *basic foods are progressively subjected to international production and marketing arrangements*. Food has increasingly become an international commodity, either at world market or concessional prices or as aid. This transition is resulting not only in a vastly increased reach of global marketing and distribution arrangements for food commodities, but also in the transformation of the basic autonomy of local production systems by global market arrangements, or aid, as the case may be.

The exact form of such incorporation into the world economy varies widely. With respect to various basic food commodities, we are concerned in particular with the ramifications of the integration of national economies into the world market for food products. This may involve imports of concessional food commodities such as cereals to supplement, substitute or compete with the production of local staple foods. Though often intended to enhance food security, such imports may actually render the production of staple foods economically unviable (Andrae and Beckman, 1985; Maxwell, 1986). Another dimension of this incorporation process relates to agricultural inputs, notably the imported production and processing technologies meant to increase outputs. In agriculture these may be patented gene banks and fertilizers for higher yielding varieties; in the livestock sector, cross-breeding technologies utilizing frozen semen and concentrated animal feed; and in the marketing sphere, advanced processing and packaging techniques based on Western consumption patterns and labour-saving devices. Many of these technologies may prove unsustainable in the long run in peasant economies.

Moreover, for many products there is a still accelerating surplus production in the North and a stagnating production in many countries of the South. Seemingly, in trying to 'bridge' this gap through donations and concessional terms of trade, complementary institutional interests have been emerging in both North and South, which have a stake in the disposal and receipt of such aid. Dairy production and products occupy a special position in this regard. Seasonality of production and perishability of milk, aside from other qualities, impose special technological requirements on the extension of international distribution chains. However, such obstacles to globalization have been progressively overcome through technological advances, which have thus placed dairy products in essentially the same category of exportable surplus commodities as meat and grains.

It is interesting to trace how the thinking about these options has been evolving within the circles engaged in international aid programmes. In 1968, a report of the Committee on Commodity Problems (CCP) of the FAO summed up the problems and the perceived possibilities in the international dairy situation in the following terms:

> For several years milk production has tended to exceed commercial outlets, more especially in Europe and recently to some extent in the United States, with a resulting increase in butter stocks which are now (early 1968) estimated to exceed normal requirements by about 250,000 metric tons. Recent analyses prepared by the secretariats of FAO, OECD, and EEC suggest that these stocks will increase further. *. . . Attempts to remedy the situation by way of encouraging consumption in producing countries have met with insufficient success.* Likewise attempts to export butter surpluses with the assistance of government subsidies have failed to ease the stock position materially and *have disrupted normal international trade. On the other hand, consumption needs in developing countries are enormous and increasing and are likely to continue to exceed supplies available from domestic production* and commercial imports for a long time. Additional supplies to these countries, if carefully planned, would stimulate development of economic

and human resources, and as their economies continue to grow, *could lead to the expansion of commercial markets* (FAO 1968; authors' emphasis).

The background for these FAO aid plans lay in the 'chronic imbalance between milk production and use' within Europe and the US, which had become critical by the late 1960s. At that time, butter stocks in the EU had reached a record level of 480,000 tons. Since a stock of some 230,000 tons was considered adequate, about 250,000 tons could be considered as surplus. The EU as a whole had thus emerged as a net exporter, though within Europe the United Kingdom, Italy and the Federal Republic of Germany were still large importers. (Japan was another significant importer.) Along with this increased stock, prices of butter, skimmed milk powder, cheese, whole milk powder and other dairy products were showing a downward trend in Western markets. It was expected that there would be an excess of milk supplies of the order of about 14.0 million tons in the EU countries, while in developing countries the shortfall in supply in comparison to increased demand (due to population increases) was calculated to be in the order of some 20 million tons. The gap could profitably be made up, it was suggested, by *donations of milk commodities under dairy aid programmes*. This would help to 'bridge the nutritional and economic gap and at the same time help to stabilize prices on international markets'. It was argued that 'traditional dairy exporters, who now face competition from subsidized exports, would benefit if those exports were replaced by organized food aid programmes'. Besides, it was anticipated that 'a saving in heavy storage costs in surplus countries and the promotion of the demand for dairy products in developing countries in the future' would be another benefit. Hence, in April 1969, the Council of EC Ministers decided to include for the first time dairy products within its food aid programme and consequently allocated during that year 35,000 tons of butter oil and 123,000 tons of skim milk powder to the World Food Programme, which channelled most of it to India's Operation Flood programme (van Dorsten, 1986).

Such was also the basis on which dairy aid, both as food aid and as a support for the development of indigenous milk production and consumption, was considered by the Committee on Commodity Problems. The aims to be realized through such aid were identified by the CCP to be the following:

1 It was anticipated that there would be shortages in supplies from local sources relative to expected demands in the developing

countries. Therefore, milk and milk components in suitable forms had to be made available for recombination and sale.

2 Such provision should in the first place meet the nutritional requirements of children, both pre-school and school age, and expectant mothers, through communal milk distribution programmes.

3 Existing dairy industries in developing countries would be strengthened by the aid programmes.

4 Resulting from the enlarged scale and diversity of dairy processing, the availability of technological resources would be broadened.

5 As local milk production would increase and local dairy industries be developed, the quantity of whole milk brought in as aid could decline from an initial high to zero over five years on the average.

In the perspective of the CCP, aid would be offered provided that donated milk could be processed by 'technically competent processors' to suit local conditions and could be locally recombined from imported materials and local milk supplies. It was expected that about 60,000–80,000 tons of EU milk fat and around 240,000–330,000 tons of solid non-fat could thus be exported annually. Such amounts were further expected to increase as the new milk plants came into being and socio-economic development cum welfare projects were enlarged.

From this brief résumé of the international dairy situation at the time that dairy aid was included in the food aid programme of the FAO, certain assumptions emerged, namely that (1) as in the case of other forms of food aid, dairy aid was considered only when mounting surpluses emerged in the major dairy producing countries; (2) dairy aid was seen as a mechanism for balancing international prices; (3) dairy aid was conceptualized in such a way as to increase milk consumption in the Third World; and (4) dairy development was conceived as involving the promotion of dairy industries in developing countries which would provide the processing infrastructure for recombining imported skim milk powder.

The exact mix of motivations prompting governments of Third World countries to develop an interest in receiving dairy food aid in the final analysis amounted to an empirical question. It was not a matter of course that they *should* be interested. Turkey at one time, for example, declined offers of dairy aid for fear that this might damage its own efforts at dairy development. But where an interest in receiving dairy aid did get articulated, it was likely to be influenced by various factors such as changing food habits (in the direction of protein-rich foods), the specific demands of middle and higher income categories for a regular supply of milk, the interests of processing plant managers in more easily available commodities so as to ensure sufficient and continuous throughput and, last but not least, the very availability of dairy commodities at attractive terms to selected Third World countries. Whatever the exact mix of these factors, the 'push' factors for dairy aid from the donor side could hardly be effective without some institutionalized expression of a corresponding interest at the receiving end.

The need to safeguard the interests of dairy corporations and farmers' lobbies on the donor side, while designing dairy aid programmes, was clearly recognized by the FAO. Their interests concerning the need to develop new markets in the developing countries for milk and milk products were firmly incorporated into the proposals of the FAO to use dairy aid as food aid:

> Until the late 1950s commercial trade in skimmed milk powder was virtually non-existent. *Donations and concessional supplies of skimmed milk powder obviously have paved the way to the rapid expansion in commercial trade during recent years.* A striking example is provided by Japan where for some years milk powder was supplied on concessional terms for school lunch programmes. As the economy developed, commercial imports expanded considerably (FAO, 1968:15, authors' emphasis).

The FAO's Committee on Commodity Problems stated that this example could be taken as indicative of the 'long term benefits that may result for international commercial trade from concessional imports'. Some of the trends reported for the 1960s for the import of skim milk powder by developing countries in Latin America, Asia and Africa similarly indicated a connection between aid and trade, in the sense that aid was preceding and apparently paving the way for trade. With roughly constant total magnitudes of imports of skim milk powder, one can note that in all three continents the aid component declined while the trade component increased (see Table 9.1). To quote again the CCP:

> At present food aid in milk products plays a rather modest role in the overall consumption of milk and milk products in developing countries, but it is of great importance to the vulnerable and low income groups for whom commercial supplies are beyond reach. *Getting these groups accustomed to milk products also paves the way for later commercial demand* (authors' emphasis).

Table 9.1   International trade in skim milk powder,
1962 and 1965–6 (in 1000 tons)

Imports (developing countries)	1962	1965	1966
Latin America:			
Commercial	30	58	76
Donations	78	74	43
Asia (excl. Japan):			
Commercial	43	46	77
Donations	86	77	73
Africa (excl. South Africa):			
Commercial	13	11	17
Donations	54	23	10
Unspecified:			
Commercial	22	4	10
Donations	2	3	2

Source: FAO, 1968:31.

It was evidently assumed at the time that 'development' would soon raise the income levels of marginal groups to a level at which they would be able to afford regular purchases of commercially imported milk. Even for the late 1960s this appears to have been an overly optimistic perspective. Still, the potential of dairy food aid for future trade was reiterated by the dairy industry as well as by the FAO. For example, an industry spokesman submitted to the 1978 International Dairy Congress that 'the supply of dairy products as aid is likely to stimulate a demand for milk or milk based foods which finally can be bought and paid for by the recipient countries' (Allum, 1978:1–2). One major concern from an industrial viewpoint, however, was the potential negative effect that aid might have on current, as opposed to future trade. From this perspective the key question was: 'how best can food aid in the form of dairy products be guaranteed in both continuity and in the optimum form required, but without severe penalty to the donor States?' Part of the answer was taken to be that dairy aid and export programmes should be developed concurrently, thus allowing 'milk production [to] be planned to fully take into account exports and food aid, thereby removing from the industry the stigma of gross over-production'. For this strategy to be possible, however, a stated precondition was a decisive involvement of the dairy industry itself. It was submitted that '[untold] danger to trade would occur should state purchases for food aid of other than intervention produce be attempted without the clear authority and advice of the industry'.

Again, in much the same vein, an EC statement in 1977 identified two major objectives of EC food aid as follows:

1 Food aid, primarily intended to meet the developing countries' needs, is only a temporary means of speeding up the economic modernization of the Third World, this process being likely to increase the external outlets of European industries later on.
2 Food aid is part of a trade policy aimed at developing regular trade and, thus, increasing possibilities of sale of community agricultural products (Commission of the European Communities, 1977:8–9).

In the light of these projections, it seems justified to assume that the promise of future sales to the Third World may have had the effect of reducing concerns about increasing overproduction of milk in Europe at the time.

Components of dairy aid

Under various early aid programmes, locally produced milk was considered as the prime source of fluid milk for direct consumption. But it was taken for granted that urban demand would increase with the growth of urban populations and that with this situation there would be competition among milk plants for available supplies. The main source for the extra supply was assumed to be recombined milk; that is, local milk combined with imported milk components. It was pointed out by the FAO that where the local milk had an especially high fat content, skimmed milk powder could be imported to be recombined with it and such imports 'should be put on a commercial basis as soon as practicable'.

The commercial forerunners for such arrangements were the milk recombination plants established in South East Asia, the Caribbean, Latin America and Africa, where plants had been installed with the help of dairy companies from New Zealand, Australia, Switzerland, the Netherlands, the United Kingdom and the United States. In addition, among the international organizations UNICEF in particular was quite active during the earlier stages in initiating dairy aid programmes involving the establishment of recombination facilities.

The key towards complementarity rather than conflict with the requirements of trade was expected to lie in the conceptualization of special aid programmes at concessional terms that would have no direct repercussions on international market prices. Such aid programmes were to be designed in particular for projects involving:

1 Recombined whole milk for commercial sale or subsidised sale to low-income groups in urban centres in connection with milk plant development projects based on fuller utilization of existing plant capacities (for example India, Pakistan, Sri Lanka).
2 Food aid linked with other social or economic development projects (such as vocational training or labour mobilization projects utilizing skimmed milk powder (SMP), condensed or evaporated milk, cheese, whole milk powder and butter or butter-fat preparations (ghee, butter oil).
3 Nutritional improvement schemes for pre-school children, expectant and nursing mothers through the provision of SMP and whole milk biscuits for distribution to children in remote areas (FAO, 1968:21).

Yet, such programmes could be called off when surpluses would no longer be forthcoming, with consequent nutritional repercussions such as effects on dietary balances. Imbalances might also occur with regard to the particular conditions and commodities available for special feeding projects. In this connection the WFP mentioned problems such as: 'shortage and irregularity of supplies, inadequate transport and storage facilities, lack of institutions and of trained personnel, consumption habits, possible health risks arising from lactose intolerance, lack of vitamins in unfortified skimmed milk powder and unhygienic treatment, potential health hazards' (Committee on Food Aid, 1976a:8).

Dairy development projects linked with other development projects were presumed to accord well with WFP priorities, which gave first consideration to projects designed to increase agricultural, and especially food, production, to improve the nutrition of vulnerable groups and which could also form part of a poverty-oriented strategy for rural development. In favourable situations they were expected to generate employment and at the same time produce milk and milk products, particularly for the urban areas where the demand for such commodities was substantial. Consistent with these priorities, according to the WFP/CFA dairy development programmes in developing countries were to be guided by three main objectives: (1) increasing milk production; (2) improving nutritional standards of the population, especially among vulnerable groups; (3) strengthening the economy and thus the incomes of small and marginal farmers and agricultural labourers. The incorporation of dairy-oriented animal husbandry into farming was therefore expected to lead to a diversification of farming and to a fuller use of crop residues. Ancillary industries could be developed which would increase employment and income levels of the community as a whole. Furthermore, 'dairying is a grass-roots activity using indigenous inputs, which lends itself to a marked degree to improvement through self-help, often through co-operative organizations and other farmer groupings, thereby making it well suited to receiving food aid' (Committee on Food Aid, 1976b:8).

In essence these points of departure provided the model or strategy on which Operation Flood has been based. This Indian dairy development strategy, in which the WFP and also the EC became heavily involved, developed into the largest single development programme of its kind. As phrased by the WFP: 'Operation Flood is the culmination of WFP experience in the field of dairy development in India and has evolved as the end-product of earlier WFP-supported projects designed to assist a varied cross-section of the dairy industry in that country' (Committee on Food Aid, 1976b:14).

Operation Flood: basic components

The origins of the Operation Flood Programme can be traced to the town of Anand in Kheda District, Gujarat, where specific forms of rural co-operatives had been quite successful in organizing rural economic activities, primarily for marketing purposes. In 1946, the first attempt by milk producers to eliminate the existing exploitative contractor system had taken the form of a co-operative movement, which succeeded in brushing aside the middlemen and becoming the main supplier of milk to the Bombay Milk Scheme. The private procurement system that had been in existence since the 1920s was taken over and since then the co-operative movement has grown stronger (Patel, 1986).

The 'Anand pattern' first developed as a three-tiered structure of village co-operatives, unions of village co-operatives and federations of these, while subsequently a fourth all-India federation of federations was added. The rationale of this structure was that it would enable member unions to benefit from a shared marketing programme managed by skilled marketing specialists. In this connection, large recombining plants, with bulk distribution through milk tankers and vending machines, were also established. In addition, the setting up of extended transport facilities between the main milk collection centres in the villages, the chilling plants and the city dairies was aimed at. In order to balance supplies, special plants were set up which could preserve the milk in different forms for use according to requirements.

The Anand Dairy Co-operative, which had been the model for this development, was considered an outstanding example of successful co-operative dairy development strategies in other parts of the Third World. Since the mid-1950s, recurrent foreign assistance from a number of sources had helped the Anand dairy co-operative to embark upon a progressive expansion of its activities, especially in the area of processing and product manufacturing. A quantum leap in foreign involvement, however, occurred in 1969, when the Indian government requested assistance from the WFP for the implementation of Operation Flood.

The then Prime Minister, Lal Bahadur Shastri, had initiated the setting up of the National Dairy Development Board (NDDB) in 1965, in order to organize dairy co-operatives all over India along the lines of the Anand model. The NDDB would be the source of technical expertise and assistance in helping to build milk producers' unions of co-operatives at village level and in seeing that arrangements were made for animal husbandry inputs.

Operation Flood aimed to improve milk production and supply, thus enabling the organized dairy sector to obtain a commanding share of the markets in India's major cities of Bombay, Calcutta, Delhi and Madras (together offering a potential milk market of about thirty million people) and at speeding up the process of dairy development by increasing milk procurement and production in the rural areas which supply milk to these cities. The project initially involved the following main lines of action:

1 Major increases in the capacity and throughput of dairy processing facilities, including the establishment of new city milk plants.
2 A diversion of the bulk of the urban markets from the traditional supplies of raw milk to the modern dairies.
3 A resettlement in rural areas of city-kept cattle and buffaloes which at present serve a large part of the city markets.
4 The development of a basic transportation and storage network to facilitate regional and seasonal balancing of milk supply and demand.
5 The development of milk procurement systems in appropriate rural areas in order to provide for raw milk a channel which is more remunerative than the traditional channel.
6 An improvement in standards of dairy farming by improved programmes for feeding and management, of animal breeding, veterinary services, feedstuff supplies and related extension services, thereby increasing milk yields per animal.

The WFP assistance to India was meant to achieve the following related objectives:

1 To make milk available at stable and reasonable prices to the bulk of city consumers, including vulnerable groups.
2 To enable the dairy organizations involved in the project to identify and satisfy the needs of consumers and producers, so that consumers'

preferences can be fulfilled economically and *producers can earn a larger share of the money paid by the consumers for their milk.*
3 *To improve productivity of dairy farming in rural areas with the long term objective of achieving self-sufficiency in milk,* thereby bringing about major increases of agricultural output and incomes with *special emphasis on improvement of the income of small farmers and landless people.*
4 *To remove dairy cattle from the cities* where they represent a growing problem in terms of genetic waste, social cost and public health.
5 To establish a broad basis for accelerated development of the national dairy industry during a period of WFP assistance and after (Committee on Food Aid, 1976, authors' emphasis).

WFP had undertaken to contribute in particular dried skimmed milk and butter oil to Operation Flood. The programme commenced in 1970, and was planned to take five years to complete. However, in 1976 it was reported that 'owing to delays in expansion of dairy plants and construction of new dairies and other organisational problems resulting from the vast size and complexity of the project, progress has not been as rapid as anticipated. However, the project is now well under way' (Committee on Food Aid, 1976).

According to the inter-agency mission which visited India in March 1975, under instructions from the Executive Director of WFP, to carry out an interim evaluation of this WFP-assisted project:

> ...the project should be reviewed against the background of historic developments. India has a large cattle population of at present about 230 million animals, out of these about 70 to 80 million may eventually come into dairy production. Cattle are looked upon mainly as a supply of draft animals and manure often used as fuel. Milk is usually kept for cattle owners' own use, for the manufacture of ghee, etc. Therefore, originally *although quite a lot of milk was produced, little entered into commercial channels* (Committee on Food Aid, 1975, authors' emphasis).

Given this situation of limited milk supplies from rural areas, city cattle keeping and private vending of milk was a thriving industry which existed side by side with the state controlled dairies which could only provide limited amounts to city consumers. From the government side, the task of cattle development in the country was left to various Animal Husbandry Departments, which functioned with varying degrees of efficiency. The organization of co-operatives was left to the realm of the state co-operative departments and already existing co-operatives were treated as private enterprises. Against this background, the official evaluation report saw Phase I of Operation Flood as a highly commendable departure and intervention:

> It must be looked upon as a revolution in thinking and organisation. It has potential not only of obtaining larger and better milk supplies for the cities, but also of bringing about some very substantial social improvements in the milkshed areas. The project attempts to condense into a few years a development which in other countries, with more favourable conditions, took 30–60 years. It is the world's largest dairy project (Committee on Food Aid, 1975:9).

Using the basic patterns of operation developed under Operation Flood I for the four metropolitan cities, Operation Flood II was launched in 1975 to replicate the Anand model throughout India in all (142) cities with a population over 100,000. These were to be incorporated in a National Milk Grid through twenty-five 'cluster' federations of dairy co-operative unions, thus making it possible, theoretically at least, to balance seasonal or other shortfalls in certain regions with surpluses from other regions. Insulated road and rail milk tankers for long distance transportation of liquid milk were to be put into operation so that, in fact, the milksheds of Bombay, Delhi, Calcutta, Madras would all become interconnected. Besides, additional storage facilities for a buffer stock of dairy commodities for recombination, largely from donations, were to be provided.

Thus the objectives of Operation Flood II were formulated as follows:

1 To enable some ten million rural milk producers' families to build a viable, self-sustaining dairy industry by mid-1965.
2 To enable the milk producers to rear a National Milch Herd of some fourteen million crossbred cows and upgraded buffaloes during the 1980s.
3 To erect a National Milk Grid linking the rural milksheds to the major demand centres with urban populations totalling some 150 million.
4 To erect the infrastructure required to support the available national dairy industry including: (a) a national frozen-semen system; (b) vaccine production and delivery system; (c) indigenous development of dairy processing and conservation methods (for traditional and modern dairy products); (d) enlarged facilities for indigenous design and manufacture of dairy equipment; (e) provision of manpower development programmes, with special emphasis on professional managerial and technical cadres for rural industries such as dairying; (f) *ad interim* programmes to supply butter oil as an affordable cooking

medium and extruded foods as the basis for infant supplementary feeding programmes, especially in integrated rural development programmes based on the Anand Pattern; and (g) erection of a Management Information System to provide timely information to local decision makers responsible for development of the National Milk Grid. And finally: 'by means of the improvements thus achieved in milk production and marketing, to enable milk and milk products to form an appropriate part of a stable, nutritionally adequate national diet (currently estimated at an average per capita availability of 180 gm of milk daily), which is to be achieved for a population of 750 million during 1980s' (*Dairy India*, 1983).

In order to bridge the still existing gap between the indigenous supply of milk forthcoming through this procurement and marketing network and the urban demand, additional foreign aid was considered to be necessary. For that purpose, large amounts of dairy surplus commodities from the EC continued to be transferred through the existing networks in India. In this connection a Memorandum of the European Commission stated that 'the development of agricultural processing units may require external contributions until such time as parallel efforts to encourage local production take over' (Commission of the European Communities, 1983:8). Besides, since the build-up of these networks was primarily being financed out of the sales of the donated commodities through the Indian Dairy Corporation (IDC), which was later to be merged with the NDDB, EC aid thus contributed to the organizational basis for Operation Flood.

Apart from aid from the EC and the WFP, Operation Flood was assisted by the UNDP, UNICEF and a number of government and national agencies for development co-operation. The UNDP/FAO provided technical and plant management expertise, while UNICEF supplied dairy equipment. The World Bank stepped in in 1975 to participate in the financing of three comprehensive dairy development projects in other areas of India. The purposes of these were: (1) to implement integrated programmes for increasing the production of milk in rural areas through co-operative development programmes (following the Anand pattern in Gujarat); (2) import of cattle; (3) quality crossbreeding; (4) animal health improvement; (5) facilities for milk collection; (6) processing, (7) marketing; and (8) training of farmers and instructors.

Analysis

Officially, Operation Flood has often been typified as a programme which is: (1) directed to the rural poor; (2) considered suitable to be replicated throughout different regions of the country; and (3) capable of promoting the development of an independent, self-sustaining Indian dairy industry, notwithstanding its reliance on very considerable inputs from international dairy surpluses and on Western dairy technology. These have been no minor claims, especially as they were made rather emphatically by the international agencies involved and the implementing agencies, the National Dairy Development Board (NDDB) and the Indian Dairy Corporation (IDC).

A basic question of interest to many observers has been whether the Operation Flood programme effectively worked out as an operationally and economically viable instrument for enhancing dairy production in India while at the same time offering scope to the poor and landless farmers to participate in dairying. Moreover, given India's striving for self-sufficiency, a related crucial issue is whether or not Operation Flood was leading to increased dependence on foreign dairy imports and dairy technology and, if so, what the likelihood would be of a continuation of European food aid to India on a longer term, given the burden it was imposing on the EC budget.

The anticipated mutuality of interests between India's poorest people and European farmers has attracted scholarly interest from several quarters, including from a group of researchers participating in the Indo-Dutch Programme on Alternatives in Development (IDPAD), a programme of co-operation in social science research between Indian and Dutch scholars. IDPAD provided a useful framework for a study of the impact of the Operation Flood programme, as it enabled fieldwork in both locations of origin and destination of the dairy surpluses. Thus in assessing the Operation Flood programme, it was endeavoured to take several important aspects into account, namely its impacts in terms of: (1) India's dependence on foreign (European) dairy products, mainly of skim milk powder and butter oil; (2) India's domestic dairy production; (3) the incomes of the participating farmers; (4) the existing 'unorganized', or informal, dairy production and marketing; (5) the nutritional levels in rural areas; and (6) the position of rural women. This section presents a preliminary overview of the findings of the IDPAD research project on these issues, while additional aspects will be taken up in Chapter 10.

1 Dependence on foreign dairy products

With respect to Operation Flood's impact on India's dependency on foreign deliveries of skim milk powder, it should be understood that India has the potential capacity to meet its domestic demand. The aid commodities from the EC in the form of milk powder and butter oil represented only a very small part (approximately 1 percent) of the total Indian milk production. Besides, the co-operative dairy industry set up in the context of Operation Flood itself produced about 60,000 tons of powdered milk products in 1983/84, which is roughly equal to twice the average annual EC donation of skimmed milk powder to India during Phase II of Operation Flood. In recent years, the Indian milk powder production has increased even further.

More significant, however, is that as far as the co-operative industry itself is concerned, the imports *do* represent an important part of the annual throughput, which for example for 1980 was estimated to be around 30 percent. Although subsequent levels of domestic milk powder production, at least technically, would allow for a completely indigenous provision of milk to the major cities, a continuous stream of aid commodities has tended to blur the effective costs of such an indigenous supply, partly as a result of the price policy which has been followed for many years. The result of this is that India has in effect become dependent on cheap foreign dairy deliveries in another respect: the availability of dairy aid has allowed the Indian authorities to maintain the so-called transfer prices for skim milk powder and butter oil at levels (far) below indigenous production costs. The main result of this has been that the margin between the price at which rural producers are prepared to supply their milk to the co-operatives and the price which urban consumers are prepared to pay became too narrow to cover adequately the costs of the milk processing and marketing system. Hence, without aid or cheap supplies from abroad, the Indian co-operative dairy industry would have to face a painful process of adjustment and it remains to be seen what part of the recently built infrastructure would then remain viable.

An alternative for the Indian government could be to start subsidizing this sector on a permanent basis out of indigenous resources, or else to pass on the costs to the urban consumers. One may appreciate that the Indian authorities have sought to circumvent the painful decisions this involves. This may also explain why after many years of aid, which was meant to make itself superfluous, there have again and again been renewed efforts – through new phases of Operation Flood – to have the aid continued. Nevertheless, the fact that in several states of India (especially Gujarat and Maharashtra) a lack of market outlets for flush season surplus milk can be observed (as evidenced by the introduction of milk-holidays), points to the necessity of a painful *internal* adjustment of supply and demand instead of a relatively comfortable reliance on donated commodities.

2   Domestic dairy production

With respect to Operation Flood's impact on India's domestic dairy production, it should be observed that (notwithstanding official claims) the growth of the indigenous dairy production, as a result of Operation Flood, did by and large remain below the expectations mentioned, for example, in the Operation Flood II project documents. Although processing capacity, both of the metropolitan and urban dairies as well as the rural feeder-balancing dairies, has rapidly increased, the required institutional build-up appears to have advanced more slowly in many other regions. With the exception of some advanced regions, the large increases in milk procurement under Operation Flood seem due mainly to a shift in marketing channels (that is, farmers switching from sales to ghee traders to co-operatives), rather than to any sizeable increase in milk production. Moreover, the figures reflecting this procurement increase also include the effect merely of an enlargement of the spatial coverage of the programme. Beyond this, in many milksheds Operation Flood has also not been able to induce co-operating farmers to enlarge dairy production along the proposed lines of modernization (improved feeding practices, veterinary care and genetic upgrading of stock).

Apart from delays in the implementation of the programme, an important reason for this low production response (which contrasts with the grand promises of the original Anand model) can be found in the nature of traditional dairying in India, which should mainly be considered as complementary to agricultural production activities. When, after having met home consumption, a certain milk surplus is still available, the decision of farmers as to how to dispose of it strongly depends on existing marketing opportunities and the prices offered on each of those markets. The case of Maharashtra, for example, showed quite clearly that if collection centres offering reasonably high prices are expanded, procurement of milk appears to be highly price elastic. But such a response in milk *procurement* does not necessarily imply an increase in milk *production*. The main condition for raising milk production is that farmers consider it an attractive opportunity for investing resources. In many parts of India this does not yet seem to be the case.

Over the past several years, there has nevertheless been a slow overall increase in national milk production, most of it due to the increasing availability of fodder (a by-product of the rise in agricultural production in the Green Revolution regions of the country). Notwithstanding opposite claims of the main implementing agencies, Operation Flood's own contribution to the increase in domestic production therefore must have been limited and in any case needs to be placed within the perspective that milk procurement within Operation Flood areas represents no more than 5–10 percent of the total national production. Referring to the official figures with respect to the production increase, the official Jha Committee's evaluation report regarding the second phase of Operation Flood thus points to 'the need for improving both the methodology and the instruments for collecting the relevant data'.

The impact of EC dairy aid on India's dairy production appears to have been twofold: while the EC's financial support for Operation Flood's investments, including the stimulating effects of increased marketing outlets, may have had a positive impact, one should also note a certain depressing impact which cheap imports (given the existing price policies) cannot but have had on the domestic price level, thereby frustrating local producers.

Operation Flood has been aiming at replicating the successful Anand pattern of dairy development in other regions, where conditions for milk production, milk marketing and co-operativization differ in crucial ways from those obtaining in central Gujarat. It should not be surprising that these major differences in conditions have been seriously hampering the replicability of the Anand pattern. The differences in performance and viability between the dairy co-operatives in Bihar and Banaskantha, for example, make it quite clear that some regions are more favourably predisposed (for example because of the existing livestock production system, prevailing milk utilization patterns and socio-political factors) to the replication of the Anand pattern than others.

3   Participating farmers' incomes

With respect to Operation Flood's impact on the incomes of participating farmers, several studies have pointed out that Operation Flood did contribute to these incomes. However, it appears that this increase in income has resulted more from (modest) price increases and higher sales of milk made possible by the new infrastructure than from production increases on the part of the participating farmers. By implication it will be clear that Operation Flood can only have had a very limited impact on the income position of the participating producers. The main impact on incomes seems to be through the creation of an alternative way of disposing of the milk which is already produced and which offers a premium in comparison to the traditional ways. Though detailed data are scarce, the secondary nature of dairying activities is mentioned by all available literature and researchers as of central importance. Agriculture remains by far the most important source of income for participating producers.

An important claim of Operation Flood has been that its implementation would help to eliminate rural poverty by giving the landless and small peasants access to additional sources of income. Since access to livestock would be easier for them than access to land, the idea was that this class of rural producers could be encouraged to take up milk production. Furthermore, given the new co-operative milk marketing structure, which would provide remunerative prices, Operation Flood was expected: (1) to eliminate the allegedly wasteful and exploitative private trade in milk; (2) to utilize unemployed or underemployed family labour (women!); and (3) to increase the available quantities of milk for rural consumption, thereby positively affecting nutrition levels.

These claims have been exaggerated. The assumption that access to livestock is relatively easy did not prove to be correct. Although the distribution of livestock assets and incomes from dairy farming was less skewed than the landholding distribution, it nevertheless remained uneven. The participation of the landless is especially quite unfavourable. Only about 10 percent of the landless labourers keep a milch animal, often of a low quality. The participation of marginal farmers (30–50 percent of whom own milch animals) is relatively stronger, but is generally estimated to remain significantly below the participation of the better-off categories. Indeed, the major problem which was faced by the landless households and marginal farmers was the sheer lack of fodder and credit. For Operation Flood, or dairying in general, to be able to contribute to the reduction of poverty among landless labourers, these harsh realities would have to be faced squarely. This does not imply that income generating activities in the dairy sector are entirely impossible for the poor. It does mean, however, that the grand expectations and claims of achievements should be toned down to more realistic assessments.

4   Informal production and marketing

With regard to Operation Flood's impact on the existing 'unorganized' or informal, dairy production and marketing, it can be observed that thus far the expansion of the 'organized' sector dairies in their efforts to capture a commanding share of the urban milk market, under Operation Flood, has not led to a significant overall loss of employment in the informal sector. The main reasons for this appear to have been: (1) the rapid growth in the urban consumer demand for liquid milk (implying that the expansion of the organized sector dairies did not necessarily result in a shrinkage in the absolute share of the informal sector); and (2) the responsiveness of the informal sector to typical Indian consumer demands. Besides, because of the low supply elasticities prevailing in the informal sector, it is quite clear that this sector in itself would not have been able to meet the expanding demand for liquid milk. In other words, without Operation Flood milk prices would have risen sharply, causing the poorest consumers to stop consuming their already tiny quantities of milk altogether. This result, however, has been achieved by relying partly on dairy aid commodities and through subsidizing the organized dairy sector, and thus also, and primarily, the middle and high income groups.

5   Nutritional levels in rural areas

With regard to Operation Flood's impact on nutritional levels in the rural areas, it should be observed that an appreciation of this impact is rather controversial, since the elimination of deficiencies in caloric intake partly depends on structural developments in agriculture and the complementary employment effects. Both critics and protagonists of Operation Flood agree that the consumption of milk and dairy products in the rural areas is lower than it was before Operation Flood was implemented. Several researchers found that the co-operative infrastructure has led to rural price increases, favouring deliveries of rural dairy products to the urban centres. Coupled with a slowly increasing milk production, the end result is a lower consumption level in the rural areas, both among producers and non-producers.

The programme's impact on nutritional levels should, however, be considered against the background of the agricultural sector as a whole (within which milk production constitutes only a secondary factor) where access to basic foods is primarily determined by income generation and employment in crop cultivation. The question then remains to what extent co-operative dairying provides an additional source of income which can outweigh the lower direct consumption of milk.

Producers *can* purchase alternative calorie-rich foodstuffs from their income from dairying, such that they *might* be able to improve their food consumption pattern as a whole. Whether this is in fact the case is difficult to establish, however, as systematic micro-studies into rural income expenditures and consumption patterns are by and large lacking. What seems clear, however, is that especially the non-producers (namely, a large number of the poor, landless labourers and marginal farmers), who do not have adequate means to participate in the production process, stand to lose as a result of the commercialization under Operation Flood. Before the launching of Operation Flood they often received free buttermilk, the by-product of ghee production. The increased sales of milk for purposes of urban consumption and the concomitant reduction of ghee production thus cannot have had a positive effect on the food consumption patterns of the poor non-producers.

6   The position of rural women

With respect to Operation Flood's impact on the position of rural women, a central question is whether female labour input in dairying has increased due to the introduction of dairy co-operatives. This question is most relevant with respect to the small-farmer and landless women because it is they who are most intensively involved in milk production. As to women on medium and large farms, it is very unlikely that their physical workload has increased due to the introduction of dairy co-operatives. Among these classes much work was already done by men or hired labourers and this tendency has probably been reinforced by the increasing commercialization of milk production. Moreover, preparation of milk products, usually the task of women, has almost certainly declined in importance due to increased marketing of milk in fluid form.

As regards the landless and small-peasant women, a distinction has to be made between: (1) those households which were already involved in milk production prior to the establishment of a dairy co-operative; and (2) those households which took up milk production or significantly increased their dairy assets as a consequence of the new possibilities created by the dairy co-operatives. The *first* category formed probably the majority of households and it is far from certain that the workload of women in these households has increased. Anand pattern dairy co-operatives might have labour-saving as well as labour-increasing effects. For example, women who earlier had to walk long distances in order to sell their milk, or who used to spend much time in ghee manufacture might have reduced their workload by selling the liquid milk now to the nearby co-operative collection centre. Also, some of them might have substituted purchased cattle feed for natural herbage, grass and fodder, which they earlier used to collect from the road side. On the other hand, they might now spend more time in watering, feeding and care of their milch animals.

For the *second* category of women the total workload has almost certainly increased. These women were found particularly among agricultural labourer households who, after the receipt of a dairy animal loan, took up milk production for the first time and combined this with wage labour. Other labourer or small farmer households might simply have expanded their already existing milk animal holdings in response to the increased demand for liquid milk and passed on the increased workload to women. Nevertheless, also among these households some women might have decreased their total daily workload, namely in the (exceptional) cases that dairy farming came to replace earlier female wage labour.

In sum, while it is clear that landless and small-farmer women bear a large share of the labour burden in dairying, it is less clear what precise effects dairy co-operatives have on their work burden. Several indications exist that women have come to enjoy less control over the dairy incomes than they did before. In all research areas women were found who indicated that with the smaller amounts earlier involved in private trade transactions, men were less interested in controlling the milk income than they now appeared to be under the co-operative system. This tendency was not only due to the comparatively attractive prices paid by co-operatives, but also to the system of bulk payments followed by most co-operatives (in deviation from the Anand model guidelines which prescribe daily payments). Moreover, most co-operatives enlisted the men as members which made it seem legitimate that they would also collect the milk payments. Notwithstanding these observations, women's control over dairy incomes in the prior situation should also not be exaggerated. In the case of loan advances by private traders or occasional sales of ghee by milk producers, there were also rather large amounts of money involved which men often found attractive to control.

Incorporation into global market arrangements

The case of Operation Flood reflects the increasingly pivotal role of international dairy aid programmes in the globalization of the production and distribution of food products. The experience with the Operation Flood programme also raises questions and issues which reach well beyond the specifics of the Indian case. In international aid circles, Operation Flood is often cited as a prime example of a successful, foreign assisted, dairy development programme, and agencies such as the FAO or World Bank have been actively propagating replication of the Indian programme in other Third World countries. Visits to the NDDB headquarters at Anand are frequently being arranged for delegations from other countries in Asia and Africa and NDDB experts have been engaged in internationally sponsored feasibility studies in such countries as Pakistan, Sri Lanka, the Philippines and China. In these – and other – cases the basic idea is to find ways of establishing linkages between international dairy commodity aid and national dairy development programmes in Third World countries. In its most general sense, the Operation Flood programme may therefore be regarded as an instance of the internationalization of processing and distribution arrangements for dairy products. In turn, this transformation forms part of wider global processes by which the production and marketing of various basic foods are being increasingly integrated into the world market, even if the specific form of this integration may be based on concessional terms. Diverse as the product-specific characteristics may be in these processes, they have important implications in common.

In view of the recurrent reference made in international circles to Operation Flood as a programme capable of promoting equity and self reliance, it will be useful to focus on it from an incorporation perspective. On the basis of the evidence presented above and elsewhere (Doornbos *et al.*,1990; Doornbos and Nair, 1990), there appear to be important reasons to question the claims advanced by many proponents of the Operation Flood programme that it (1) can ensure equity of benefits; (2) can provide a replicable model for different contexts and conditions; and (3) can promote autonomy of India's dairy sector. In fact, a contrary assertion might well be made, and probably on stronger grounds, to the effect that the programme, whatever its merits, cannot realistically be expected to meet these particular policy criteria. It will be recognized that the issues addressed here are essentially those thrown up by various incorporation processes, namely, problems of differentiation and marginalization affecting (1) local social strata; (2) regional categories; and (3) the prospects of possible dependency at the national level. *Ipso facto,* one must doubt whether Operation Flood can represent a model of self-reliant dairy development.

What transpires from the Operation Flood debate is that it registers so many qualifications of different kinds that by itself this may already be taken as an indication that the programme essentially represents a mixed bag of experience. By implication this underscores a basically differentiating impact as a key characteristic for the project's record at macro- and micro-level. The paradox is that differentiational impacts have tended to be officially ignored or denied while instead the programme has been propagated as having social benefits only. In the world of development planning, however, Operation Flood is by no means the only example of a 'success story' partly achieved along with a trend towards marginalization beyond the programme's confines.

Beyond the level of more or less tangible, and measurable, impacts upon which so much of the discussion on Operation Flood has focused, there have been basic differences in perspective on the key premises of

Operation Flood. These differences themselves strongly influenced the emerging debate around the programme. In particular, contrasted assessments of the implications of the linking up of India's organized dairy sector with an international milk grid account for much of the heat that this discussion generated. Almost in any case, however, if Operation Flood *did* represent a step calculated to preserve or achieve autonomy and self-sufficiency in Indian dairying, it surely implied a calculated risk as well. For it must have been quite hard if not impossible to conceive whether in the end one would be in a position to point to a viable, self-sustaining dairy sector while having avoided becoming absorbed into an incorporating network, and/or afflicting a severe measure of aid-addiction.

The differentiating effects involved appear to have been strongly enhanced by the availability of foreign aid. The aid connection of Operation Flood I, II and III, and earlier of the Anand-based Dairy Co-operative (Amul), is a longstanding and diversified one which has involved many different donors. In particular, the enlargement of scale that has occurred since the beginning of the EC involvement has been massive and in fact almost unprecedented as far as development programmes are concerned. The irony is that in its scale of operation in India, the National Milk Grid represents an institutional white elephant which is basically unprecedented in the donor countries' own experience, where decentralized operations in dairying have been more common practice. Indirectly, this has had another effect. Without the claim to a pivotal intermediate function between foreign aid (from whichever donor) and India as the recipient country and without the claim to a central co-ordinating role in allocating resources and managing a national milk grid system, the executive leverage of IDC/NDDB *vis-à-vis* other bodies in the Indian institutional infrastructure (Ministry of Agriculture, Planning Commission, state governments and others) would have been severely reduced. Indeed, it appears that the propagation of the much-praised Anand model as the single recipe for India's dairy planning may also be understood in terms of the needs of a centralizing counterpart agency to foreign donors to have a legitimizing 'model' to justify its mission and monopolistic position.

Beyond analysis of the programme's performance with respect to its impact on different production aspects, therefore, a consideration of the programme's distinctive features and mode of operation is necessary within a wider institutional perspective, reviewing Operation Flood against the background of the Indian policy context.

Institutional strategies and the politics of evaluation

It is by no means uncommon for complex organizations to engage in strategies of institutional maintenance and enlargement. In fact, it is an often observed tendency for large organizations, in particular public bureaucracies, to try and ensure continued involvement and institutional legitimation through either expansion or redefinition of tasks. As one policy analyst put it: 'organisations may go on the offensive by growing bigger instead of better ... We are all familiar with the salesmanship involved in moving to new technologies or larger structures where internal dynamism and grandiose conceptions are mistaken for new ideas' (Wildawsky, 1972:518). However, special concern in this regard is necessary in the case of organizations which are basically run as project implementing bodies and thus, in principle, temporary organizations. In the case of the Operation Flood structure, it appears that the availability of foreign funding has enabled the growth of a sizeable command complex which will be very difficult to dismantle or reduce to size upon the termination of the project's duration.

In addition, other institutional factors may strengthen the staying power of the Operation Flood structure. To see these, it will be necessary to consider the Indian political-institutional context within which they have emerged. Notwithstanding the extremely detailed rules and regulations with which the Indian government bureaucracy has often been perceived by the outside world, paradoxically, there is also a relative ease with which new voluntary organizations appear to have been set up in India – be they small non-governmental grassroots organizations or institutional complexes which may grow into large corporate bodies such as IDC/NDDB. To be sure, as Kothari points out, the category comprises considerable heterogeneity and polarization:

> Voluntary action has spread today from the activity of those agencies which are the most dominant sectors of government and corporate policy, destroying democratic institutions, natural resources and natural communities, to the actions of social movements concerned with restructuring society towards greater control of the people on their destinies on the basis of justice and non-violence (Kothari, 1986:26).

Of the particular Indian context in which these diverse institutional innovations occur, one may say either that it provides a relatively permissive climate which may even seem to encourage the rapid establishment and proliferation of new institutions within the non-government sphere, or alternatively that it does not actually provide adequate countervailing checks on the emergence of new and powerful bodies.

In actual fact, if India were viewed in terms of its administrative grid, it must be recognized that the grid is increasingly under pressure. State governments tend to claim increasing shares of government business, while non-government institutions also take over a growing number of functions. Counter-efforts at political centralization are usually directed at (and often have a way of contributing to) the most divisive and explosive political issues and do little to reinforce an innovating and leading role of central planning in Indian development (Kaviraj, 1984), or to initiate new approaches and structures through which the diversified political base can effectively relate to the centre. Thus, semi-public organizations have increasingly been able to take up institutional 'space' and the autonomy which they may succeed in forcing government to grant them may later well be turned against the latter, as it may serve as a basis from which to claim additional powers. Especially semi-public and different kinds of non-government institutions which can rely on foreign connections for resources and support have thus been able to gain in power and room for manoeuvre. The Operation Flood structure presents a prime example of this phenomenon.

Of special interest in this connection is the way in which non-representative semi-public institutions seek to gain and strengthen an image of public legitimation. One question that has thus often been asked regarding the Operation Flood structure is how co-operative actually are the co-operatives? Equally often, the rhetorical insistence on producer-control has been interpreted as a reflection of the need for organizational legitimation. As a perceptive institutional analyst once remarked, 'policymakers have their needs, too' (Schaffer, 1985). But surely, whenever the notion of co-operative participation tends to be reduced to the (obligatory) delivery of inputs such as milk, only conceptual confusion can arise.

Similarly, past events concerning Operation Flood have been (re)constructed so as to give legitimacy to the present. Several myths of origin have developed around certain events and have been incorporated in the background history of Operation Flood: references to the celebrated night that Prime Minister Shastri spent at Anand, declaring the next morning that there should be an Anand-replicating programme for all of India; counts of heroic battles against exploitative middlemen, adding purpose to the producer-co-operative image of the Operation Flood structure; and last but not least, the reported 'threat' of the EC intending to dump surplus dairy products on India, which was reputedly turned into a blessing on the basis of an ingenious management formula. Each of these elements in the Operation Flood narrative serves as an ingredient in a political myth of origin: basically unverifiable and lacking in plausibility as concrete facts, their basic function is to provide legitimacy to the whole operation. To be sure, to a greater or lesser degree many large organizations in their quest for public support, and/or publicity, may have a need for such myths and cultivate them accordingly. But an organization's urge to cultivate legitimizing myths is likely to be stronger if its formal status and continued existence is less clear or self-evident on other grounds.

Connected to this, not the least noteworthy feature of the Operation Flood structure had been its handling of the politics of evaluation. The key question in this regard is why the assertions about the programme's function as an instrument capable of promoting equity of benefits and participation were being made with such persistence and on what were they based: selective evidence, wishful thinking, inadequate understanding of social processes, or an anticipation that this was what donors would like to hear? Admittedly, donor agencies too must sell projects to their constituencies. And surely, a programme that in one stroke can reach the poor, landless and women and in addition helps to break down caste barriers, can rely on solid constituency support in donor countries. Yet, none of this should be a reason to take the question of evidence and verification too lightly.

The question gets added salience precisely in view of the fact that independent research into the social effects of Operation Flood on rural producers has never been particularly welcomed, let alone facilitated, by the project authorities. The highly sensitive reaction of NDDB to most independent research and researchers has more often than not led to controversy and conflict (Baviskar, 1984). Notwithstanding the magnitude and the ostensibly public nature of the Operation Flood programme, on quite a number of occasions the project authorities have been noted for their lack of co-operation and hostility towards scientists interested in analysing the programme's alleged success.

In the final analysis it appears that the official claims about Operation Flood's performance with respect to rural participation and equity are perhaps best understood in terms of the *politics of evaluation* that has come to characterize so much of the evidence and discussion on the programme. For example, over several years there was a notable controversy about Operation Flood in the Indian press and in Parliament. This controversy was noteworthy first of all for its intensity. Few subjects outside those where the politics of the nation are directly at stake were treated in such heated terms as the presumed merits and demerits of Operation Flood. One of the examples of this was the exchange between Dr. Claude Alvarez and Dr. V. V. Kurien in the *Illustrated Weekly* in 1985, which led the Government of India to decide on the installation of the Jha Commission of Enquiry into the programme. Other instances were to follow (Doornbos and Terhal, 1993).

One point to note in this connection is an apparent contradiction between the very intensity and vehemence of the Operation Flood debate in the Indian press and in Parliament, as opposed to the mundane issues that were at stake. At both ends of the debate the positions have tended to be stated in unusually strong terms. The programme, for example, was often acclaimed as a monumental success story of global significance and its leaders credited for their far-sighted vision. In contrast, in critical press reports, the Operation Flood authorities were more likely to be depicted as a power-hungry gang whose activities had more resemblance to those of a private industrial corporation than of a public body and which, in its unresponsiveness to government or even farmers' interests, would not shy away from double-talk and unconventional means in pushing through its course of action (Baviskar and George, 1988).

Confronted with these contrasted images, the casual observer trying to come to grips with the 'realities' concerned, might well have difficulty finding points of recognition for either the height of praise or the depth of blame bestowed on Operation Flood or its executors. Instead of it constituting either a shining model or a glaring disaster, the observer might find it representing a project with a characteristically mixed experience: one whose promoters are trying hard, but against various odds – ecological, economic and other – to keep it going, yielding some modest achievements to its credit, but remaining largely unfulfilled as far as several of its major objectives are concerned. Again, this is not unlike many other development projects. Also, our onlooker might be struck by the apparent absence of corruption eroding the project organization and be rather surprised about the magnitude of accumulated foreign funding in the project.

But the discrepancy between the spectacular 'debate' and the less spectacular 'reality' suggests that there has been an autonomy of sorts to the debate about Operation Flood, propelled by other factors than (or in addition to) any contrasted readings of the empirical evidence. As a matter of fact, one should consider the possibility that the indictments of 'failure' may not be unrelated to the claims of 'success', and vice versa. To see this, it is important to consider the position of the NDDB as the key consulting agent executing the Operation Flood programme on behalf of the WFP, EC, World Bank and other donors. Its continued involvement in Operation Flood and the assurance of follow-up project phases – Operation Flood I, II, III and so on – critically depends on proven 'success' that can convince donor agencies. 'Success', however, is a matter of evaluation and, indirectly, of criteria employed and is notoriously difficult to measure objectively. In the final analysis, 'success' thus becomes what evaluation reports, press coverage, visitors' impressions and so on will say it is. Clearly, then, for a body so largely dependent for its own upkeep on positive evaluations, the importance of maintaining an image of success – *vis-à-vis* donors as well as politically influential categories – is vital: hence an almost natural institutional inclination to try and promote evaluation studies or press reports which will reiterate the image of success and to prevent, or counter if necessary, any assessments whose final outcome is less predictable or might result in a mixed or negative account.

This strategy appears to have worked well in the case of Operation Flood, confirming that '...(ad)ministrators have significant resources to bring to this [evaluation] struggle...They collect the basic information that is sent upward in one form or another. They can drag their feet, mobilize clientele, hold back information, etc.' (Wildawsky, 1972: 513). However, if all too actively pursued, calls for positive evaluation may have a boomerang effect. Critical journalists spotting repeated glamour articles about a 'best of both worlds' aid and development programme are likely to become intrigued and in the end perhaps determined to make their own search for the project's Achilles heel. Researchers interested in doing their own independent enquiry will get irritated at trivial hurdles put in their way to obstruct their project.

Glancing over the intense controversy about Operation Flood that has been raging in the Indian press for several years, it appears that the Operation Flood programme did indeed become a prime subject of the politics of evaluation. High praise followed by profound critique provokes additional praise in an increasingly sensitive publicity spiral. Once set in motion, the pendulum has difficulty gravitating back to its centre point. Only a more reflexive attitude to critique, and indeed to one's own achievements, could have prevented the swing from getting out of control. Deliberate authority involvement in suppressing unwanted evaluation results and in sponsoring 'objective' but assuredly positive studies, however, adds to an impression of the prime importance given to the politics of evaluation. One thing this cannot fail to do is in the longer run to make much of the official project reporting suspect. All this is clearly a far cry from any reasonably objective monitoring and evaluation in order to arrive at a realistic and relatively accurate assessment of the project's progress. The result has been a dearth of independent data on the performance of the world's largest dairy aid and development programme, as has been evinced through numerous calls for such data, including, not without irony, from donor organizations.

10
Sustainability, Technology and Corporate Interest in India's Modern Dairy Sector

with Liana Gertsch

Introduction

One key question thrown up by global institutional arrangements governing food production, food processing and access to food is whether in the end they will enhance or endanger food security as well as productive employment in the countries involved. Will reliance on international food commodity flows provide greater food security than dependence on autonomous production structures? Does the answer lie in free market mechanisms, in autarchy, or in a complex interplay of subsidized surplus disposal combined with technology-based interventions to raise productivity? And what role and interest would the latter option imply for the intervening institutions? The present chapter addresses some further aspects and issues of the Indian dairy development programme Operation Flood in order to highlight how it has grappled with these questions.

As noted in Chapter 9, over the past few decades this programme enjoyed massive material support from the World Food Programme and the European Community, out of the latter's dairy surpluses, as well as more limited support from the World Bank and several other international donor agencies. In the course of its development the programme extended its command over dairy production and processing in a majority of Indian states, and incorporated an ever-growing number of primary producer co-operative societies within its organizational matrix on the basis of detailed standard regulations governing membership and performance. Nonetheless, for a proper perspective it remains important to note that the programme encompasses no more than approximately 8 percent of total Indian milk production. This chapter reviews several aspects of the programme which reflect the extension of internal and external linkages found in the Indian co-operative dairy sector. Following a discussion of various dimensions of the programme in the light of these linkages, the implications of its distinctive institutional features are re-examined.

The context

The origins of the Operation Flood programme may be located in a particular structural problem in the supply and demand of dairy products. By one estimate, it was claimed that, prior to India's initiation of Operation Flood, 18 percent of the country's milk production was in urban centres, 10 percent in villages near to urban centres and the remaining 72 percent in distant villages (Mellor and Ponteves, 1964:133). Although the bulk of production was rural, it was in urban and metropolitan areas that demand was increasing, due to urbanization and urban middle class income growth. India's existing resource base included one-sixth of the world's cattle and goats and over half its buffaloes. Due to capital and infrastructural constraints, the traditional private milk traders have not been able to fully bridge the gap between rural supply and urban demand. At the same time, up until 1989 the EC was carrying very large dairy surpluses. Simply transferring those resources as donations or subsidised exports to India would most likely have depressed the local incentive to produce milk. Instead, as discussed in Chapter 9, through Operation Flood a plan was developed to sell donated dairy commodities at competitive local prices in order to develop the indigenous dairy industry. The EC would not lose in this arrangement as it could not find ways of increasing consumption within the Community or of expanding commercial dairy exports profitably. Politically the EC would also gain by demonstrating globally the developmental use realized from its dairy surpluses. Besides, as noted, at the early stages there was some thought of future market creation.

Operation Flood, hailed as a 'white revolution', indicated by its name the optimism that accompanied its inception. As already discussed, a host of social benefits were expected to accompany the achievement of its mission of providing milk to urban areas from rural milksheds. Of the twin agencies responsible for implementing the plan, the National Dairy Development Board (NDDB) was to serve as a technical consulting body, while the Indian Dairy Corporation (IDC) handled the financial aspects of the scheme. The NDDB was (and is) a registered society, which gives it a parastatal status with most of its activity conducted in the private arena. The IDC, on the other hand, was strictly a public body with the authority to receive and sell dairy aid. Recently, the two have been merged under the general umbrella of the NDDB, which continues to operate with substantial autonomy due to an organizational charter which permits broad interpretation of its accountability and powers of intervention. Public relations documents of Operation Flood have claimed social benefits while, officially, the programme's main priority has been economic viability. This duality of purpose may, however, act as a double-edged sword. On the one hand the programme avoids stringent accountability to either the government or any kind of shareholders; on the other hand it receives criticism for not sustaining independent commercial feasibility and for not honouring its social claims.

It is clear that, by public sector standards, Operation Flood has intervened to an unusual degree into civil society, while by private sector standards it has very strong political connections at all levels. Prima facie, the strategy of extending an autonomous network of institutionalized linkages from the local, village level up to the national centre appears to transcend the constraints and limitations commonly experienced by government and non-government agencies. Operation Flood has grown to command an awesome amount of material and human resources. A voluminous literature has attempted to establish the effects of the programme (for a review see Doornbos *et al.*, 1990). The size and likely longevity of the project, and continued institution building by the NDDB, justify careful external scrutiny.

Like any development effort, Operation Flood operates within constraints and opportunities, in this case largely relating to the limits of the resource base and the possibilities of replication of the model through mobilization of material, human and financial resources within and outside India. India's population represents 15 percent of the world's total, living on 2.5 percent of the earth's surface (Parisot, 1990:190). India ranks third in world milk production, which it accomplishes with 17 percent of the world's cattle and over half of its buffaloes (Parisot, 1990; George, 1985a:31; citing CED, 1982; Mascarenhas, 1988:53). However, this large number of livestock is responsible for only six percent of global milk output and India possesses only 0.5 percent of global pasture land (George 1985a:36; citing Crotty, 1980). Between 1970 and 1985 total milk production in India increased at a rate of 5.5 percent per annum. By 1985, six percent of total milk production was handled through dairy co-operatives (Alderman *et al.*, 1987:6). Cattle productivity in India is relatively low. A 1976 estimate puts the average annual milk yield of an Indian cow at 157 kg, while that of a cow in the West is estimated to be somewhere between 3,000 and 4,000 kg (NCA, 1976). Buffaloes are the main milch animals and are of limited use for draught and work purposes. These figures are of obvious significance when considering India's chosen strategy of dairy development.

The model

As discussed in Chapter 9, the co-operative model adopted by NDDB to organize dairying nationally, known as the 'Anand Pattern', comprises a four-tiered vertical structure consisting of village societies, district unions, state federations (within each of India's federal states) and a national, all-India federation. Producers group into dairy societies, a number of which form a district union. All the unions within a state (usually around six to seven) form a state federation. The logic of this arrangement is to have all the functions relevant to the dairy sector performed within the co-operative framework and hence eliminate the potentially exploitative role of commercial intermediaries. Village societies organize individual producers into a production base. District unions organize milk collection, process it and manufacture products, which requires transport and storage facilities as well as processing and marketing equipment. State federations market the dairy products and ensure that the dairy supply is balanced geographically. The federations also investigate further opportunities in the product line according to their market information. The whole structure has recently been extended into a fourth tier – the National Co-operative Dairy Federation of India (NCDF). From its vantage point at the top, the NCDF can co-ordinate activities among state federations, attempting to manage the dairy infrastructure in such a way that supply is balanced across the country throughout the year, despite seasonal swings in supply. State level and national federations are also expected to co-ordinate with government agencies and 'lobby' for co-operative interests.

In the original Anand pattern, village producers were the notional owners of the co-operative (union) assets. In subsequent extensions of the programme, juridical control over assets has been vested in the state federation. The producer-members of primary societies receive a fixed price for their milk. Cattle feed is made available at a reasonable price, veterinary services are provided either free or at a moderate rate, and aid is sometimes offered in obtaining finance from banks or other agencies. Farmer training and the extension of cross-breeding technology are also part of the input package. At each tier, representatives are elected to the next higher tier in an effort to ensure that policy decisions are influenced by input from the bases. In addition to the representative structure, the co-operative organization (at the union level and above) hires professional managers to guide policy. As employees of the co-operative, managers are accountable in principle to the elected board in the district union or state federation in which they work.

The strategy of co-operative organization as envisaged by the NDDB is to vertically integrate all operations relating to a particular commodity from producer to consumer. Through this structure, inputs and extension services are made available to producers. Moreover, the value added at various stages of processing and manufacture is kept within the co-operative enterprise so that profits may end up as increased dividends for members, bonuses or reinvestment funds. Individual producers are expected to benefit from economies of scale in all stages of product preparation despite the single producer's very small base of operations. Rather than representing universal practice in India, however, it is best to perceive the 'Anand pattern' co-operative model as an ideal from which in reality many deviations are found, particularly in relation to 'ownership' of assets, decision-making and representation.

In asking why the NDDB chose the Anand pattern as a universal model in India, the answer would be because it was successful at a given time and place; but, when asking why it was successful, one finds the reasons do not rest on the co-operative structure alone. In documenting the history of the Kheda District Co-operative Milk Producers' Union (KDCMPU) which was the precursor to the NDDB and provided the Anand model, Patel (1990) provides a number of factors contributing to its success. The Patidar caste in the region, who were owner-cultivators of medium-size holdings, were a highly entrepreneurial and skilled group, exhibiting considerable caste solidarity *vis-à-vis* the Kshatriyas, who were tenants and agricultural labourers. Agricultural surplus realized by the Patidars was put into dairying as a subsidiary activity. The early Kheda co-operative was formed as a joint effort of producers mobilized in order to boycott a private dairy (Polsons) which earlier had been organizing the milk trade in the district. After a sustained effort, the Patidars were able to gain significant control of the Bombay milk market, partly through cultivating political support in Bombay and at the state level. In addition to the relative spatial proximity of the Bombay market, the producers benefited from good infrastructural connections to the city.

Outside events also benefited the co-operative. Nationalist ideology at the time of independence championed co-operative organization and this proclivity was subsequently carried through in the first two five-year plans which encouraged and offered incentives to co-operativisation. As Patel notes, the Patidars, who by independence had consolidated their economic and political position, could claim a very impressive array of government figures, both at the centre and at the state, who either directly represented Patidar interests or who were sympathizers. Funds which started flowing to the co-operative even before independence from the Bombay state government increased over time as the central government and international agencies added to the dairy's resource base. International aid started in the mid-1950s from UNICEF and later came from New Zealand, the American PL 480 programme, the World Food Programme, World Bank, EC/EU and Oxfam.

The Patidar community consolidated their control at various levels by actively participating in dairy co-operatives, the Congress Party at local, state and national levels, various co-operative institutions such as banks, industrial societies, village industry associations and others. With these channels at their disposal, Patel suggests, the Patidar lobby at the centre could encourage and facilitate an NDDB strategy to institutionalize and universalize the Anand pattern. One compelling reason to do so was that the obvious influence of Patidar dairy interests was alienating potential co-operative members in areas where Patidars were not a dominant group or were unpopular. The Kheda union relied on a steady milk supply from outlying areas where Patidar influence was weak. Hence, as Patel argues, an effort was made to professionalize the management image by hiring technocrats who were projected as technically competent but politically neutral and removed from the fray surrounding the Patidar associations. Whether these new managers acted independently of the Patidar community is debatable, although their influence in terms of the dairy structures has been very much in evidence.

In the course of organizing dairy producers and resources to more effectively increase production and implement a long-distance milk supply system, NDDB/IDC made plans for the creation of a National Milch Herd and a National Milk Grid. The National Milch Herd, under the second phase of Operation Flood (1978–85), was meant to comprise cows crossbred with high-yielding exotic breeds and upgraded buffaloes in order to raise milk production (George, 1990). It was intended to include 14 million cross-bred cows and upgraded buffaloes representing one-sixth of India's milch animals and yielding an estimated one-fourth of production. The National Grid's purpose was to even out differences in the supply of milk due to seasonal fluctuations and regional variations in production. This was to be accomplished by maintaining a buffer stock and a system for moving the commodity from areas of surplus to areas of deficit. The grid would allow consumers throughout India to enjoy a stable supply of milk throughout the year. This structure entails a complex network of storage facilities, tankers, chilling plants, feeder balancing dairies, urban dairies and bulk vending outlets.

The applicability of this standard model under diverse conditions is questionable. As Shanti George (1990) argues, the centralized structures of Operation Flood (the Herd, the Grid and the producer co-operatives) do not adapt to differences among livestock, people and regional environments. In every case, basically the same plan is used to organize the cattle, producers and resources even if the conditions in a specific case cannot utilize, let alone benefit from, the structure. Examples are the introduction of foreign breeds of livestock in climatic conditions unsuitable for their optimal welfare or the establishment of settled procurement facilities among societies where the livestock owners are semi-nomadic (see also Joshi, 1990).

Replication

The original task of Operation Flood, as stated in the charter in 1965, was clear: to replicate the Anand model throughout India. In the beginning of the process, replication took place in Gujarat state. Only with the advent of a large EC dairy surplus channelled through the IDC (1970) did expansion take off on a national scale. This has been accompanied by an increasing level of bureaucratization. Robert Chambers, in his article 'Bureaucratic Reversals and Local Diversity' (1988), lists three main bureaucratic tendencies: (1) centralization in a hierarchy; (2) standardization of rules and activities; (3) simplification. Connected to these he also mentions centralization of programme planning, of financial allocations and audits, of personnel policy, and of control of transfers of middle level staff. Except for the last two points, the rest of these characteristics hold true for Operation Flood. The apex implementing agency propagates the Anand pattern in a manner which tries to minimize the complexities arising from local differences. The NDDB is responsible for programme blueprints and resource allocation. For the Anand model to yield similar results in disparate conditions, it would be necessary to also create the conditions of success that existed in the original case. In other words, the model which has been replicated (1) is not truly the Anand model which arose spontaneously from grassroots organizing; and (2) is a relatively rigid construct imposed from above and therefore not always appropriate for local circumstances.

The motivation to replicate is not simply a desire to be visible in the public eye in order to attract support, although this is certainly an important consideration. The tendency is fed by evaluation reports and research which sustain the belief that bigger is better and regard replication itself as a main criterion of programme success (Paul, 1982). Once started, replication tends to develop its own momentum which may lead quickly in unforeseen directions. Any attempt to regulate and hold accountable a rapidly replicating programme will require a strong analytical capability in order to perceive potential trends within a time frame that allows time for action to influence events. Moreover, the interests and processes associated with replication may not be the same as those of the original programme cadre and agenda. In some cases – and Operation Flood is an example – in which competition for a limited supply of a product is intense, replication is used to try and edge competitors out of the market. Alternative outlets for milk, such as household processing into indigenous products, are discouraged or marginalized by the increasing coverage of one particular programme.

Some authors assert that Operation Flood has neglected, or conceivably discouraged, the possibility of upgrading household technology in the production of traditional products such as clarified butter and milk solids, yoghurt, cottage cheese and so on. Taking a household strategy further might have enabled the development of decentralized, small-scale factory processing with some amount of appropriate technology and investment (Doornbos *et al.*, 1990; Bachman, 1981a, 1981b). It is worthwhile investigating whether this is a viable alternative to the current capital intensive strategy. No conclusions can be drawn at present in the absence of information on the optimal economic scale of small(er) enterprises.

Evidence shows that throughout the Operation Flood programme, the state of Gujarat has received preferential treatment in the allocation of resources and has consequently been able to consistently produce the best results in dairying (see Map 3). Under the first phase, Gujarat received 30 percent of expenditure although a sophisticated co-operative infrastructure already existed in five districts prior to the programme (Doornbos *et al.*, 1990:Ch. 4). Indeed, the purpose of the programme was to extend this success. In 1984–85, 32 percent of milk collection and processing potential and 33 percent of total milk consumption were located in Gujarat (European Court of Auditors, 1988:6). Forty-two percent of milk powder production capacity and 64 percent of actual production took place in Gujarat (European Court of Auditors, 1988:6). One-sixth of the total capacity of all dairy and milk powder processing projects under execution on 31st January 1985 was also found in Gujarat. Two-fifths of the cattle feed factories operating in March 1985 were located in Gujarat, where 76 percent of capacity was used, compared to 10–32 percent in plants located in ten other states (European Court of Auditors, 1988: 10). During the first phase of the programme, 79 percent of the total number of co-operatives were found in three states: Gujarat (43 percent), Tamil Nadu (24 percent) and Maharashtra (12 percent). By September 1985, the proportion of all co-operatives found in these three states had decreased to 39 percent. Nevertheless, the degree of spatial concentration is high enough to indicate the difficulty of truly replicating nationwide the Anand model.

In replicating itself, Operation Flood operates within constraints established by its main competitor – the private sector – and various other affected interests. In marketing milk, the co-operative sector must confront the private 'unorganized' milk trade. Small and medium private milk traders are often in a position to make fast decisions based on the situation at a given moment. Their operational costs are low compared with the organized sector. They often bind milk suppliers to them by lending money to cover working capital and daily consumption needs. As a matter of policy, Operation Flood does not offer credit, claiming that it breeds corruption and that it can be obtained from other agencies. (In some cases co-operatives may offer forms of credit such as advancing cattle feed against milk supplied but this is not a feature of the original Anand model). The co-operative dairy is constrained in changing the producer price of milk partly due to the high fixed cost element of the processing-distribution-marketing infrastructure and partly due to the preference for maintaining a constant price for farmers in a continually expanding catchment area where cost of procurement may vary significantly. Once a reasonably stable price balance is established, it is difficult to alter. Private traders have more flexibility in pricing and product line, offering a higher price for milk in lean season and a lower one in flush season. The ability of the private trader to cater to particular consumer and producer preferences, as well as to provide services such as moneylending, door-to-door delivery and end of the month bill payment, means that their hold on their market share is not easily eroded by Operation Flood, if at all. Evidence of this is found in a study of milk-vending in Mehrauli District in the Delhi region by Batra (1990).

Dairy development policy affects producers, middlemen, consumers, several levels of politicians (who may oppose the programme as a threat to local autonomy or support it as a source of patronage), dairy technocrats, bureaucrats and foreign agencies. Their respective claims may be balanced differently depending on the arrangement negotiated between the NDDB and state governments. The Anand pattern does not and cannot determine this balance, which is the outcome of a process of political manoeuvring.

Case studies document the shifts which have occurred in the Anand pattern as it was extended. Writing about the Rajkot Dairy in Saurashtra (Gujarat), Joshi (1990) states that the milk producer societies were formed by the state level federation in top-down fashion. The dairies are owned by the union instead of the producers. Overall the contribution to policy making of producer societies, relative to processing (district) and marketing (state) agencies, is very small, leading to a programme resembling more a processing and marketing structure than a producers' co-operative.

Shekawat's (1990) research in Western Rajasthan shows the difficulty of trying to integrate Operation Flood with a pre-existing public institutional structure. In some cases the implementation of Operation Flood does not take advantage of past wisdom culled in state dairy agencies which have adjusted to local needs over time. In Rajasthan the state dairy federation, in conjunction with the state government, emerged as an authoritative apex agency managing most of the vital dairy functions, for example, planning, channelling of resources, implementation, control of marketing, manufacturing and processing and so on. The union has been restricted to innocuous technical tasks such as milk collection, provision of feed, health care and artificial insemination. The state federation controls dairy co-operatives, makes most important decisions, owns and operates the plants. Co-operative members do not participate in decision making or own any of the assets. Elected representation has been increasingly replaced by the appointment of state government officials to the board of directors of the state dairy federation. Even the chairman of the board has become a nominee of the state government. Anand-pattern by-laws have been continually amended to further enhance the role of state government members on the board of directors.

Mitra (1990) has looked at the effect of replicating the Anand pattern on caste/class relations in Bihar. Corruption in the co-operative, where members acted as middlemen, buying milk from non-members at a low price and selling it at a high price to the co-operative, defeated the objective of using the co-operative to eliminate exploitation. Mitra concludes that policies of resource allocation and commodity exchange have a differential impact on different rural classes. Overall, Mitra states that co-operatives do not end inequality if membership is not restricted to more or less equally placed persons. Small and marginal producers face a critical resource constraint when trying to take advantage of the co-operative dairy programme, in that they usually lack access to sufficient land on which to grow their own fodder. Moreover, old patterns of inequality and exploitation have been replicated by Operation Flood in Bihar. Dairy co-operatives are not an opportunity for lower classes or castes to catch up with more privileged groups. Membership is not restricted to disadvantaged groups, and co-operatives also admit very strong groups who can manipulate the organizations to their own advantage. The co-operative has not specifically or systematically addressed the problem of distribution of benefits.

Overall, Baviskar (1985) finds that the NDDB replaces local initiative through centralized and bureaucratic 'co-operative' management. Co-operative members do not significantly influence policy but are subordinate to managers and technocrats whose power is increased by the lack of direct and meaningful communication between union managers and dairy producers (Baviskar, 1985, 1990). Lower-level bureaucrats are able to control co-operative management while at a higher level co-operative representatives play a symbolic role, as the European Court of Auditors (1988:10) has also observed.

A critique from a different angle by Shanti George (1985a; citing CED, 1982:6; World Bank, 1978:22) suggests that the focus of the programme is misplaced because the institution operates more as a joint stock company than as a co-operative. As support for this argument, she points to the relatively low price paid to producers and the allocation of profits which go primarily to capital reserves for future investment rather than to producers as bonuses or dividends. All these tendencies seem even less justifiable within a co-operative when the cost of production is decreasingly compensated by sale price.

The task of replicating the Anand pattern on a large scale confines the process to a very limited time frame compared to the original co-operative, which evolved in tune with local needs and rhythms. The Jha Report admits the shift of initiative from producers to state federations:

in some States it became necessary to set up a federation in the first instance in order to take up the responsibility of forming cooperatives and unions for implementing the project. This attempt to build up the Cooperative structure from the top rather than the bottom was fraught with difficulties, particularly in States where there was no tradition of a healthy cooperative movement . . . Competition from the private sector was also often intense and there were disagreements between the IDC and the State Governments on how to proceed. Moreover . . . in some instances [States] . . . the Anand pattern was accepted, without any genuine commitment to it (GOI, 1984:78).

An effort to prioritize interests is revealed by the programme's differential treatment in favour of those elements which can meet the conditions of Operation Flood, at the expense of elements which do not fit the mould (for example, urban herds, non-organized producers, nomadic producers and those owning milk-bearing animals other than cows or buffaloes). Organizing the market has necessitated demonstrating that other sectors of the economy relevant to dairying, such as general agriculture and animal husbandry and feed/fodder production, are compatible with an emphasis on large-scale co-operative dairying. It has also involved integrating the dairy market itself and the multiple interests within it. Both these efforts have given rise to as yet unresolved debates. The local co-operative base provides the kind of legitimacy through representation and participation that a development agent with foreign linkages needs to have. Nevertheless, the NDDB remains unequivocally on the top as overall mediator.

The resource constraint

The limits of the dairy economy in India, whether public or private, are very clearly drawn by what the resource base (labour, capital, land and livestock) is able to support. How the resource base is utilized in the context of the Operation Flood programme reflects the overall fundamental strength or weakness of the dairy development strategy, including the institutions. The first condition to consider is that dairying cannot be carried on unless agriculture is sufficiently well developed to provide at least minimal food security for the farmers. The surplus beyond this level in India is often too low to permit investment in dairy cattle (Vaidyanathan *et al.*, 1982, cited in Nair and Dhas, 1990). This also means that agriculture will be the primary activity and dairying secondary for a large majority of farmers. First preference in livestock selection is for draught cattle (bullocks) to help in farm operations and transportation rather than for milch cattle (Nair and Dhas, 1990). Participation in dairying, even as a secondary activity, is usually a risk to producers for a variety of reasons but mainly because of limited land and capital. Surpluses are often invested in more secure activities.

Co-operative dairy planners are basically concerned with how to meet the growing urban demand for milk within the unavoidable feed and fodder limitations. Three possible strategies were considered: (1) keeping the size of the national herd constant and increasing feed inputs per milch animal; (2) increasing the size of the national herd and keeping feed inputs per milch animal constant; and (3) keeping the size of the national herd constant, replacing 10.2 million local milch animals by the same number of genetically improved animals, and feeding each group at economic rates (NDDB, 1980). An optimal feeding rate optimizes the animal's genetic potential for production. Economic feeding maximizes financial returns to the milk producer but may not enable the animal to produce at its full potential.

The third option was chosen, because the first reduced farm level profits (through high input costs) and the second required a large increase in all types of feed (NDDB, 1980). However, the third strategy does imply a significant break with traditional modes of production and requires a series of technical interventions in order to extend crossbreeds into the local cattle population. The NDDB's success of meeting its goals in this regard has been very limited. By 1984–85 Operation Flood expected the national herd to contain 10–20 million cross-bred cows and improved buffaloes which would replace an equal number of local nondescript cattle. This segment of the herd would constitute 11 percent of the total milch animal population, consuming 21 percent of available concentrates, 8 percent of green fodder, 7 percent of dry fodder (crop residues) while 6.4 percent of a total population of nine million milch animals in Operation Flood were crossbreeds (Achaya and Huria, 1986). At most 12 percent of India's milch animal population is covered by Operation Flood (Achaya and Huria, 1986), other estimates being closer to 6–10 per cent. The Jha Report also criticizes the inadequate performance of the artificial insemination programme.

Introducing a significant number of high-yielding crossbred cows into Indian stock in order to increase the milk production base has significant side-effects. Male progeny of milch cattle are less suited for draught and general work functions. Crossbreeds require more and better feeding. Indigenous cattle have developed important qualities of adaptation over centuries such as disease resistance, heat tolerance, a lower metabolic rate given certain temperatures and feeding conditions and a more efficient feed conversion ability given scarce resources. Crossbreeding them with exotic animals may undermine those qualities. As Nair and Dhas (1990) mention, this model derives from countries which are able to provide adequate manufactured cattle feed and cultivated green fodder; not from countries like India where provisions for livestock compete for the same resource base that sustains people. It would appear likely that, in the long term, Operation Flood would lead to a 'segmented' cattle population, with the existing low-yielding animals left to produce milk and draught power to the extent made possible by feeding primarily on crop residues and natural herbage, and a small 'élite' herd of high-yielding crossbreeds being fed on higher amounts of scarce feed such as green fodder and concentrates which they convert to milk more efficiently (George, 1985a).

Nair and Dhas' research (1990) indicates the varying degree to which crossbreeding has penetrated various states. The proportion of adult female cattle which are crossbreeds range from 56 percent in Gujarat to 9 percent in Himachal Pradesh. Given that crossbreeds are raised for milk production, it is logical that the sex ratio (males per 100 females) will shift in favour of females; that of indigenous cattle will shift in favour of males for draught purposes. Nair and Dhas confirm this trend. If crossbreeds occupy an increasing share of the total cattle population and the composition of the herd shifts towards females, will the supply of draught power through indigenous cattle be adversely affected? Eighty-seven per cent of crossbreeds are female. Male progeny usually do not survive to adulthood. The data indicate that the draught animal population has either stagnated or decreased.

The consequences of intensified dairying on pre-existing interdependencies between food, energy and cattle systems have been investigated by Nair and Dhas as well as by Parisot (1990). Milk is an important source of animal protein in the Indian diet, both vegetarian and non-vegetarian. Some animal proteins cannot be substituted by vegetable sources. By one estimate, 30 percent of protein in India comes from animal sources and 70 percent of that is from milk (Nair, 1987). Nair and Dhas suggest that the expansion of cross-breeding technology may increase milk production but it will do so at the expense of draught power availability for small and marginal farmers and will entail increased fossil fuel usage. Their argument is that small and marginal farms are increasing in number and these farmers keep cheap, poor quality animals. A number of factors may favour milch animal investment over that of work animals: decreasing availability of draught animals alongside increasing availability of crossbred milch cattle (if the programme succeeds) will lower the cost of the latter; increasingly commercialized milk production (and crossbreeding) will exert an upward pressure on feed costs which are already rising in any case, making the sustenance of inferior work animals too expensive. If substitution of draught for milch animals does occur, draught power will need to be provided, possibly by increasing mechanization and/or a rental market of draught animals. Mechanization is likely to lead to concentration of landholding by larger landholders and a rental market for the machinery in order to make economic use of the technology. Small and marginal farmers who opt for mechanization may choose to co-operativise the ownership and sharing of tractors.

Parisot's argument is more ecological. She concludes that intensified dairying is leading to land degradation and fodder scarcity. While the animal population has been increasing, grazing land has not. Overstocking the land with livestock degrades the land and further diminishes fodder. Neglecting the need for grazing land in order to maintain or extend agriculture creates a situation where forced migration of livestock will bring land degradation to larger areas. High yielding breeds exacerbate these tendencies by requiring larger amounts of green fodder and concentrates. According to Parisot, dairying based on cross-bred cows breaks the former interdependence between agriculture and livestock, essentially because the animals take in too much without giving enough back to the ecosystem.

Other resource bases relevant to milk production and consumption are income, access to and privatization of communal lands, and the cultivation of green fodder for cattle feed. Because milk is an income elastic commodity, consumption is higher in urban areas where incomes are higher and distribution patterns become increasingly skewed towards urban centres. Commercialization of milk production may induce rural producers to moderate their consumption in order to supplement income and purchase cheaper foodstuffs. (As milk has traditionally been a luxury consumption item, the process suggested above does not necessarily worsen the welfare of low income producers). Lower classes are disadvantaged by the increasing privatization of communal grazing lands either through land grabbers or through questionable methods of land reform. Co-operativization of communal land as suggested by the NDDB is not a solution as it excludes those producers who are not co-operative members.

Furthermore, research on labour resources in dairying has produced contradictory evidence as to whether organized dairying is labour-generating or labour saving (Shah and Bhargava, 1982; Singh and Das, 1982; Doornbos *et al.*, 1990:Ch. 7). Constraints in dairying such as green fodder, labour and credit have not been shadow priced so it is difficult to gauge the value of these factors in the production process (Alderman *et al.*, 1987:28). In the absence of this data, macro-policy formulation is lacking important information.

The NDDB's strategy to raise production, as stated in its Operation Flood phase III document, has been to place greater emphasis on marketing of liquid milk and the associated infrastructure. The logic behind this is that, the greater a union's command of its milk market through its possession of an adequate supply through the grid, the stronger its position will be as the most effective outlet of milk. A synergism should develop between procurement and marketing. Marketing, thus, becomes 'the driving force to improve procurement' (NDDB, 1985:22–3). Beginning from this premise, the document then projects the need for increasing dairy capacities in urban centres and marketing infrastructure. Despite repeated criticism from various sources of an expenditure bias in favour of processing and marketing at the expense of production (for a review see Doornbos *et al.*, 1990:Ch. 4), the NDDB continues to hold to this line.

The state of milk production in India remains contentious, partly because of poor statistics. There are wide regional variations. Milk production levels mainly reflect milch animal numbers and their productivity; but these in turn are affected by the requirements of draught animals in agriculture, size of landholdings, cropping patterns, levels of mechanization, demand for milk and dairy products, the commercialisation of milk production, the availability of feed and fodder, the introduction of exotic breeds or the upgrading of indigenous ones, and the profitability of milk production. There is no quick and easy method to produce a big increase in dairy productivity. Any intervention to promote productivity is bound to have repercussions elsewhere. One must question the wisdom of building a vast modern processing and marketing infrastructure on a traditional production base which has received proportionally less priority in planning and resources in budgeting.

Welfare and equity issues

The welfare sentiments espoused by Operation Flood authorities are often claimed by its critics to reflect the need to attract funding and legitimation. The litany is laudable: promises of income and employment generation; the ability to mitigate social inequities found in class, caste, power and gender constructs; participation by everyone regardless of economic position; benefits which are scale neutral and are dispersed equally throughout regions and among social groups. Highlighting these aspects at its inception, Operation Flood could purport to take seriously the task of poverty alleviation. Programme officials hoped to achieve reform through the back door, expecting benefits to permeate society without eliciting a direct confrontation with incompatible interests.

Despite programme claims, subsidized consumer prices for milk are mainly set by state and municipal governments, and pressures to keep prices low limit producer income. Such prices also do not consider total opportunity costs, generally failing to factor in the value of non-cash inputs such as family labour, for which dairying must compete with other income-earning or subsistence activities.

Furthermore, the relative profitability of dairying is not consistent across the nation. Producer prices vary according to local conditions such as competition, farmer efficiency and proximity to markets, both from state to state and even district by district (Nagabrahmam, 1983: 15).

The Jha Report states that producers receive a relatively high share of the consumer price (73 percent). However, the Jha Report also notes that consumer subsidies in metropolitan cities play a significant role in depressing prices. George (1985b:2166) claims that the producer share of the consumer price could be greater. She argues that high costs in the organized dairy sector and inefficiencies in milk collection and marketing lower the producer price, and that traditional household processing and distribution by women is a more economic processing system which has the added benefit of allowing women greater control of the proceeds of their labour. However, traditional systems have scale limitations that must be recognized.

On the issue of participation of the poor in dairying, a mixed picture emerges. Operation Flood I claims that 50–70 percent of co-operative members were recruited from small and marginal farmers and that 10 percent were landless. A further breakdown of the 'small and marginal' category would be useful. Evidence shows that in Operation Flood co-operatives, the landless compose 39 percent of all households but produce only 11 percent of the milk (NDDB, 1982). The bottom 10–20 percent of the population are under-represented in terms of milch animal ownership as well as in their rate of participation (Verhagen, 1990). Wealthier landowners can also afford to keep better quality animals.

Contrary to the Operation Flood claim that its benefits are scale neutral, the landless are disadvantaged from the outset. Land is essential to dairying. Sufficient dry and green fodder and natural herbage is prerequisite to raising the productivity of milch animals. Without land, it is impossible to grow fodder and to plan pasturage. The poor cannot increase their dairy profits by purchasing feed. The need for land in dairying undermines the assertion that advantages will accrue equally to member producers irrespective of their landholding. Co-operative structures, veterinary services, provision of feed, the introduction of crossbreeds and so on, Verhagen argues, are of minimal use if the basic input – land – is unavailable. By not confronting the land issue, social reform through the back door is not effective.

Other resource constraints for the poor relate to capital. The co-operative dairy provides no credit; medium and large farmers know how to obtain access to other credit facilities, while poorer farmers cannot. Larger milk producers are able to reinvest their surpluses and sustain dairying as a profitable enterprise. For others, the factors noted above, together with macro-economic policies in favour of consumers, make dairying unremunerative. Furthermore, the poor are less able to tolerate investment risks. However, neither credit nor risk constraints have been empirically studied to gauge their effect on the participation rate in dairying, especially among the poor (Alderman *et al.*, 1987:58). The poor find it particularly difficult to participate in the cross-breeding strategy as envisioned by Operation Flood, and this, in turn, is likely to marginalize petty producers (Verhagen, 1990). Cross-breeding may effectively exclude the poor, because it means the end of multi-purpose livestock. This is likely to lead to a correlation between landholding and the breeding of specifically milch animals, which implies restructuring the production base as an élite herd located where conditions are optimal (Verhagen, 1990).

From a consumer perspective, a different aspect of the dairy market becomes important (Batra, 1990; Parisot, 1990; July 1975). Milk is both income and price elastic. Consumption of milk has traditionally been skewed toward upper-income groups, even before Operation Flood. Geographically, consumption levels also vary widely. Price moderation of milk is most directly to the benefit of higher and middle income groups. Other prices affected by intensified dairying impact on consumer welfare (Alderman *et al.*, 1987:60). Dairy development may raise the price of other commodities such as coarse grains since they are used as animal feed. As the poor also consume coarse grains, an increase in their price will be most disadvantageous for that group. Likewise, decreased production of clarified butter due to increased marketing of liquid milk has meant a drop in buttermilk availability which is a side-product of clarified butter production (George, 1985b:2168). As buttermilk is also a consumption item of the poor, decreased availability again disadvantages them. In short, then, the total basket of prices related to dairying needs to be considered in determining consumer welfare.

Lipton (1985:107) argues that aid depresses milk producer prices by at least 10 percent. Terhal and Doornbos (1983) suggest that food aid mitigates the pressure on municipal and state governments to set prices at real market value. For political reasons, governments prefer to keep down the consumer price of milk, and dairy aid, sold at concessional prices, makes this possible. Consequently, aid creates a price disequilibrium.

One of the key features of Operation Flood I in the Plan of Operations was the subsidized distribution of double toned milk among vulnerable groups (Doornbos *et al.* 1990:Ch. 4). As the programme progressed, however, milk was regarded as too expensive to distribute according to the scheme. Indeed, over time, the focus of Operation Flood in official documents has shifted away from statements of social uplift to an emphasis on the programme as primarily a milk production and marketing strategy.

As Baviskar notes, dairying is part of a profit-maximizing strategy for big farmers, whereas among small ones it tends to be related to survival. Verhagen, van Dorsten and Baviskar (all 1990) agree that while the poor have benefited to some degree from dairying, the problem lies in the increasing gap in the rate of benefit between marginal and large producers. This gap is mainly due to the resource constraints of the former group. For example, Savara (1990) claims that tribals in Surat (Gujarat) continue dairying despite its precarious viability because there is little alternative. Their dairying is subsidized through the state and loans are made available to purchase animals, through the combination of a special tribal welfare scheme pursued by the government in conjunction with Operation Flood. There are also other cases of public welfare programmes latching on to the dairy programme but, as a subsistence pursuit, such small-scale dairying cannot sustain itself without subsidies.

Expectations of social change through widened participation in the management of dairy co-operatives have been disappointed. The few studies that have investigated the composition of the management committees of the village dairy co-operatives indicate that the larger farmer/upper-caste members control them (Patel, 1982; Chakravarty and Reddy, 1982). According to Shah (1981), the chairmen and secretaries of Kheda co-operatives are generally from the local dominant castes, a finding which corresponds with the information provided by the NDDB study of Sabarkantha and Rohtak co-operatives on the socio-economic background of the members of the managing committees (NDDB, 1983:Exhibit 40–51). Moreover, the studies which investigate this aspect further reveal factional divisions which affect the functioning of the co-operatives (Rajaram, 1983; NDDB, 1977; Jain, Prasad and Gupta, 1982). In fact, even the village Ode, described in such positive terms by Somjee and Somjee (1978), is an example of divisive factionalism. Administrative employees of village dairy co-operatives, thought to wield more power than those elected to office in these co-operatives, usually come from the same caste and class as large farmers. It is not unusual for locally powerful individuals to become co-operative secretaries.

Women's co-operatives have also been unable to avoid caste, class and gender inequalities (Mitra, 1990). Baviskar (1990) describes the co-operative dairy structure as paternalistic, where managers act and speak on behalf of members in the belief they know better the appropriate course of action. Domination by managers is highly unconducive to member participation. These studies indicate that the dairy co-operatives are neither immune to factional divisions and conflicts nor particularly suited to successfully overcoming barriers of caste, class and gender. The only study that attempts to verify empirically the assumption that co-operative dairying is positively correlated with the adoption of a broad range of 'modern' values and practices could not find evidence of this (Shah, 1981). In fact, a negative correlation appeared to exist. In sum, therefore, there is a lack of empirical evidence supporting the claim that co-operatives act as powerful 'instruments of change' in the direction of a more equitable, less exploitative, rural social structure.

Operation Flood's main priority was to develop a sophisticated, effective procurement system to satisfy rising urban demand from rural production. The co-operative structure facilitated this process, but did not live up to its rhetoric about poverty alleviation and enhanced social consciousness. This is not to imply that poor milk producers have not been helped. In hindsight, however, reduction of poverty – even while advocated as a goal in official documents on Operation Flood – never functioned as a decisive criterion for resource allocation and project design. In the absence of a specific agenda to aid the poor, which would require bold changes in power and ownership patterns, existing social gaps are expected to remain or possibly be widened by projects mainly concerned with economic growth.

Economic viability and aid

For foreign donors, aid can be regarded as an investment, a means of surplus disposal, or an instrument of development. When providing technical inputs and/or expertise to a recipient country, the donor can expect to benefit later, either by securing a market for its exports, or through some other type of spin-off effect. For example, during the 1950s New Zealand provided technical and human resources to India at advantageous terms, then benefited as a steadily increasing share of its milk powder exports followed that technology to India (Chatterjee, 1990). Generally, this type of arrangement implies that inputs for a given project, such as skim milk powder or cross-breeding technology, will be exclusively purchased from the donor. Thus aid can represent a convergence of interests between donor and recipient agencies.

Originally, India viewed food aid as an opportunity to improve its balance of payments situation and to strengthen its dairy sector with a view toward achieving self-sufficiency. At the time of Operation Flood's Phase I implementation in 1970, India was importing dairy products. The NDDB favoured aid since it could be used to further the NDDB model of dairy development.

The EC originally saw Operation Flood as a way to dispose of surpluses and promote exports, although subsequently EC interest shifted to the need for indigenous dairy development in India, to the extent that the EC became reluctant to continue the high level of aid. Nevertheless, by then Operation Flood became a politically expedient demonstration of how 'good surplus disposal' might promote development.

The European Court of Auditors (ECA) concluded in connection with the negotiations surrounding Operation Flood III that the EC had largely accomplished its task in enabling India to meet solvent demand for milk (and products) and that India could sustain the process in the future with its own production levels and technology. It also concluded that Operation Flood objectives had not been effectively met, although EC aid continued to be supplied partly because the EC had been relying too heavily on overly optimistic Indian documents (ECA, 1988:13–15). The decreased mountain of surplus milk products made possible by a deliberate effort of the EC to bring down overproduction may have also lessened the pressure on the EC to find a means of disposal.

The funds generated by the sale of donated commodities have become essential for maintaining the financial viability of the system. Although self-financing is a statutory requirement of the NDDB, this criterion is not consistently applied either for capital investment or for operating capital loans. Subsidised capital has become virtually indispensable to the 'private' dairies. The constant need for fresh money constitutes one of the most pressing reasons for continuation of aid. One may well wonder how this arrangement will fare in the current neo-liberal economic climate, which seeks to eliminate various sorts of subsidies and to allow more unfettered competition. The donated commodities also remain intrinsic to the functioning of the National Milk Grid, which aims to keep supply constant in conditions where regional variations and seasonal fluctuations occur. The Grid's central problem is the underutilisation of installed capacity (Doornbos *et al.*, 1990:Ch. 4). Capacity must be high enough to ensure the processing of milk during flush season and to allow the possibility of increased supply over time. Underutilisation has been attributed to competition from the private sector, mismanagement, mishandling and overexpenditure – over and above seasonal variations. The resulting increased overhead costs constrain capital generation within the various co-operative institutions. Hence imbalances in the Grid affect the financial health of the dairy and the milk supply.

Other financial pressures on the Grid include poorly marketed cattle feeds (leading to underutilisation of feed plants), debts and losses inherited by dairy federations from the public dairies, political pressure to expand capacity, and inappropriate milk pricing policies. Moreover, the IDC/NDDB sells donated dairy aid below the domestic cost of production, which depresses milk prices. Finally, the losses one would expect in such an enterprise limit the ability of the IDC/NDDB to finance new investments or working capital despite the considerable reserves generated by aid (Alderman *et al.*, 1987:30–1).

Throughout the co-operative structure and in the IDC/NDDB itself, financial weaknesses are obscured by the availability of additional resources through aid. The IDC/NDDB's statutory obligation to be self-financing applies to all the institutions of Operation Flood. Yet 30 percent of the funding state federations receive from the IDC/NDDB for milk processing, marketing and production enhancement programmes is received as grants. (If one takes into account other expenditures which the IDC covers itself – for example development, labour development, research and development, creation of centralized facilities and services and so on – then the assistance roughly works out to 50 percent loan and 50 percent grant although this amount varies widely from state to state depending on their pattern of expenditure (GOI, 1984:69). Village co-operative societies obtain 80–90 percent of their capital from the IDC/ NDDB as grants; the rest is share capital and member deposits (Alderman *et al.*, 1987). These figures contradict the self-financing principle. The programme remains affordable due to the enormous financial reserves from the sale of EC dairy commodities. And there are additional complications. The availability of grants, political pressures, the underpricing of donated commodities, and the failure to fully cost unwaged labour and the services performed by unions results in consumer prices that are too low. The artificially low sale price in turn makes it difficult for the federations to repay their loans.

Seasonality can be *partly* avoided by the introduction of crossbred cows which are not seasonal breeders (but whose milk production still varies somewhat seasonally as they are more sensitive to temperature than local cows and buffaloes). Supply can be evened out by processing flush season surpluses into milk powder to cover lean season shortages or by transferring milk from surplus regions to deficit regions. These, however, are expensive solutions (in particular the first one) with implications for participants in the dairy industry as well. While for some years emerging indigenous surpluses in several Indian states have seemed to suggest that Indian stocks are available for this purpose, milk prices would have to be adjusted to sustain this shift, and this transition will inevitably be slow, as Baviskar and Terhal (1990) point out. Instead, imported commodities are used to maintaining an even supply of milk, while the domestic resources are used for unrestricted (luxury) products. Aid keeps the grid running smoothly and relatively inexpensively. In the absence of dairy aid, large amounts of financial resources would be cut off and indigenous supply and demand would have to be readjusted – a potentially painful process, so far averted.

Nevertheless, there are signs of improvement. Baviskar and Terhal (1990) report that Calcutta is receiving milk powder from surplus areas inside India, thereby enhancing interdependency inside India rather than external dependence. Also, in keeping with a more general reorientation of EC policy since the mid-1980s, the amount of dairy commodity aid under Operation Flood III is substantially less than under the second phase. Commenting on this, Clay (1985:44) observed that 'this move, reflecting management considerations and widespread concern about the developmental and institutional effectiveness of the uses of these commodities, indicates some degree of autonomy from agricultural surplus disposal in food aid policy-making within the EEC'.

The European Court of Auditors (ECA, 1988:6) has pointed out that high production costs and low consumer incomes mean that few market opportunities will be available for Operation Flood once effective demand has reached its limit, despite increasing supply. This is not to say demand will have been satisfied; lack of purchasing power will limit market expansion. When confronted with income-constrained demand or price controls on milk, the dairy industry responds by promoting investment in processed luxury products which are not subject to the price regulations imposed on milk.

India, according to the ECA, has virtually reached self-sufficiency in dairy supplies at current consumer prices, particularly in the liquid milk market (ECA, 1988). Although India could now produce enough skim milk powder to satisfy demand during the dry season, it continues to solicit EC dairy commodity aid. Using reconstituted EC commodities to supply the liquid milk market releases indigenous supply for product manufacture (for example, ice cream, cheese, butter, infant food). This specialized market, besides avoiding price controls, is not in direct competition with the traditional dairy sector. The ECA now considers India to be in a position to satisfy the milk needs of those who can afford to buy liquid milk, thus undermining justification for further provision of skim milk powder by the EC (ECA, 1988:13).

Since income levels and the cost of milk production are stable, there are few opportunities to increase solvent demand. Producer prices cannot be lowered any further. No radical reduction of processing, transportation or marketing costs is projected. Income shifts upwards take place slowly. As for aid in the future, its role may largely be to permit an investment pattern oriented towards the manufacture of luxury items. Its original purpose – to satisfy solvent demand for liquid milk – has essentially been achieved (ECA, 1988:14). Unfortunately, as the European Court of Auditors report observes (1988:15), this does not resolve the issue of insolvent demand. There is still a need for satisfying the nutritional requirements of a large number of people who lack financial resources. For this sector of the population, dairy products would need to be distributed on concessional terms. As Operation Flood is concerned with preserving the solvent dairy market, concessional distribution would need to go through alternative channels, either public or private (NGOs). Interestingly, the Indian authorities have not displayed much interest in this form of food aid from the Community, in contrast to their active pursuit of continued aid for a third (and now a fourth) phase of Operation Flood.

What, then, have been the advantages of dairy aid through Operation Flood? First of all, without access to large amounts of donated skim milk powder and butter oil, the programme would neither have been designed, nor *a fortiori* implemented at its present ambitious scale. By distributing the donated commodities themselves, NDDB has efficiently exploited the twin advantages of dairy commodity aid. It has been able to invest in facilities for collecting, processing and marketing indigenous milk, and to even out local imbalances in the indigenous marketing process.

But easy access to enormous amounts of dairy aid has also obscured the precarious economic viability of this type of processing and marketing system. The aid flowed partly as subsidies to urban milk consumers, while on the other hand giving distant producers easy access to a new marketing channel. Hence gains were realized in both sectors. However, these gains were not sufficiently based on an indigenous breakthrough in productivity, which would have required either higher producer prices than the downward political pressure on consumer prices would allow, or even larger amounts of subsidies or aid. Clearly the price that consumers would have to pay in order to cover the full costs of a year-round supply of milk would be prohibitively high for poor slum dwellers. Indeed, the ECA Report (1988:31) contends that even the middle-class consumers would find such prices unaffordable. With subsidies, the present system favours mainly middle and upper classes. And while aid has helped many producers by facilitating enlarged sales, the benefits have mainly accrued to favoured regions (for example, Gujarat, Punjab, Maharashtra) and larger, better-off producers.

Institutional transformations

Operation Flood has changed the relationship between NDDB and the state governments. When the Anand pattern was extended from village and district level to the creation of state-level federations, these needed to integrate pre-existing state dairy departments. As a result, the state government has actually withdrawn from the dairy sector.

Once a state has in principle accepted the programme package, the state government drafts a dairy development plan that conforms to Operation Flood objectives (Nagabrahmam, 1983:7, 15; Subramaniam *et al.*, 1989:14; Doornbos *et al.*, 1990). When the IDC/NDDB approves the plan, it makes resources available. The new state federation (or other temporary implementing agency), can apply for a loan if it has sufficient collateral. If not, the state is expected to guarantee the loan. The state is not allowed to audit the federation through its own institutions but is required to establish an independent auditing board. According to the agreement, the federation controls pricing policy at both the producer and consumer ends. In actual practice, prices are established in consultation with state officials and in conformity with the national government's overall pricing policy. For example, the co-operative dairies have been compelled to observe government-ordered price freezes on milk. The agreement also requires the states to transfer state dairy plants to the co-operative sector, preferably free of outstanding debts and, if necessary, renovated. State governments at times have felt politically pressured into conforming to the needs of a centralized programme and unable to achieve compromises that could acknowledge their autonomy and specific priorities.

On the national level, dairy affairs came under the jurisdiction of both the NDDB and the Ministry of Agriculture, leading to a certain amount of duplication and conflict. While the NDDB had been created as technical advisory body, Operation Flood transformed it by infusing it with power and wealth. Essentially, Operation Flood broke the connection between NDDB dairy planning and state-centred dairy development. As George (1990) puts it, the NDDB abandoned its original function to develop dairying in general to become the implementing arm of Operation Flood. The centre has relinquished more and more control in dairy development to the NDDB. Efforts to place the NDDB/IDC under the Ministry of Agriculture Dairy Division have been politically tricky and sensitive (Jha Report, 1984; Lok Sabha Debates, 25th August 1987). Whether this feat can be accomplished by including the dairy industry in the framework of the Technology Missions (which are ultimately managed by the sectoral ministries) is by no means certain. However, no such restructuring will reduce the incorporation of India's dairy industry into the global linkages which the Operation Flood institutions have been instrumental in extending. As George observes, this has been partly facilitated by focusing attention on the 'Anand Pattern' as a generalized concept that conjures images of ultimate rural autonomy. Inevitably, the reality is much more complex.

At the most general level, the relationship between specific resources, their use, and the nature of institutional interventions through Operation Flood is one of increasingly centralized planning of Indian dairy development. Not enough is known about the dynamics of participation and representation in the various tiers of the current structure, and especially their failure to extend to the highest level. The NDDB has purported to create a representative co-operative structure, but has not itself been subjected to scrutiny by farmers' representatives. For all intents and purposes the NDDB enjoys a remarkably autonomous position: non-representative, non-governmental, yet vested with vast policy-making powers that enable it to intervene in some of the most vital aspects of India's agricultural sector.

Within the co-operative framework, the contracting of foreign linkages appears to have given a decisive boost to the roles of technocrats and managers. The current trends of growth and centralization run parallel to a trend towards stronger managerial control – federations and district unions are for farmers rather than of farmers. As the roles of technocratic managers and representative organs on each tier shift, the relative power of the executive positions and the nature of their interactions are changing. Their relationship to third parties follows a similar pattern. As already noted, Baviskar (1990) and Patel (1990) offer instructive, though different, observations on this phenomenon and its politico-historical background.

The special status the Anand dairy co-operative (AMUL) and the Gujarat Co-operative Milk Marketing Federation enjoy within the national dairy development strategy also appears to be difficult to reconcile with a policy of replication of a standard package. A fourth tier, the National Co-operative Dairy Federation of India (NCDF), responsible for an integrated and rational co-operative dairy policy, has been created. In recent years the NCDF has witnessed and facilitated closer regional co-ordination of production and marketing, within which Gujarat retains a strong position but has to count with an increasing role of some other regional producers.

As noted earlier, the dairy sector has been included in the Technology Missions since August 1988. At the time, the key question was whether inclusion would bring the NDDB more closely under the control of the Ministry of Agriculture, given that the NDDB had managed to dominate its public financial arm (IDC), which was the only legal link to public accountability. One must not exclude the same happening with the Technology Mission, resulting in another 'arm' of the NDDB serving to augment the influence and resources of the NDDB without imposing substantive accountability. Evidence of the mission's potential fate could be its relocation, early on, to Anand, home of AMUL, NDDB and Operation Flood, whereas all other missions are headquartered in Delhi, where their respective ministries are located (Kothari, 1989).

In 1992, a mid-term evaluation of Operation Flood III appeared (Commission of the European Community, 1992). Undertaken under the auspices of the EC and with the express agreement of NDDB as to the mission's terms of reference and composition, the evaluation, in emphasizing two main concerns – the relative weakness of the milk production base, and the inadequacies of the information kept by the programme – is remarkably critical of several structural shortcomings in the programme previously noted by independent researchers since the early 1980s. The report concludes, nonetheless, by recommending that the programme be extended for two years – Operation Flood IV.

Why did this critical document argue for yet another phase? As discussed in Chapter 9, NDDB has been hypersensitive to critique from researchers, journalists and government agencies; the EC even suppressed the report of an official EC/World Bank mission in 1986 at the insistence of NDDB. While we can only speculate, it seems likely that during previous applications for project extension, external critique was considered damaging to the success story of the Anand dairy co-operative, which was crucial to the project's viability. The second phase used this argument to propose extending the project throughout India; the third phase proposals were argued on the need for further expansion and consolidation. Consistent with the politics of evaluation, each proposal claimed to be the last, and denied the growing dependence on dairy aid. Because this rationale for extension (success, replication and consolidation) was getting exhausted, NDDB had to find a new strategy. Ironically, criticism of structural weaknesses in the project then seemed to provide the justification needed; what once was stifled became serviceable. In this way, another final round of EC aid was proposed, this time under the banner of 'viability and sustainability'.

Concluding remarks

Operation Flood has become the saga of a 'success story'. The 'success' has been a case of institution-building at a virtually dazzling scale. Yet, in as far as its aims of dairy development are concerned, India has come to critically rely on dairy commodity aid, and a form of dependence on external aid was in fact engendered (Baviskar and Terhal, 1990; Batra, 1990). It can be argued that this dependence has been created to a significant degree by the indigenous Indian institutions in charge of dairy policy. Although the government of India has been officially involved at each successive step in this process, formally authorizing or ratifying programme proposals, agreements, investments and so on, it has by and large relegated the initiative for policy making for the overall dairy sector, explicitly including even its international aid and trade dimensions, to autonomously operating public corporate bodies. An issue to address is the extent to which sector-oriented institutions have become able to tie the interests of their consumer constituents to international commodity arrangements, at the expense of local producers, as well as with long-term implications for India's balance of trade position and her capacity to be self-sufficient in dairying.

Looking at the other side of this arrangement, the foreign aid linkage could be the greatest stumbling block to decentralized planning for livestock and dairying in India. Probably more than any other single factor, dairy commodity aid appears to have been indirectly instrumental in the centralization of planning and the establishment of a single institutional channel for the handling of aid commodities. As it happens, this is quite advantageous for donors, who now need to have contact with only one receiving channel instead of a variety of state and other agencies. Operation Flood as a single complex rather than as a number of disaggregated projects reduced the institutional capacity donors require to negotiate, process and evaluate project proposals and progress reports. At the same time, it fostered a strong negotiating capacity on the Indian side, which at times seemed capable itself of setting the terms of new agreements with the EC/EU, in turn reinforcing its domestic position.

When asking what particular institutional qualities and characteristics enabled the NDDB to play the pivotal role it did, or how these features were acquired, a few elements stand out. First of all, within the NDDB and throughout the co-operative dairy structure, there has throughout been a strongly managerial-bureaucratic approach. This provides managers and bureaucrats with a considerable amount of leeway in decision-making and, indeed, autonomy of action in relation to both government and internal representative organs. Perhaps more importantly, these institutions also enjoy considerable autonomy *vis-à-vis* other institutionalized or non-institutionalized interests within or outside the sector; for example, private milk traders, feed/food cultivators, users of communal lands, cattle owners, ministry departments, planning bodies, state governments and so on.

Secondly, the key dairy institutions have certainly occupied a key position between the donor agencies on the one hand and the various state governments and dairy federations on the other, adding scope for manoeuvre and opportunities for brokerage to their role, and this in turn has strongly enhanced their autonomous powers. NDDB contributions to policy making not only reflect a 'balancing' role but constitute a very active effort to shape the direction of dairy development policy. Indeed, a basic aspect of its function seems to have been the linking of India's dairy sector into an international milk grid and the world market for dairy products. The final paradox is that the relative loss of autonomy thus incurred by India's dairy sector did not fundamentally contradict the substantial autonomy of NDDB itself.

11
Revisiting the Food Aid Debate: Taking a Closer Look at the Institutional Factor

Introduction

While the previous chapters have focused on various differentiating effects that tend to come with the institutionalisation of development policies, projects and programmes, it is equally of interest to note how some of the key actors engaged in these processes have themselves become institutionalized, and what their specific institutional foundations may imply for their mode of operation and strategies of institutional continuity. As discussed in the Introduction to this volume, institutional longevity and survival can become a powerful motivating factor in the strategizing of institutions, at times overriding and thus reorienting the basic purposes for which the institutions concerned were set up.

Some of the tendencies concerned were observable already in the keen eye for institutional self-interest with which, as discussed in Chapters 9 and 10, the organizations engaged in receiving dairy aid and promoting dairy development in India went about their business. Significantly, however, parallel institutional interests have emerged also at the donating side of the world of actors engaged in the distribution of food aid. The present chapter takes a closer look at the patterns and implications concerned, starting out with a brief appraisal of continuities and change in the international food aid debates.

The debates

Revisiting the debates around food aid, as was amply illustrated at the EADI Workshop on Food Aid and Human Security in Oslo in April 1998, is instructive in several regards. At one level, the debate as it is conducted towards the end of the millennium, remains strongly reminiscent of that of the 1970s and 1980s. In fact, continuity and repetition of arguments produce a kind of '*déjà vu*' effect: there is ongoing discussion about 'additionality' versus 'fungeability' of food aid; about food aid as a 'resource' as opposed to a 'tool'; on food aid for 'relief' as opposed to 'development'; on the pros and cons of monetization; on the risks of disincentive effects and chronic aid dependency as opposed to enhancing agricultural self-sufficiency and national food security; and on a range of related questions. Significantly, these debates have followed parallel tracks even though the specific food aid commodities at issue – grains, milk, meat – might be different. With respect to most of the issues, the arguments advanced have remained essentially the same and appear to have become routinized; when revisiting the discussion one is struck to note how little the debate has moved forward over a period of roughly two decades. Significantly, also, one notes that food aid continues to be a topic that has its 'supporters' and 'critics'.

At another level, though, there is noticeable change in the terms of the debate. This has less to do with changing appreciations of the merits or demerits of food aid *per se* (though a 'critical' shift of emphasis has seemed manifest in this respect), but rather with changes in the broader context and conditions under which the discussion is being conducted. In particular, the availability of food aid out of agricultural surpluses in Northern countries is no longer as assured a given as it had been during earlier periods, and hence an element of fundamental uncertainty about the future of food aid as it has come to be constituted has entered the equasion (Clay *et al.*, 1998a:5–8). Evidently, this uncertainty has at once an unsettling effect on the arguments used in the debate so far, for if the lifeline to the practice of aid is itself endangered, any debate about it becomes necessarily more abstract and academic.

In addition to the basic factor of the prospect of surplus commodities running out (and concurrently the alternative of buying food aid commodities on the market becoming too expensive), contextual changes also include shifts in the nature of donor–recipient relations governing food aid. Among other things, questions have increasingly been targeted at the role earmarked for food aid as a development tool in the hands of donor organizations (Fritschel, 1998:7). Recipient countries have become increasingly vocal and critical at being relegated to the receiving end of the line, and would like to have a stronger say in the preconditions under which food aid programmes are to be executed. Various receiving countries also now have their own expertise available for assessing needs and issues, which they feel should be engaged into the dialogue. Besides, food aid in its classical sense of concrete commodities being donated has evolved in many different directions, with concessional imports, triangular commodity purchases, monetized commodity inputs on food markets, and other such forms having been developed. Several such forms have actually become rather difficult to distinguish from 'normal' imports, especially if government agencies are still involved in the latter. Again, as compared to the patterns prevailing some decades ago, other more sophisticated support arrangements are now available for aid-receiving countries, such as the annual meetings for budget support (which could well include an item for food purchases if deemed necessary) organized for various countries in Paris or other venues. In principle these meetings allow for more wholesale approaches to issues of aid, besides being more 'chic'. Several of these changes have sharpened the questioning of whether there is still a place for international food aid at the end of the millennium, or whether one should prepare for a fresh start without it in the next one.

The institutional factor

Even though there is increasing discussion, and questions being raised, about the future of food aid, it is important to be quite specific as to what is meant by this, and what exactly is at issue. Food aid per se is actually a time-honoured phenomenon, with the first recorded food aid dating from the time of the Crimean War, and with other instances possibly being even older. In this respect, one would seem to be quite justified in assuming that food aid, already with a respectable historical record, will have a future in many instances where there is a pressing need for it. One point of consensus today is indeed that relief aid in emergency situations is, and must remain, beyond question (Clay *et al.*, 1998b:41–3).

Current questions about the 'future of food aid', however, appear to carry a more restricted and specific connotation. Food aid in the late twentieth century has come to denote a whole complex of institutional arrangements involving donor–recipient relations with numerous countries in the South, which finds (or, perhaps, found) its point of departure in the availability of surplus agricultural commodities in the North in need of an outlet for disposal. It is this availability, which for many years could be taken for granted, which is now no longer guaranteed, and by implication questions about the future come to concern the entire range of institutional structures and their modes of operation which have been developed towards the allocation, distribution and dispatchment of food aid.

This general set-up was based on several premises, which themselves have been subject to continuous debate. Central has been the belief that the world is producing sufficient food to provide nutrition to the entire global population, so that what would be required would essentially be to have suitable bridging mechanisms between supply and effective demand. In this perspective, it was believed that food aid could serve as one such mechanism, until such time that global market integration could effectively replace its role. In the end, though, the operational starting point was that food aid was a disposable resource at the discretion of donor agencies, meaning that with this resource at hand they attempted to search for appropriate applications, looking for 'the best way of making use of it' (Fritschel, 1998:1, 6). In practice this meant trying to identify recipient countries where donor criteria and conditionalities could be expected to be met, or where wider policy objectives as formulated on the donor side might seem attainable with the use of aid commodities as an incentive. This practice of food aid has hence been essentially resource- and donor-driven. It has also led to prolonged debates about its potential disincentive effects on local production and other implications and the extent to which these could be overcome.

'Crisis' and resource patterns

The impending changes in context with regard to the continued availability of food aid commodities naturally could not but provoke profound uncertainties in various quarters involved with its provision. Indeed, these prospects have already been prompting reactions ranging from directly defensive postures to readiness to re-examine missions and objectives. A closer look at actual and potential reactions may thus be useful with an eye on reconnaisances of future roles.

First, when examining the situation of such organizations it is important to bear in mind how closely several of them – such as the World Food Programme (WFP) and NGOs like CARE and Catholic Relief Services – have been tied up institutionally with the above patterns and mechanisms of food aid procurement and disbursement (Christian Michelsen Institute, 1993). The tie is so complete and direct, especially on the North American scene, that without agricultural commodities to be disposed of, the agencies concerned at once tend to lose their basic rationale, as well as their means of survival.

What do institutions do when under threat of losing their key functions? Several strategies may ordinarily be expected. Predictably, one immediate response is almost certainly a defensive one, namely of arguing 'we have always done right'. To substantiate this, the affected institutions will produce figures and feedback meant to underscore their record of institutional effectiveness in accomplishing their mission. Significantly, the need to do this may be felt particularly strongly in cases where such effectiveness in the past had remained unclear or had not been entirely undisputed.

A second line of defence, potentially closely related to the first, is to seek strategic support from relevant bodies: parliaments, the press, real or imagined constituencies at the receiving and/or giving side (among the latter, for example, farmers' lobbies, shippers' organizations, church bodies, experts). The messages being formulated at this level are likely to be loud and clear, leaving no doubt about the vital role the organization in question is performing, and pointing to the untold dangers that would follow if its operations were to be ruptured.

Sooner or later, these lines of response, may be followed by seemingly even more serious and 'objective' efforts to set the record straight: mobilization of (positive) evaluations, ostensibly neutral, meant to produce the kind of base-line documents that will impress funders or political decision-makers and thus help to give the institutional activity a new lease of life. As the stakes are high in institutional evaluations, there are strong chances of complex 'politics of evaluation' syndromes coming into play. Sensitive points in these engagements tend to arise around questions such as who is to appoint whom as evaluators, who is to formulate and decide on the terms of reference, what conclusions and recommendations are to be put forward, either with or without amendments, and whether these should be accepted as legitimate and politically acceptable outcomes. As institutional survival itself may be at issue, such instances of micro-politics may at times become notably tense and conflict-ridden, as has in fact been illustrated more than once within the broader area of international food aid arrangements (Doornbos and Terhal, 1993). Multi-donor engagement in the programmes concerned, and multi-agency involvement in their assessment, may at once render these processes even more complex, but make their outcomes nonetheless more assured given the likelihood of a mix of interests playing a role on the donor cum assessors side.

At times, defensive strategies may recognize the impending demand for more radical reorientation, but try to get away with marginal adaptations. In such instances it may be worth reading between the lines and trying to decipher the codes: the message may contain distracting measures of 'reform', claims of 'novel' approaches, and the praise of wise men in evaluations. But once the documents are filed, there may be an intention to try and get back to business as usual.

More serious, though not necessarily more common, is a basic preparedness and determination among institutions to have a honest look at their role in the face of changing circumstances, and to try and strike out in new direction on the basis of radical adaptations of their mandate and programme activities. The most courageous among the latter type of reaction, yet by far the most rare, would be for some institutions to decide to wind up in the light of contextual changes which have rendered their core role superfluous or problematic. The problem with either of this kind of resolution is that they depend on being formulated and proposed from within the respective institution itself, which goes against normal institutional survival instincts.

Various such strategies, in different possible combinations, are presently already becoming manifest on the food aid front. Indeed, several international NGOs, some UN agencies, and particularly WFP appear to have good reasons to re-examine their mandates in the light of changing circumstances. For many such agencies, the issue is as much one of institutional longevity as about the safeguarding of food aid as such. It is ironic that such struggles are often particularly pronounced in the case of organizations that were set up as temporary bodies to begin with. The latter may have been readily set up, with broad initial enthusiasm and institutional support from various sides, and seemingly clear original objectives, but in the end turn out to be extremely difficult to dismantle, especially in the case of multilateral agencies with their rather diffuse ownership. Again, one factor tending to enhance the 'staying power' of such institutions is the practice of multi-donor evaluations, which often includes one or another party ready to neutralize any proposals for radical re-orientation.

Reversing the order?

In rapidly changing contexts, such as the one the world of food aid is currently facing, there may be a need for far more radical reorientations or restructuring than have been under consideration thus far. Paradoxically, some such initiatives may actually better help the institutions concerned to stay in business. Dutch NGOs, for example, have for some time been studying options for 'aidless' NGO activities, anticipating a time when there will be less finance available to sponsor international aid programmes in the South. For NGOs and other organizations specifically operating in the field of food aid, it may similarly be worthwhile to consider other options related to their present activities. One pre-condition to any such re-appraisals becoming meaningful, must how-ever, almost certainly be their serious consideration of severing their own direct 'dependency' on food aid commodities as a basis for their operations.

As an alternative scenario to the predominant way in which food aid has been disbursed thus far, which basically laid the initiative for pro-ject activities in the hands of food aid donor agencies, the possibility of reversing the key steps might be given due consideration. A reverse order might start (and might in the past have started), from a reconnais-sance of priorities in terms of enhancing food security in a given situation (e.g. through raising productivity, improving marketing possibilities, con-sidering additional technological or financial imputs, safeguarding equit-able distribution, etc.). Such an alternative starting point might allow more reliable determination of possible needs for temporary or longer-terms food aid support, based on careful scrutiny of the conditions under which aid might be 'safe' and useful, and possibly in conjunction with other interventions. Calls for support which would thus emanate from situations in need of food supplements, in turn would presuppose donors being prepared to take on a more 'recipient' role, ready to receive such kinds of requests. Such alternative scenarios have been followed in rare instances only, however, and it seems without much enthusiastic support from the key institutions engaged in handling food aid. Still, there may be a point in giving them a closer look.

Essentially, reversing the order might entail one or more of the fol-lowing elements and steps, in different possible combinations:

(1)   Reversing the donor–recipient hierarchy, and for donor agencies to accept a role of being 'on demand' rather than 'in command'; particu-larly in regard to the food aid and food security field, genuine part-nership should replace sensitive notions of 'donors' and 'recipients'.

(2)   For donor agencies themselves dependent on the food aid lifeline, to consider merging or at least closely liaising with other organiza-tions which have a different entry point into the overall prob-lematique, as a way of enhancing the potential for institutional and operational responsiveness; for example, WFP might seek to liaise or integrate its activities more closely with those of FAO, among others, on the productivity side; precisely because it is a 'single-commodity' organization, a merger of WFP with others might make it easier to weigh different alternatives and determine when food aid might be resorted to, if at all, in conjunction with other strategies;

(3)   Significantly widening (even after any possible mergers) the dialogue on operational priorities and choices in the field by including other actors, internal as well as external, in principle including all those that would be relevant towards the identification and resolution of a complex set of issues; in practice this could mean fora in which Ministry of Agriculture staff within a country concerned as well as farmers' bodies, marketing organizations, NGOs with an interest in the area concerned, and other multilateral agencies might participate, each bringing in their own expertise and comparative advantage;

(4)   To collectively study and define key issues and strategies towards attaining food security, with a broadened focus on relevant variables such as employment and income-generation, enhancing agricultural production, paying due respect to rural as well as urban nutrition aspects, and other factors; such collective involvements should yield more informed views as to when and how it might be advisable to find recourse to food aid to temporarily compensate for inescapable gaps or setbacks in attaining food security, and how a possible food aid intervention is likely to impact on other policy efforts being made in this regard.

A reorientation in this vein might bring about a number of things at once, namely (1) to give due recognition to the complexity of the interplay of factors affecting food security, which has often been highlighted in critical reviews of food aid practices; (2) by juxtaposing different lines of expertise and resources on a common set of problems, to avoid undue reliance on one specific type of intervention, such as food aid, towards solving problems which may require more multi-stranded approaches. By implication one would minimize the risk of one-track interventions in the end prolonging rather than serving to attenuate the problems faced. One would also have the benefit of being able to draw on a sizeable literature that has already focused on several of the complexities involved, and thus to make 'positive' use of analyses and commentaries that too often have been regarded as 'negative'.

Towards alternative scenarios: an example

It has become a commonplace to note how inert the UN and other multilateral agencies have been *vis-à-vis* urgent needs and calls for reform. Normally, therefore, there would be little chance of re-orientations such as the above being given much serious attention. At the present time, though, the 'threat' of disappearing surpluses may have the interesting effect of 'far-fetched' ideas being taken more seriously. As regards the above suggested reversals, experiences to date with a modest precursor project, namely the *War-torn Societies Project* (*WSP*) initiated by the United Nations Research Institute for Social Development (UNRISD) in 1995, suggest that these would not necessarily be a step in the dark.

The focus of WSP projects, which to date have been undertaken in Eritrea, Mozambique, Guatemala and Somalia, has been on post-conflict reconstruction, and WSP seeks to make a contribution to this through action-oriented research activities meant to lead up to informed policy dialogue (UNRISD, 1994). In each country, research was initiated on what were perceived to be the key issues in reconstruction – mapping out what was being done, and what needed to be done, in such areas as demobilization, returnee integration, provision of food security and basic needs, establishment of justice and governance structures, and other areas. The choice of themes would be made by a Project Group, comprising of all interested parties, national and international as the case might be, in the project as a whole; invariably, though, national views would get priority in the making of these choices. The ensuing research would be carried out in several successive phases according to a particular common scenario, and would be carried out exclusively by teams of well qualified and well accepted national researchers (Doornbos, 1999).

Around each chosen research theme, a working group of up to 10–12 members would be formed, consisting of representatives of national and international agencies taking a special interest in the respective theme. On food security, for example, a working group might comprise members from the Ministry of Agriculture, from farmers' organizations, the food processing industry, NGOs involved in the provision of food aid and rehabilitation schemes, FAO or World Food Programme representatives wherever applicable, the World Bank country mission, etc. On refugee resettlement issues, similarly, one would have representatives from the main national organizations responsible for returnee programmes, UNHCR, international and national NGOs engaged in resettlement schemes, UNFPA, and others with an involvement or interest in the field. These working group would meet regularly, approximately once a month, giving both direction to the research activities and feedback to the field data and results. In this sense, the research was a kind of participatory action-research, but here with the active participation of people from various agencies with a stake in the broad policy field, and thus more a matter of participation at a macro rather than the usual micro level of participatory action-research.

In these various pilot projects, the set-up of working groups associated with selected research themes became significant in two major ways. First, the research material gathered often constituted the first compilation and stock-taking of relevant and up-to-date information on the given field in the country in the new situation, and thus had a direct relevance to many parties involved (e.g. Doornbos and Tesfai, 1999). But second and at least as important, was the dialogue that ensued in most working groups in connection with the research. This was dialogue fed by research, and in turn feeding into the research, but it was also a research-induced dialogue among various stakeholders in the respective policy area itself, which in several cases turned out to be highly valuable. Indeed, involvement in informal WSP working groups enabled representatives from different ministries, agencies, political parties or other organizations to compare notes, get a better understanding of other members' involvements and perspectives, of the rationale for certain policy positions, or of the shortcomings of particular policy measures. In several instances these confrontations with new perspectives and research data did actually lead to adjustments or rethinking of policy. In Mozambique, for example, local-level research data gathered through the project on the impacts of structural adjustment on agriculture and food security gave the actors concerned, notably the World Bank, reason to adapt their policy approaches. In Eritrea, WSP discussions and research helped clarify an enduring policy stalemate between external and internal actors that had arisen over the government's monetization policy of food aid commodities. Invariably, the dialogue aspects in all four pilot cases, judging by numerous expressions of interest by participants concerned, has turned out a striking feature of these WSP projects.

From the experience with these projects, therefore, there does indeed appear to be scope for action-oriented research playing a constructive role in generating policy dialogue and better understandings. While the focus here has been on societies emerging from prolonged conflict and devastation, there does not seem to be any a priori reason why similar kinds of approaches should not be applicable to other policy contexts with important external as well as internal involvements, or to certain sectoral areas in which similar kinds of issues recur. The particular modalities to follow might need to be quite different in other areas, but the key element would be to build on action research as a strategy towards broader deliberation with the inclusion of all relevant actors whose inputs it would be important to have.

Returning specifically to the food aid field, adopting this kind of approach might (1) help alter the external–internal actor dichotomy from which it appears to suffer so pronouncedly, and (2) by bringing in other relevant actors, local and external, it might provide a better basis for determining optimal mixes of agricultural production incentives and aid components – as long as the latter can be made available. It would certainly not be true, as has sometimes been suggested, that no relevant counterparts would be available and ready to participate in any such common endeavours, in turn leaving the field basically open to donor-initiated actions. To the contrary, it would be essential not to bypass potential counterparts, but to engage them in the process from the beginning. The WSP pilot projects seem to have demonstrated that it is in principle possible to generate meaningful policy dialogue on the basis of collective action-research at a macro level. Having passed this basic viability test, it may now be useful to develop appropriate methodologies for different kinds of policy contexts, notably also that concerned with issues of food security.

Concluding remarks

Looking back again at the debates about food aid over the past several decades, one cannot fail to notice a certain shift in the nature of these debates. First, during the post-war dawn of food aid arrangements, much of the discussion was on technical and operational aspects, though by and large remaining non-controversial in nature: the pros and cons of particular approaches were largely debated from a basic acceptance of the need for food aid in a number of circumstances. Almost imperceptibly, though, food aid subsequently became a more 'permanent' proposition, and areas for possible application of food aid were extended as Northern surplus commodities made this possible if not compelling. In debate, these links to overproduction – of grains, milk and meats – were seriously questioned, and the nature of the exchanges became increasingly adversary and controversial. From the side of the industry during this episode, critique and alternative suggestions were not particularly welcomed. They would hardly be listened to, and rather stood a chance of being dismissed out of hand or being accused of having been inspired by ulterior motives to damage a 'just' cause.

Presently, with the imminent decline of available surpluses for disposal as food aid, a change in the climate for discussion again appears to be in the making. Already, one senses a greater preparedness to reconsider issues and involvements, priorities and alternatives, at least among some of the staff and sections of the agencies involved. Others, however, remain as sensitive to critique as before, if not more so.

As suggested above, this is not too surprising but appears perfectly explicable in terms of struggles for institutional survival (be it that these often happen to be focused on a short rather than a longer horizon). Nonetheless, more meaningful internal dialogues on alternative futures may come to ensue within the key agencies engaged in food aid activities. If these came off, then conceivably they might instil a broader orientation on food security with correspondingly new approaches by the organizations involved, thus allowing suitable institutional complementarities within the limited space for policy engagement that is left.

Conclusion: Assessing Institutional Interventions

The explorations undertaken in the previous chapters into the institutional factor in development theory and praxis have highlighted several core questions: they have looked critically at normative and analytical approaches, at different kinds and levels of interconnections between political and institutional processes, and at different examples of the politics of institutional design. Several convergences and common implications significantly emerge from these analyses, including the recurrent clashes around the 'neutral' and 'universalist' claims for the role of various kinds of institutions, the socially differentiating tendencies and capacities that seem virtually inherent in the institutionalization of development programmes and policies, and the importance of recognizing the intricacies of 'institutional design' in relation to patterns of resource competition. Above all they underscore the need to develop a proper analytical grasp of what essentially are political processes. Beyond this, it is equally important to recognize key shifts occurring in regard to the basic conceptual categories with which we tend to approach the analysis of development institutions. In particular, it will be instructive to revisit some theoretical perspectives on the state in the light of the preceding analyses.

Revisiting theoretical perspectives on the state

It is a commonplace now to say that the role and position of the 'state' has been subject to pervasive change, requiring a new understanding that will include recognition for the relevant aspects of the global institutional context enfolding it. Closely related to this, theoretical propositions in which the state, specifically the 'developmental' state, played a key role, call for revision. Significantly, however, the fact that certain theoretical approaches tended to be 'state-focused' does not necessarily make them obsolete: in some instances, in fact, part of their baggage may be as relevant as before, possibly even more so, if one shifts the focus to other institutional levels than that of the state.

To illustrate this, in theories of the state and development, three different themes in recent decades had been attracting considerable attention and debate: *corporatism, the relative autonomy of the state* and *dependency*. Though clearly leaving their imprint on development research, each of these themes and debates has tended to dissipate over time, perhaps largely because, at the level of the state, too many divergent variables and political forces were identified which seemingly undermined some of the basic tenets in the debates. The current retreat of the state from various key areas in many countries has enabled private or quasi-private interests to fill the spaces falling vacant. These may include or be linked to public corporate bodies operating with a substantial degree of autonomy, creating new forms of corporatist practice at a sectoral level. The implications of these trends, theoretically as well as substantially in the context of the present discussion, are of first order importance. They may be illustrated, for example, by the institutions responsible for Indian dairy development, reviewed in Chapters 9 and 10. However, the essence of their role would seem exemplary for not a few mega-institutions in India and other countries at the present time.

When revisiting the earlier debates alluded to, first of all, the contours of the *corporatist state* that seemed to be emerging in Western as well as developing countries until some decades ago, have faded. This is true even in those state systems which first provided the context of the debate. However, it does not necessarily mean corporatism has been eclipsed. The main corporate institutions connected with the Indian dairy industry may indicate the existence of alternative routes towards a type of *meso-sectoral corporatism* as it is now known in corporatist literature (Williamson, 1989:17–18; Schmitter, 1989), appearing in non-state, sectorally disaggregated forms. The strong inclination of these institutions to present a unified front, to exercise a firm and unchallenged line of command over the entire sector, and to reconcile potentially conflicting interests between producers and consumers under the guise of programmatic unity of interest, all point to the practice of corporatist-type management. Other corporatist indications include the middle-class bias among programme beneficiaries, the emphasis on modern large-scale organization, the militant way in which other agents operating within the sector run the risk of getting marginalized, and the effort to restructure the market into compatible, functionally related compartments. The dairy industry's nominally representative institutional framework, as well as strongly centralized, executive structure directly linked to the centre of power in India, and its inability or unwillingness to engage in policy dialogue about its programme also appear consistent with corporatist praxis.

With respect to corporatism, the significant evolving trends in the Indian Operation Flood programme appear to have been: the attempts by the co-operative sector to promote the idea of a convergence of interests between dairy producers, consumers, policy makers and aid donors; the effort to bring activities functionally relevant to dairying into a common organizational nexus; the emphasis on a nominally representative organizational structure at lower levels while maintaining power in a centralized executive structure which cultivates close contact with public policy makers at the centre; a biased distribution of benefits in favour of specific groups and geographic areas; and the way discipline and conformity is achieved among the programme participants and between the programme and other relevant actors.

Operating within the grey area of public and private enterprise, disguised as private and based on the sectoral association of relatively small producers, this brand of corporatism has had a long history in industrialized capitalist countries. Experience elsewhere, such as in Italy, has demonstrated that this form of corporatism can sweep small producers out of the picture, while corporate financial and technocratic interests receive most of the profits and benefits and consumers must finally pay the bill through higher product prices or taxes. Evidence from the Indian dairy institutions suggests that the tendencies towards corporatism may have been exacerbated by the extremely rapid growth of the institutional dairy complex, the lack of effective countervailing power either from other interest groups or from the side of government, and the lack of experience with policy dialogue.

The debate on *relative autonomy* is a related issue. The discussion as it was initiated by Hamza Alavi (1972) focused on the relative autonomy of the state *vis-à-vis* different powerful interests: rural landlords, the urban industrial bourgeoisie, and an absentee (metropolitan) ruling élite. According to one version of the hypothesis, the state was able to exert itself, mediate some conflicts, and play its own autonomous role precisely because of latent conflicts of interest. Another version stressed the overdeveloped bureaucratic apparatus of post-colonial states relative to representative politics as an explanatory factor of the relative autonomy of the state. Again, however, the hypothesis, though drawing considerable attention and running the risk of becoming reified, in the end seemed unable to account for many of the complexities and variations of contemporary Third World states and consequently became eclipsed by newer debates (cf. Fox, 1993).

Yet, if brought one level further down, the notion of relative autonomy has a certain heuristic value. When considered in the context of non-market, sector-oriented institutions, the notion of relative autonomy does seem to grasp some essential characteristics of their operations. To a remarkable degree, this tendency – and capacity – was demonstrated by the institutions responsible for India's dairy development programme Operation Flood, which had placed themselves between 'metropolitan' aid-giving institutions like the European Union and its predecessors, the World Bank and numerous other donors on the one hand, and India's agricultural sector, urban consumers, metropolitan dairies and the federal government on the other. It is important to note that this positioning already occurred during the 1970s and 1980s, a period during which the Indian government saw itself as broadly 'in charge'. Today, several other bodies, each with their 'own' external linkages and sphere of 'autonomous' operation within India or other countries, could similarly illustrate the position. Among others, the Bangladeshi mega NGO BRAC and the much publicized Grameen Bank similarly appear to have attained positions of considerable autonomy *vis-à-vis* the state and other key actors.

Relative autonomy partly emerged through the managerial-bureaucratic-technical élite of Operation Flood, whose authority and autonomy increased over time in relation to the representative organs of the co-operative and the state. Moreover, the intermediary position that officials of the NDDB occupied between metropolitan donor agencies on the one hand and Indian state governments and dairy federations on the other points to another crucial aspect of their relative autonomy. Besides brokering and manoeuvring between these interests, the NDDB actively participated in influencing sectoral policy at the centre. The institution managed to turn any possible constraints to its own advantage by exploiting the room for manoeuvre these still entailed – thus recreating, in Alavi's phrase, a 'relative autonomy of the state', though now at its own, sectoral level. In addition to this specific example, however, as Shaw and Carlsson show, various other new patterns of 'relative autonomy', now among the Newly Industrializing Countries (NICs), have recently also presented themselves within the context of the changing international political economy (Shaw and Carlsson, 1988:7–10).

Finally, as regards the *dependency debate*, as noted in Chapter 1, this essentially revolved around assessing the extent to which structural determinants in the world economy which are controlled by hegemonic powers restrict the room for manoeuvre, policy options and growth potential of Third World economies. The debate remained at a highly generalized level, referring to whole states and economies and leaving little room either for differentiation among them or for possible alternative routes. This allowed it to be bogged down in intricacies, specificities and exceptions, until it finally dissipated without addressing the possibility of alternative routes not only *out of* but also *into* dependency.

A sector-specific approach may provide a stronger basis for examining dependency relationships, and again the Indian dairy development case seemed to offer a good illustration. Regardless of whether India is 'generally' in a state of dependency, India's domestic market is crucially important and basically able to defy the question of dependence. Within the dairy sector, India's old milk culture has over time developed numerous solutions to the demands imposed on it, and today again is technically in a position to meet the country's essential requirements from its own resources (Baviskar and Terhal, 1990). Structural determinants, in this case of the world market in dairy commodities, *need* not have any effect on this basic capacity. However, there appear to be ways, rarely explored in research, whereby institutions operating on behalf of particular sectors of the economy can themselves initiate a dependent relationship. This does not imply that the mediating institutions become dependent, but that by creating linkages they expose certain sectors to external conditions, and, if continued on a long-term basis, these linkages may assume a structural character. Thus, although the dairy institutions may themselves remain relatively autonomous, by linking the internal market to external aid they may have rendered the indigenous dairy sector vulnerable to external conditions. Over time, as vested interests develop around this arrangement, the structural ties will be increasingly difficult to cut, despite India's potential to produce enough milk for herself.

This particular example, which could be amplified by others from comparable 'linking' organizations in other sectors and countries, is significant in several respects. One is that it calls for important revisions to the theoretical perspectives with which we look at political and institutional processes, and that we should indeed learn to perceive the world around us as one in which not only 'states' but other key actors play the primary roles. Second and closely related is a fuller appreciation of the changed global context within which new types of institutional linkages and interventions are devised. And last but not least, the case itself is an example of how differentiating institutional interventions may be initiated at even a mega-scale.

Institutional transformations and the global context

The need to modify state-focused theories in development studies evidently invites further exploration of the largely uncharted territory defined by the unfolding of new state and non-state forms of political management and control as well as, in that context, by the proliferation of new kinds of partnerships and/or patterns of competition between state and non-state agencies. In part, therefore, this involves an exploration of shifting boundaries: not of state boundaries in any conventional sense, but of the changing boundaries of state functions and the state's 'reach', coupled to an interest to explore what lies beyond those boundaries.

There are indeed numerous signs that pervasive processes of transition are occurring in this regard, essentially leading up to *changing forms of organization of collective activities* in many parts of the world. The 'visible' side of these processes are patterns of 'top-down' deregulation and de-institutionalization, the disintegration or fragmentation of political entities, and the proliferation of arms among non-state political actors. Other levels of manifestation of these processes include 'everyday forms of state formation', referring to the micro-world of 'bottom-up' shifting allegiances to alternative power-holders (state, anti-state, and non-state forms as locally represented). At yet other levels again there is ample evidence of supra-state re-alignments, of pervasive integration and incorporation of transnational institutional structures, and of a rapidly widening scope of organizational devices. In short, the transitions around us invite re-examination, among other things, of what states are about, and of degrees or kinds of 'state-ness'.

That the range of these transitions is vast and with far-reaching implications is beyond dispute. Nonetheless, it will be important to avoid any premature teleological perspective, either about the future of the state or its possible successor-bodies, or about the nature of the transformation processes (e.g. 'democratization', 'liberalization') to which it is being subjected. While the future of 'the state' as we have known it is uncertain and evidently deserves a question mark, it would be unwise at this stage either to read the signs as pointing to its demise, or alternatively to underestimate their potential significance. In a dynamic perspective, for example, we might see the state as a 'project', expanding or contracting at different time intervals, to be succeeded or superseded by other such 'projects' in due course. Such an approach might possibly have some merits in examining current tendencies. But actually we cannot even be sure about the validity of such dynamic perspective, if this were to presuppose a kind of iron cyclical movement in which the state might temporarily recede but would inevitably be expected to come back in (Azarya, 1988). Instead, we might need to be more alert, as suggested above, on 'changing forms of organization of collective activities'. A new institutional 'grey zone' appears to be opening up, which it will be of crucial importance to try and map out.

Thus, while there is no lack of intrinsic interest in exploring the political parameters of institutional infrastructures, dramatic changes in their current contexts make a revisit to some of these issues all the more compelling. The role of the state has continually evolved, partly in response to the logic of internal dynamics, but also in relation to trends, pressures and shifts in priorities at the global level. The latter changes, as noted, in recent decades have accelerated at an unprecedented scale. In particular, the world-wide wave of conservative economic policy advocating privatization and public austerity, carried to fresh shores by highly influential international agencies, has brought pressure to bear on the state in favour of greater freedom for the market mechanism. Thus, highly diverse types of regimes have been withdrawing from direct control over various vital aspects of their economies. This trend has reinforced, and been reinforced by, internal political pressures to curtail the public bureaucracy in various instances.

As discussed in Chapter 1, it is not just that the state in most parts of the world has been forced to surrender a good deal of the space it occupied in favour of markets and civil society. What is of equal importance is that states, markets and civil societies alike have themselves all become largely dependent upon larger and more powerful forces at the global level. These linkages and pressures are by no means single-directed, but often pose contrasting demands on states and institutions at the receiving end – such as of market-oriented efficiency versus socially-oriented equity. At times different agencies within the UN system, for example, have been known to confront member-states seeking assistance in post-conflict rehabilitation with entirely opposite conditionalities (Boyce, 1996).

While the final outcome of these processes remains indeterminate, one question they throw up is whether the time has not come for a substantial reassessment of the traditional ensemble of concepts of 'state' and 'state formation'. It is by no means suggested here that these concepts have had their day. However, the vastly changing global context within which they figure does require critical reflection on the properties and capacities that can and cannot now be associated with them. The growth of new political and institutional linkages globally and the establishment of new norms for the reorientation of state structures by dominant global centres, may themselves be viewed as processes of institution-building and of 'state' formation, but now on a kind of mega-scale. Formally sovereign state structures are increasingly becoming integrated within larger regional and global supra-state frameworks, in the process shedding several layers and attributes of their erstwhile autonomy. Trends towards globalization in this respect, with increasing emphasis on the introduction of a kind of standardized institutional norms and structures, many of which derived from Western models, are unmistakable. States themselves, in Europe as well as in other world regions, are subject to significant shifts in their primary functions.

Generally, though, such trends should primarily be viewed as affirmations of newly emergent global power relations rather than as any evolution towards global unity or the emergence of a democratic political world order. A priori they imply neither cultural homogenization nor democratization at the level of global institutions, however desirable the latter may be held to be (Held, 1992). In many respects the trend instead goes together with increased tension and manifestations of diversity, and appears to comprise tendencies towards what might be termed global *'de-democratization'* as well as *'democratization'*. Democratization at a global level could refer to the strenuous efforts being undertaken in numerous instances to try and make institutions operating in the transnational orbit more responsive and answerable to representative bodies and the popular voices of global citizens. 'Global civil society' is the key phrase and focus for the relevant debates (Waterman, 1993). De-democratization on the other hand comes with the rapid proliferation of new institutional constructs that assume or are given power and authority over vast areas of international public policy and concern, though often with surprisingly limited accountability to constituent national governments, let alone to civic representations (Scholte, 1998). The two trends parallel those exemplifying the creation as well as the destruction of social capital at a global level: on the one hand the creation of social capital as the attainment of new and meaningful institutional structures with clearly laid out civic accountabilities, but on the other the destruction of social capital through the erosion of once relevant institutions into redundant entities in the wake of the introduction of supra-level bodies of institutional command. What we saw happening in Chapter 5 as regards the fate of a once relevant institution like the Ankole kingship, could well be the destiny of various contemporary institutions currently still held in high esteem by its constituents. Trends towards 'global' civic democratization and de-democratization may thus be found in a continuous race and competition, with democratizing forces trying hard to catch up with de-democratizing initiatives, but on balance, it appears, losing out more often than catching up in the process.

When considering the role and performance of particular development institutions in the 'grey zone', therefore, the context is evidently no longer one defined by a simple state-society paradigm, but one in which external agencies and global processes play decisive roles. (Shaw, 1996). At the same time, international agencies should not only be looked at in terms of their relation to the state. One of the most significant and revealing aspects of their current role concerns the particular manner in which they seek to extend their institutional identities, competing for the control over 'functional' territories and spheres of involvement. Indeed, a certain shift in emphasis from the classical kind of state territoriality to functionally defined 'territories' claimed by global agencies, each with their characteristic claims and different kinds of boundary demarcations, appears to be one key dimension in what goes under 'globalization' today. The implications of these tendencies for understanding relevant political relationships and interactions, and indeed for spotting and locating the political element in the first place, are momentous but appear as yet to have been insufficiently recognized and studied.

If these various transformations in the significance of the 'national' and the 'international' demand corresponding adjustments in our research foci, current shifts in the major analytical perspectives likewise tend to put political and institutional linkages in a different light. As argued in Chapter 1, one possible consequence of the relative demise of the major paradigms, which had accorded a central role to the state and had attached a particular normative quality to their respective perspectives, is that development-oriented institutions and institutional arrangements of various kinds may come to be assessed more 'autonomously', so to speak, and possibly with greater regard for their intrinsic merits, than was often the case previously, when their role was largely judged in terms of the broader political–ideological context this formed part of.

Nonetheless, any enhanced autonomy with which we might *focus* on the role and performance of institutions does not necessarily imply increased autonomy of *action* for the institutional actors concerned. In fact, similar to how state governments may be confronted with contradictory pressures from different UN agencies, as noted above, one of the implications and contradictions of the changing political context on a global scale is that development institutions may find themselves pulled in quite opposite directions, due to the contrasted expectations and demands that different external and national agencies and 'clients' might attach to their role. Development agencies of various kinds, for instance, may find themselves caught between conflicting demands: their own funders may want them to check on compliance by their counterparts with criteria of efficiency and other conditionalities, while the latter (many of them voluntary and self-help organizations) expect basic support and space for experimentation in a spirit of mutual trust (Fowler, 1998). Institutional ambiguity and role conflicts may thus arise from either the initial or the acquired charters of development institutions, and become part of their institutional design. Also, criteria of proper financial management and accountability have tended to become more enhanced within the overall set of changing interrelationships and priorities. At the same time, these ambiguities may help explain the increased attention which actor-oriented approaches have recently been drawing for purposes of analysing different institutional roles in complex chains of interdependent social and economic transactions (Long, 1988).

When attempting to appreciate the nature and impact of development interventions, therefore, it is essential to situate them within the wider global context, itself subject to continuous and pervasive change. At the level of specific policies and programmes, meanwhile, one may note various instances of deliberate strategies of institutional concentration and integration at play. With more limited time-spans, fairly concretely spelled out objectives and, in particular, quite a keen idea as to what parts or aspects of a production or marketing cycle are earmarked for closer co-ordination, compliance and control, many policy designs in essence are strategic programmatic statements meant to establish or deepen incorporative links. Implicit or explicit incorporation strategies underlie various development projects and programmes that emphasize technological innovation and economies of scale and establish new centres of co-ordination and control. This has been the case for example in the international dairy development strategies discussed in Chapters 9 and 10, but also in new land tenure arrangements, range management, and pastoralist development policies (Chapters 6, 7 and 8).

Other tendencies concerning the institutional development of development institutions in the global context appear to point in different directions. One is a notable tendency to grant extensive autonomy of action, if not of jurisdiction, to strategically placed sectoral institutions in various developing countries. This approach appears to be favoured internationally as a way of safeguarding the institutional centres from the vagaries of local politics. On the face of it, this strategy appears to strengthen autonomy, promote 'capacity-building', and favour administrative decongestion and decentralization. By the same token, it facilitates these institutions becoming incorporated more easily into broader, transnational structures. While these tendencies may entail the development of transnational institutional chains, enabling closer collaborative rapport between different levels and segments, they may also signify the extension of pervasive powers through the mechanisms which connect different institutional levels. None of this is commonly very visible, but these incorporative linkages form a crucial element in ongoing processes of 'grey globalization'. Among other things, the latter may entail the reshuffling of institutional hierarchies and patterns of differentiation that tend to be associated with them.

As the scope of intervention of the institutions and institutional arrangements concerned can be extremely vast, there is clearly a need for a proper understanding of the contextual conditions as well as the modalities of their operation. The drastically changed role of the developmentalist state and the surrender of its primacy in the delineation and execution of development strategies, must surely be a point of departure (Ellis, 1996). Besides, any autonomy of action bestowed upon new development-oriented institutional constructs needs to be assessed against the possibility that institutional self-preservation and aggrandizement may lead to new supra-forms of entrepreneurship, which might possibly be effecting a diversion of the revenue further away from the production base to new central institutions. Often operative within the grey area between public and private management, some of the programmes concerned represent quite novel institutional variations within the non-state public sphere. Thus, by implication, they tend to raise additional questions about the relativity of the public/private dichotomy, as well as about the changing role and position of the state. Evidently, this underscores the need for a theory of institutions in the context of shifting political parameters within the global setting.

References

Achaya, K. T. and Huria, V. K. (1986) 'Rural Poverty and Operation Flood', *Economic and Political Weekly*, 21 (37), pp. 1651–6.

Adam, H. M. (1968) 'A Nation in Search of a Script: The Problem of Establishing a National Orthography for Somali', unpublished MA Thesis, University of East Africa.

Adam, H. M. and Ford, R. (eds.) (1997) *Mending Rips in the Sky: Options for Somali Communities in the 21st Century*, Lawrenceville, N. J.: The Red Sea Press.

Alavi, H. (1972) 'The State in Postcolonial Societies: Pakistan and Bangladesh', *New Left Review*, 74, pp. 59–81.

Albert, E. M. (1960) 'Socio-political Organization and Receptivity to Change: Some Differences Between Ruanda and Urundi', *Southwestern Journal of Anthropology*, 16 (1), pp. 46–74.

Alderman, H., Mergos G. and Slade, R. (1987) *Cooperatives and the Commercialization of Milk Production in India: a Literature Review*, IFPRI Working Papers on Commercialization of Agriculture and Nutrition. No. 2, Washington, DC: International Food Policy Research Institute.

Allum, D. (1978) 'A Commercial View of Food Aid in the Form of Dairy Products', in *Proceedings of the Twentieth International Dairy Congress* (sessions on dairy economics), Paris: International Dairy Congress.

Almond G. A. and Bingham Powell Jr., G. (1966) *Comparative Politics: A Developmental Approach*, Boston, Toronto: Little, Brown and Company.

Almond, G. A. and Verba, S. (1963) *The Civic Culture: Political Attitudes and Democracy in Five Nations*, Princeton: Princeton University Press.

Anderson, B. R. O'G. (1978) 'Studies of the Thai State: the State of Thai Studies', in Ayal, E. B. (ed.), *The State of Thai Studies: Analyses of Knowledge, Approaches and Prospects in Anthropology, Art History and Political Science*, Athens, Ohio: Ohio University Centre for International Studies, Southeast Asia Programme, pp. 193–248.

Andrae, G. and Beckman, B. (1985) *The Wheat Trap: Bread and Underdevelopment in Nigeria*, London: Zed Books.

Ankole Government and District Administration (1964) *Report of the Ankole Kingdom Customary Law's Committee*, Mbarara.

Ankole Government (1965a) *Report, Commission of Enquiry into Ankole Mailo Land*, Mbarara.

Ankole Government (1965b) White Paper on *Report of Commission of Enquiry into Ankole Mailo Land*, Mbarara.

Anyang'Nyong'o, P. (1992) 'Discourses on Democracy in Africa', CODESRIA Seventh General Assembly on Democratization Processes in Africa: Problems and Prospects, Dakar.

Appiah, K. A. (1991) 'Is the Post in Post-modernism the Post in Post-colonial?', *Critical Enquiry*, Winter.

Apter, D. E. (1965) *The Politics of Modernization*, Chicago: University of Chicago Press.

Apthorpe, R. J. (1959) *From Tribal Rule to Modern Government*, Lusaka: Rhodes-Livingstone Institute.

Apthorpe, R. J. (1960) 'The Introduction of Bureaucracy into African Polities', *Journal of African Administration*, 12 (3), pp. 125–134.

Apthorpe, R. J. (1968) 'Land Law and Land Policy in Eastern Africa', unpublished paper, Kampala: Makerere University.

Azarya, V. (1988) 'Re-ordering State-Society Relations: Incorporation and Disengagement', in Donald Rothchild and Naomi Chazan (eds.) *The Precarious Balance: State and Society in Africa*, Boulder and London: Westview Press.

Bachman, M. R. (1981a) 'How to Approach Food Technological Problems in Developing Countries', *LWT-Report*, 14 (6), pp. 348–50.

Bachman, M. R. (1981b) 'Technology Appropriate to Food Preservation in Developing Countries', in S. Thorne (ed.), *Developments in Food Preservation* , 1, London and New Jersey: Applied Science Publishers.

Balbus, I. D. (1971) 'The Concept of Interest in Pluralist and Marxian Analysis', *Politics and Society*, 1 (2).

Bangura, Y. (1994) 'Intellectuals, Economic Reform and Social Change: Constraints and Opportunities in the Formation of a Nigerian Technocracy', *Development and Change*, 25 (2), pp. 261–305.

Banton, M. (ed.) (1966) *The Social Anthropology of Complex Societies*. London: Tavistock Publications.

Barya, J.-J. B. (1992) 'The New Political Conditionalities of Aid: An Independent View from Africa', paper presented at EADI Symposium, Vienna (April).

Bascom, R. M. and Herskovits, M. (eds.) (1962) *Continuity and Change in African Cultures*. Chicago: University of Chicago Press, Phoenix Edition.

Batra, S. M. (1990) 'Operation Flood: Impact on the Delhi Milk Market', in M. Doornbos and K. N. Nair (eds.) *Resources, Institutions and Strategies: Operation Flood and Indian Dairying*, New Delhi: Sage.

Baviskar, B. S. (1984) 'Operation Flood and Social Science Research', *Economic and Political Weekly*, 18 (27), pp. 1203–1204.

Baviskar, B. S. (1985) *Milk and Sugar: A Comparative Analysis of Cooperative Politics*, Discussion Paper No. 208, Institute of Development Studies, University of Sussex, UK.

Baviskar, B. S. (1990) 'Dairy Cooperatives and Rural Development in Gujarat', in Doornbos and Nair (eds.) *Resources, Institutions and Strategies: Operation Flood and Indian Dairying*, New Delhi: Sage.

Baviskar, B. S. and George, Shanti (1988) 'Development and Controversy: National Dairy Development Board, *Economic and Political Weekly*, 23 (13), pp. 35–43.

Baviskar, S. and Terhal, P. (1990) 'Internal Constraints and External Dependence: EEC and Operation Flood', in Doornbos and Nair (eds.) *Resources, Institutions and Strategies: Operation Flood and Indian Dairying*, New Delhi: Sage.

Beattie, J. (1964) *Other Cultures: Aims, Methods and Achievements in Social Anthropology*. London: Cohen and West

Binder, L. *et al.* (1971) *Crises and Sequences in Political Development*, Princeton: Princeton University Press.

Boeninger, E. (1991) 'Governance and Development: Issues, Challenges, Opportunities and Constraints', World Bank Annual Conference on Development Economics paper, Washington DC.

Boyce, J. (1996) *Economic Policy for Building Peace: The Lessons of El Salvador*, Boulder and London: Lynne Rienner Publishers.

Bratton, M. and Rothchild, D. (1992) 'The Institutional Bases of Governance in Africa', in Goran Hyden and Michael Bratton (eds.) *Governance and Politics in Africa*, Boulder and London: Lynne Rienner Publishers.

Brock, B. (1968) 'Customary Land Tenure, "Individualisation" and Agricultural Development', Rural Development Research Paper 65, Kampala: Makerere University College.

Bunting, A. H. (ed.) (1970) *Change in Agriculture*, London: Duckworth.

Carlsson, J., Kohlin, G. and Ekbom, A. (1994) *The Political Economy of Evaluation: International Aid Agencies and the Effectiveness of Aid*, International Political Economy Series, Basingstoke: Macmillan.

Centre for Education and Documentation (1982) *Operation Flood: Development or Dependency?*, Bombay: Centre for Information Technology and Education.

Chakravarty, T. K. and Reddy, C. O. (1982) 'Dairy Development Programme: Process and Impact: A Study at Village Level in Anantpur', *Journal of Rural Development*, 1 (4) July, pp. 459–512.

Chambers, R. (1988) 'Bureaucratic Reversals and Local Diversity', *IDS Bulletin*, 19 (4) Oct., pp. 50–56.

Chatterjee, S. (1990) 'Aid, Trade and Rural Development: A Review of New Zealand's Assistance to Indian Dairying', in Doornbos and Nair (eds.) *Resources, Institutions and Strategies: Operation Flood and Indian Dairying*, New Delhi: Sage.

Christian Michelsen Institute (1993) *Evaluation of the World Food Programme. Final Report*, Bergen.

Claessen, H. J. M. and Skalnik, P. (eds.) (1978) *The Early State*. The Hague: Mouton.

Claessen, H. J. M., van de Velde, P. and Estellie Smith, M. (eds.) (1985) *Development and Decline: The Evolution of Sociopolitical Organization*, South Hadley: Bergin and Garvey.

Clay, E. J. (1985) *Review of Food Aid Policy Changes since 1978*, World Food Programme Occasional Papers, No. 1, Rome: WFP.

Clay, E. J. *et al.* (1998a) *The Future of Food Aid: A Policy Review*, London: Overseas Development Institute, June.

Clay, E. J. *et al.* (1998b) 'Food Aid and Food Security in the 1990s: Performance and Effectiveness', *London: Overseas Development Institute, Working paper* 113, (1998b) September.

Coleman, J. S. (1977) 'The Concept of Political Penetration', in L. Cliffe, J. S. Coleman and M. R. Doornbos (eds.) *Government and Rural Development in East Africa: Essays on Political Penetration*, The Hague: Martinus Nijhoff.

Commission of the European Communities (1977) 'Food Aid: Progress, Problems and Prospects', *Information: Development Cooperation*, 165/77E, Brussels: EEC Commission.

Commission of the European Communities (1983) 'Food Aid for Development', Communication to the Council COM (P3) 141 final, Brussels: EEC Commission.

Commission of the European Communities (1992) *India – Operation Flood III Mid Term Evaluation Mission, CC/ALA/930/A/2/91/323 (Request No: 2245) Final Report. Main Report*, Joint Venture of Dangroup International (Denmark) *et al.*

Committee on Food Aid (CFA) (1975) 'Milk Marketing and Dairy Development', Second interim evaluation of WFP-assisted Project India, 618, Rome: FAO World Food Programme (April).

Committee on Food Aid (CFA) (1976a) 'Food Aid Policies and Programmes', Rome: FAO World Food Programme, 2/7-c (October).

Committee on Food Aid (CFA) (1976b) 'WFP Assistance to Dairy Development: Report to the Executive Director', Rome: FAO World Food Programme (September).

Crotty, R. M. (1980) *Cattle, Economics and Development*, Slough, UK: Commonwealth Agricultural Bureau.

Dairy India Yearbook (1983) New Delhi: P. R. Gupta.

Das, A. (1992) *India Invented: A Nation in the Making*, New Delhi: Manohar.

Deutsch, K. W. (1961) 'Social Mobilization and Political Development', *The American Political Science Review*, 55 (3) pp. 493–514.

De Waal, A. (1997) *Famine Crimes: Politics and the Disaster Industry in Africa*, London: James Currey Publishers.

Diamant, A. (1959) 'Is There a Non-Western Political Process?', *The Journal of Politics*, 21, pp. 123–127.

Doornbos, M. (1969) 'Political Development: The Search for Criteria', *Development and Change*, 1 (1), pp. 93–115.

Doornbos, M. (1970) 'Kumanyana and Rwenzururu: Two Responses to Ethnic Inequality', in Robert I. Rotberg and Ali A. Mazrui, (eds.) *Protest and Power in Black Africa*, New York: Oxford University Press.

Doornbos, M. (1975) *Regalia Galore: The Decline and Eclipse of Ankole Kingship*, Nairobi: East African Literature Bureau.

Doornbos, M. (1978) *Not all the King's Men: Inequality as a Political Instrument in Ankole, Uganda*, The Hague: Mouton.

Doornbos, M. (1980) 'Over de Grenzen van de Macht: het Vroege Koningschap in Nkore', in R. Hagesteijn (ed.) *Stoeien met Staten*, Leiden: ICA Publications, no. 37.

Doornbos, M. (1983) 'Role de l'Etat en Afrique de l'Est', *Revue Tiers-Monde*, 24 (93), pp. 143–152.

Doornbos, M. (1986) "Big Man" and his Big Brother: Some Notes on Incorporation' in M. A. van Bakel, R. R. Hagesteijn and P. van der Velde (eds.) *Private Politics: A Multidisciplinary Approach to 'Big Man' Systems*, Leiden: Brill.

Doornbos, M. (1990) 'The African State in Academic Debate: Retrospect and Prospect', *Journal of Modern African Studies*, 28 (2), pp. 178–198.

Doornbos, M. (1992) 'Foreword', *Development and Change*, Special Issue on Emancipations: Modern and Postmodern, 23 (2), pp. 1–4.

Doornbos, M. (1993a) 'Le Retour des Rois', *Politique Africaine*, 52.

Doornbos, M. (1993b) 'Pasture and Polis: the Roots of Political Marginalization of Somali Pastoralism', in Markakis, J. (ed.) *Conflict and the Decline of Pastoralism in the Horn of Africa*, Basingstoke: Macmillan.

Doornbos, M. and Kaviraj, S. (eds.) (1997) *Dynamics of State Formation: India and Europe Compared*, New Delhi: Sage.

Doornbos, M. (1999) 'New Research Directions in Post-conflict Contexts: The Scope for Action Research Based Policy Dialogue', paper prepared for Workshop on 'Living in Wartimes – Living in Post-War Times', University of Hanover History Department, Melsungen, 22–24 January.

Doornbos. M., van Dorsten, F., Mitra, M. and Terhal, P. (1990) *Dairy Aid and Development: India's Operation Flood*, New Delhi: Sage.

Doornbos, M. R. and Lofchie, M. F. (1971) 'Ranching and Scheming: A Case Study of the Ankole Ranching Scheme', in Michael F. Lofchie, (ed.) *The State of the Nations: Constraints on Development in Independent Africa*, Berkeley and Los Angeles: University of California Press.

Doornbos, M. and Markakis, J. (1994) 'Society and State in Crisis: What went wrong in Somalia?', in M. A. Mohamed Salih and Lennart Wohlgemuth (eds.) *Crisis Management and the Politics of Reconciliation in Somalia*, Uppsala: Nordiska Afrikainstitutet.

Doornbos, M. and Mwesigye, F. (1995) 'The New Politics of Kingmaking', in Holger Bernt Hansen and Michael Twaddle (eds.) *From Chaos to Order: The Politics of Constitution-making in Uganda*, Kampala: Fountain Publishers and London: James Currey.

Doornbos, M. and Nair, K. N. (eds.) (1990) *Resources, Institutions and Strategies: Operation Flood and Indian Dairying*, New Delhi: Sage.

Doornbos, M., van Stuijvenberg, P. and Terhal, P. (1987) 'Operation Flood: Impacts and Issues', *Food Policy*, 12 (4), pp. 376–383.

Doornbos, M. and Terhal, P. (1993) 'The Limits of Independent Policy Research: Analysing the EEC-India Dairy Aid Nexus', in A. Hurskainen and M. Salih (eds.) *Social Science and Conflict Analysis*, Helsinki: Helsinki University Press.

Doornbos, M. and Tesfai, A. (1999) *Post-conflict Eritrea: Prospects for Reconstruction and Development*, Lawrenceville, N. J.: The Red Sea Press.

Dwivedi, O. P. (1995) *Development Administration: From Underdevelopment to Sustainable Development*, International Political Economy Series, Basingstoke: Macmillan.

Easton, D. (1965) *A Framework for Political Analysis*, Englewood Cliffs, N.J.: Prentice-Hall.

Eckstein, H. (1963) 'A Perspective on Comparative Politics, Past and Present', in H. Eckstein, and D. E. Apter, *Comparative Politics: a Reader*, New York: The Free Press of Glencoe.

Eisenstadt, S. N., (1964) 'Breakdowns of Modernization', *Economic Development and Cultural Change*, 12 (4), pp. 345–367.

Ellis, S. (ed.) (1996), *Africa Now: People, Policies, Institutions*, The Hague: Ministry of Foreign Affairs and London: James Currey.

Epstein, A. L. (ed.) (1967) *The Craft of Social Anthropology*, London: Tavistock Publications.

European Court of Auditors (ECA) (1988) 'Special Report No. 6/87 on Food Aid Supplied to India Between 1978 and 1985 (Operation Flood II) accompanied by the Replies of the Commission (88/C 31/01, *Official Journal of the European Communities*, No. C 31, Luxembourg.

FAO (1968) 'Milk Products as Food Aid', Document No. CCP 68/8/1 Rome: FAO Committee on Commodity Problems, 43rd session.

Fallers, L. A. (1956) *Bantu Bureaucracy: a Study of Integration and Conflict in the Political Institutions of an East African People*, Cambridge: W. Heffer and Sons.

Finkle, J. L. and Gable R. W. (eds.) (1966) *Political Development and Social Change*, New York, London, Sydney: John Wiley and Sons Inc.

Fortes, M. and Evans-Pritchard E. E. (eds.) (1940) *African Political Systems*, London: Oxford University Press.

Fowler, A. (1998) 'Authentic NGO Partnerships in the New Policy Agenda for International Aid: Dead End or Light Ahead', *Development and Change*, 29 (1).

Fox, J. (1993) *The Politics of Food in Mexico: State Power and Social Mobilization*, Ithaca and London: Cornell University Press.

Fritschel, H. (1998) 'The Changing Outlook for Food Aid', *2020 Vision News and Views*, Washington DC: International Food Policy Research Institute, November.

Garcia, R. (1984) *Food Systems and Society*, UNRISD Food Systems and Society Series 83.5., Geneva: UNRISD.

Gasper, D. (1993) 'Entitlements Analysis: Relating Concepts and Contexts', *Development and Change*, 24 (4).

Geertz, C. (1963) 'The Integrative Revolution: Primordial Sentiments and Civil Politics in the New States', in C. Geertz (ed.) *Old Societies and New States: the Quest for Modernity in Asia and Africa*, New York: The Free Press.

George, Shanti (1985a) *Operation Flood: An Appraisal of Current Indian Dairy Policy*, Delhi: Oxford University Press.

George, Shanti (1985) 'Operation Flood and Rural India: Vested and Divested Interests', *Economic and Political Weekly*, 20 (49) Dec., pp. 2163–70.

George, Shanti, (1990) 'Operation Flood and Centralised Dairy Development in India', in Doornbos and Nair (eds.) *Resources, Institutions and Strategies: Operation Flood and Indian Dairying*, New Delhi: Sage.

George, Susan (1976) *How the Other Half Dies*, Harmondsworth: Penguin.

Ghai, Y. 1994 'Human Rights and Governance: The Asia Debate', The Asia Foundation, Center for Asian Pacific Affairs.

Ghai, Y. (1998) 'Autonomy with Chinese Characteristics: The Case of Hong Kong', paper presented at Consultation on Federalism and Diversity, Institute of Social Studies, The Hague.

Gibbon, E. (1779) *The History of the Decline and Fall of the Roman Empire*, Basil.

Gibbon, P. (1993) 'The World Bank and the New Politics of Aid', in G. Sorensen (ed.) *Political Conditionality*, London: Frank Cass.

Giddens A. (1979) *Central Problems in Social Theory: Action, Structure and Contradictions in Social Analysis*, London: Macmillan.

Giddens, A. (1984) *The Constitution of Society: an Outline of the Theory of Structuration*, Cambridge: Polity Press.

Government of India, Ministry of Agriculture (1984) *Report of the Evaluation Committee on Operation Flood II* (Jha Report), New Delhi: GOI Press.

Gregory, K. E. (1963) *The USAID Livestock Survey Team Report*, University of Nebraska.

Hall, A. (1988) 'Community Participation and Development Policy: A Sociological Perspective', in Anthony Hall and James Midgley (eds.) *Development Policies: Sociological Perspectives*, Manchester and New York: Manchester University Press.

Harriss, J. (1992) 'Between Economism and Post-Modernism: Reflections on Research on Agrarian Change in India', Rural Development Studies Research Seminar, Institute of Social Studies, The Hague, September.

Harts-Broekhuis, A. and Verkoren, O. (eds.) (1994) *No Easy Way Out: Essays on Third World Development in Honour of Jan Hinderink*, Utrecht: Koninklijk Nederlands Aardrijkskundig Genootschap/Faculteit Ruimtelijke Wetenschappen Universiteit Utrecht (Netherlands Geographical Studies 186).

Healey, J. and Robinson, M. (eds.) (1992) *Democracy, Governance and Economic Policy: Sub-Saharan Africa in Comparative Perspective*, London: ODI Development Policy Studies.

Healey, J. and Tordoff, W. (1995) *Votes and Budgets: Comparative Studies in Accountable Governance in the South*, International Political Economy Series, Basingstoke: Macmillan.

Heaver, R. (1982) 'Bureaucratic Politics and Incentives in the Management of Rural Development', World Bank Staff Working Papers 537, Washington, D.C.

Held, D. (1992) 'Democracy: From City-States to a Cosmopolitan Order?', *Political Studies: Special Issue on Prospects for Democracy*, 40, pp. 10–39.

Herren, U. (1988) 'Pastoral Peasants: Household Strategies in Mukogodu Division, Laikipic District', Working Paper 458, Institute of Development Studies: Nairobi.

Hobsbawm, E. and Ranger, T. (eds.) (1983) *The Invention of Tradition*, Cambridge: Cambridge University Press.

Huntington, S. P. (1965) 'Political Development and Political Decay', *World Politics*, 17 (3) pp. 386–430.

Hutchful, E. (1997) 'The Institutional and Political Framework of Macro-Economic Management in Ghana', UNRISD Discussion Paper 82, UNRISD, Geneva.

Hyden, G. (1980) *Beyond Ujamaa in Tanzania: Underdevelopment and an Uncaptured Peasantry*, London: Heinemann Educational Books.

Hyden, G. (1992) 'Governance and the Study of Politics', in Goran Hyden and Michael Bratton, (eds.) *Governance and Politics in Africa*, Boulder and London: Lynne Rienner Publishers.

International Bank for Reconstruction and Development (1961) *The Economic Development of Uganda*, Entebbe.

Jain, J. L., Prasad, A. and Gupta, G. N. (1982) *Organized Milk Marketing in India, Socio-Economic Impact (A Case Study of the Delhi Milk Market Scheme in N. W. Rajasthan)*, Jaipur: Kumarappa Institute of Gram Swaraj.

Jamal, V. (1988) 'Somalia: Understanding an Unconventional Economy', *Development and Change*, 19 (2), pp. 203–266.

Jha Report – see Government of India, 1984.

Jones, G. A., (1998) 'Resistance and the Rule of Law in Mexico', *Development and Change*, 29 (3)

Joshi, V. H. (1990) 'Operation Flood: Constraints and Potentialities in Saurashtra', in Doornbos and Nair (eds.) (1990) *Resources, Institutions and Strategies: Operation Flood and Indian Dairying*, New Delhi: Sage.

Jul, M. (1975) *Nutritional Impact of Dairy Development in India*, Ernaering Manuskript nr. 133, Landbrugsministeriets, Copenhagen.

Karp, M. (1960) *The Economics of Trusteeship in Somalia*, Boston.

Kaviraj, S. (1984) 'On the Crisis of Political Institutions in India', *Contributions to Indian Sociology* (July–December).

Kilson, M. L. (1963) 'Authoritarian and Single-Party Tendencies in African Politics', *World Politics*, 15 (2), pp. 262–294.

Kothari, R. (1986) 'The NGOs, the State and World Capitalism', in W. Fernandes (ed.) *Voluntary Action and Government Control*, New Delhi: Indian Social Monograph Series.

Kothari, R. (1989) 'The Problem', *Seminar*, 354 Feb., pp. 12–17.

Landau, M. (1971) 'Linkage, Coding and Intermediacy: a Strategy for Institution-Building', *Journal of Comparative Administration*, 2 (4).

Landell-Mills, P. and Serageldin, I. (1991) 'Governance and the External Factor', World Bank Annual Conference on Development Economics paper, Washington DC.

Lappé, F. M. and Collins, J. (1977) *Food First: Beyond the Myth of Scarcity*, Boston: Houghton Mifflin.

Laswell, H. (1936) *Politics: Who Gets What, When, How*, New York: McGraw-Hill Book Company.

Lawyer, K. (1993) 'The Political Ecology of Degradation in Mbarara, Ntungamo and Bushenyi Districts (Ankole), Uganda', MA Thesis, Institute of Social Studies, The Hague.

Leach, E. R. (1954) *Political Systems of Highland Burma*, London: Bell.

Leach, M., Mearns, R. and Scoones, I. (1997) 'Environmental Entitlements: A Framework for Understanding the Institutional Dynamics of Environmental Change', IDS Discussion Paper 359, IDS, Brighton.

Lipton, M. (1977) *Why People Stay Poor: A Study of Urban Bias in World Development*, London: Temple Smith.

Lipton, M. (1985) 'Operation Flood and Other EC Aid to India' in W. Calliewaert (ed.), 1985, *India and the EC*, Brussels: Center for European Policy Studies.

Lofchie, M. (ed.) (1971) *The State of the Nations: Constraints on Development in Independent Africa*, Berkeley, Los Angeles and London: University of California Press.

Lok Sabha Debates (1987) 'Part II, Proceedings Other than Questions and Answers', 25th Aug. 1987 continued on 26th Aug.

Long, N. (1988) 'Sociological Perspectives on Agrarian Development and State Intervention', in Anthony Hall and James Midgley, (eds.) *Development Policies: Sociological Perspectives*, Manchester and New York: Manchester University Press.

Long, N. (1992) 'From Paradigm Lost to Paradigm Regained? The Case for an Actor-oriented Sociology of Development', in Norman Long and Ann Long, (eds.) *Battlefields of Knowledge: The Interlocking of Theory and Practice in Social Research and Development*, London and New York: Routledge.

Lynch, O. and Talbott, K. (1995) *Balancing Acts: Community-based Forest Management and National Law in Asia and the Pacific*, Washington D.C.: World Resources Institute.

Lyons, T. and Samatar, A. I. (1995) *Somalia: State Collapse, Multilateral Intervention, and Strategies for Political Reconstruction*, Brookings Occasional Papers, The Brookings Institution, Washington D.C.

Mackintosh, W. L. S. (1938) *Some Notes on the Abahima and the Cattle Industry in Ankole*, Entebbe: Government Printer.

Macridis, R. C. (1955) *The Study of Comparative Government*, New York: Random House.

Mair, L. (1967) 'Busoga Local Government', *Journal of Commonwealth Political Studies*, 5 (2).

Manor, J. (1996) 'Recent Trends in the Study of State-Society Relations', in Mette Halskov Hansen and Arild Engelsen Ruud, (eds.) *Weak? Strong? Civil? Embedded? New Perspectives on State-Society Relations in the Non-Western World*, SUM Report No. 5, Center for Development and the Environment, University of Oslo.

Manor, J. (ed.) (1991) *Rethinking Third World Politics*, London: Longman.

Markakis, J. (ed.) (1993) *Conflict and the Decline of Pastoralism in the Horn of Africa*, Basingstoke: Macmillan.

Martin, D.-C. (1991) 'The Cultural Dimension of Governance', World Bank Annual Conference on Development Economics Paper, Washington DC.

Mascarenhas, R. C. (1988) *A Strategy for Rural Development: Dairy Cooperatives in India*, New Delhi: Sage.

Maxwell, S. (1986) *Food Aid: Agricultural Disincentives and Commercial Market Displacement*, IDS Discussion Paper 224, Brighton: Institute of Development Studies.

Mazrui, A. A. (1968) 'From Social Darwinism to Current Theories of Modernization', *World Politics*, 21 (1), pp. 68–83.

Mead, M. (ed.) (1953) *Cultural Patterns and Technical Change: a Manual*, Paris: UNESCO.

Mellor, J. W. and Ponteves, D. B. (1964) 'The Effect of Growth in Demand for Milk on the Demand for Concentrate Feeds, India, 1951–76', *Indian Journal of Agricultural Economics*, 19 (3 and 4), pp. 131–46.

Michels, R. (1962) *Political Parties: A Sociological Study of the Oligarchical Tendencies of Modern Democracy (1915)*, New York: Collier Books.

Mitchell, J. C. (1966) 'Theoretical Orientations in African Urban Studies', in M. Banton, *The Social Anthropology of Complex Societies*, London: Tavistock Publications.

Mitra, M. (1990) 'Profiles of Women Dairy Producers in Andhra Pradesh', in Doornbos and Nair (eds.) *Resources, Institutions and Strategies: Operation Flood and Indian Dairying*, New Delhi: Sage.

Mkandawire, T. (1992) 'Adjustment, Political Conditionality and Democratization in Africa', CODESRIA Seventh General Assembly on *Democratization Processes in Africa: Problems and Prospects*, Dakar.

Moore, M. (ed.) (1993) 'Good Government?', Special Issue of *IDS Bulletin* 24 (1).

Morris, H. F. (1964) *The Heroic Recitations of the Bahima of Ankole*, Oxford: Clarendon Press.

Mudimbe, V. Y. (1988) *The Invention of Africa: Gnosis, Philosophy and the Order of Knowledge*, Bloomington: Indiana University Press.

Nagabrahmam, D. (ed.) (1983) 'The Role of a Dairy Federation', Papers and Proceedings of the Top Management Seminar held on 7th–8th, March, 1983, Anand: Institute of Rural Management.

Nair, K. N. (1987) 'Animal Protein Consumption and the Sacred Cow Complex in India', in M. Harris and E. B. Ross (eds.) *Food and Evolution: Toward a Theory of Human Habits*, Philadelphia: Temple University Press.

Nair, K. N. and Dhas, A. C. (1990) 'Cattle Breeding Technology and Draught Power Availability: An Unresolved Contradiction', in Doornbos and Nair (eds.) *Resources, Institutions and Strategies: Operation Flood and Indian Dairying*, New Delhi: Sage.

National Commission on Agriculture (NCA) (1976) *Report of the National Commission on Agriculture*, Part VII, 'Animal Husbandry', New Delhi: Government of India.

National Dairy Development Board (NDDB), (March 1977) *Pilot Project on Comparative Study of Milk Producers' Socio-Economics, Productivity and Production Practices*, Anand: NDDB.

NDDB, September (1980) *Breeding and Feeding for Milk Production in Operation Flood II*, Anand: NDDB., September.

NDDB (1982) *Dairying in India*, Anand: NDDB.

NDDB (1985) *Operation Flood Phase III*, Anand: NDDB.

Nederveen Pieterse, J. (1992) 'Emancipations: Modern and Postmodern', *Development and Change*, 23 (3).

Netherlands Ministry of Foreign Affairs, Inspectie Ontwikkelissamenwerking te Velde (Development Cooperation Evaluation Unit) (1990) *Voedselhulp en Ontwikkeling: Een evaluatie van de Nederlandse Voedselhulp met nadruk op Sub-Sahara Afrika in de periode 1980–1989* (Food Aid and Development: An evaluation of

Dutch Food Aid with emphasis on Sub-Saharan Africa in the period 1980–1989), The Hague.

Nyerere, J. K. (1973) *Freedom and Development: a Selection from Writings and Speeches 1968–1973*, Dar-es-Salaam: Oxford University Press.

O'Brien, D. C. (1972) 'Order and the Erosion of a Democratic Ideal: American Political Science 1960–1970', *Journal of Development Studies*, 8 (2) pp. 351–378.

Ostrom, E. (1992) *Crafting Institutions for Self-Governing Irrigation Systems*, San Francisco: Institute for Contemporary Studies Press.

Ottenberg, S. (1962) 'Ibo Receptivity to Change', in Bascom, R. and M. Herskovits (eds.), *Continuity and Change in African Cultures*, Chicago: University of Chicago Press.

Overseas Development Institute (1992) *Aid and Political Reform*, briefing paper (January).

Packenham R. A. (1964) 'Approaches to the Study of Political Development', *World Politics*, 17, pp. 108–120.

Parekh, B. (1992) 'The Cultural Particularity of Liberal Democracy', *Political Studies: Special Issue on Prospects for Democracy*, 40, pp. 160–175.

Parisot, R. (1990) 'Cattle Development, Nutritional Requirements and Environmental Implications', in Doornbos and Nair (eds.) *Resources, Institutions and Strategies: Operation Flood and Indian Dairying*, New Delhi: Sage.

Patel, R. M. (1982) 'Glimpses of Change and Development in Borsad Taluka (Kheda district, Gujarat)', Anand: Sardar Patel University, Agro-Economic Research Centre, Vallabh Vidhyanagar.

Patel, S. (1990) 'The Anand Pattern: A Socio–Historical Analysis of its Origin and Growth', in Doornbos and Nair (eds.), *Resources, Institutions and Strategies: Operation Flood and Indian Dairying*, New Delhi: Sage.

Paul, S. (1982) *Managing Development Programmes: The Lessons of Success*, Boulder: Westview Press.

Payne, J. H. (1992) 'Economic Assistance to Support Democratization in Developing Countries: A Canadian Perspective', *Development* (1992/93).

Peters, B. G. (1987) 'Politicians and Bureaucrats in the Politics of Policy-making', in Jan-Erik Lane, (ed.), *Bureaucracy and Public Choice*, London: Sage Publications.

Platteau, J.-P. (1996) 'The Evolutionary Theory of Land Rights as Applied to Sub-Saharan Africa: A Critical Assessment', *Development and Change*, 27 (1).

Post, Ken (1997) *Revolution's Other World: Communism and the Periphery, 1917–39*, Basingstoke: Macmillan.

Power, J. and Holenstein, A. (1980) *The World of Hunger*, New Delhi: Heritage.

Pye, L. W. (1958) 'The Non-Western Political Process', *The Journal of Politics*, 20 pp. 468–486.

Pye, L. W. (1962) *Politics, Personality and Nation Building: Burma's Search for Identity*, New Haven: Yale University Press.

Pye, L. W. (1965) 'The Concept of Political Development', *The Annals*, p. 358.

Pye, L. W. (1966) *Aspects of Political Development*, Boston, Toronto: Little, Brown & Company.

Rajaram, N. (1983) 'The Structural Linkages of a Crisis in a Milk Cooperative in Kheda District, Gujarat', paper presented at the *Workshop on Cooperatives and Rural Development*, Delhi University, March.

Randall V. and Theobald, R. (1985) *Political Change and Underdevelopment. A Critical Introduction to Third World Politics*, London: Macmillan.

Review of African Political Economy (1990) *Special Issue on Democracy and Development,* 49.

Review of African Political Economy (1992) *Special Issue on Democracy, Civil Society and NGO's,* 55.

Richards, A. I. (ed.) (1959) *East African Chiefs,* London: Faber & Faber.

Roscoe, J. (1923) *The Banyankole,* Cambridge: Cambridge University Press.

Rudebeck, L. (ed.) (1992) *When Democracy Makes Sense: Studies in the Democratic Potential of Third World Political Movements,* Uppsala, AKUT Working Group for the Study of Development Strategies.

Rutten, M. M. E. M. (1992) *Selling Wealth to Buy Poverty: The Process of Individualization of Landownership Among the Maasai Pastoralists of Kajiado District, Kenya, 1890–1990,* Saarbrucken–Fort Lauderdale: Breitenbach Publishers.

Said, Edward W. (1978) *Orientalism,* London: Routledge & Kegan Paul.

Samatar, A. I. (1989) 'The Demise of Somali Traditions: The Politics of Development and Reform', in *Proceedings of the 3rd International Conference on the Horn of Africa,* Center for the Study of the Horn of Africa, New York, pp. 5–12.

Saul, J. (1997) 'Liberal Democracy vs Popular Democracy', *Review of African Political Economy,* 24 (73).

Savara, M. (1990) 'Dairy Development amongst the Tribals in Surat District', in Doornbos and Nair (eds.), *Resources, Institutions and Strategies: Operation Flood and Indian Dairying,* New Delhi: Sage.

Schaffer, B. (1980) 'Insiders and Outsiders: Insidedness, Incorporation and Bureaucratic Politics', *Development and Change,* 11 (2), pp. 187–210.

Schaffer, B. (1985) 'Policymakers Have Their Needs Too: Irish Itinerants and the Culture of Poverty', *Development and Change,* 16 (3), pp. 375–408.

Schaffer, B. (ed.) (1975) 'The Problems of Access to Public Services', Special Issue, *Development and Change,* 6–2.

Schaffer, B. and Lamb, G. (1981) *Can Equity be Organized?,* Paris: Gower–Unesco.

Schmitter, P. C. (1989) 'Corporatism is Dead! Long Live Corporatism!', *Government and Opposition,* 24 (1), pp. 54–73.

Schneider, H. K. (1962) 'Pakot Resistance to Change', in R. Bascom, and M. Herskovits, *Continuity and Change in African Cultures,* Chicago: University of Chicago Press.

Scholte, J. A. (1998) 'The International Monetary Fund and Civil Society: An Underdeveloped Dialogue', *ISS Working Paper* 272, The Hague: Institute of Social Studies.

Scott, J. (1985) *Weapons of the Weak: Everyday Forms of Peasant Resistance,* New Haven: Yale University Press.

Shah, T. and Bhargava, M. (1982) *Impact of India's Dairy Cooperatives: Analysis Based on an In-Depth Study of Six Villages in the Districts of Sabarkantha (Gujarat), Periyar (Tamil Nadu) and Bikaner (Rajasthan),* Anand: Institute of Rural Management Anand.

Shah, V. P. (1981) *Role of Milk Cooperatives in Articulating Rural–Urban Interactions: Experiences in Gujarat, India,* Research Report, Ahmedabad: UNESCO.

Shaw, T. (1996) 'Contradictions between Extra-African Policies and African Needs: From National to Human Security? From Structural Adjustment to Peace-building?', draft paper, Dalhousie University.

Shaw, T. M. and Carlsson, J. (1988) 'Introduction: Newly Industrializing Countries and South–South Relations: Concepts, Correlates, Controversies and Cases', in Jerker Carlsson and Timothy M. Shaw, (eds.), *Newly Industrializing Countries and the Political Economy of South–South Relations*, International Political Economy Series, Basingstoke: Macmillan.

Shekhawat, P. S. (1990) 'Operation Flood in Rajasthan: Replication and Institutional Issues in a Regional Context', in Doornbos and Nair (eds.), *Resources, Institutions and Strategies: Operation Flood and Indian Dairying*, New Delhi: Sage.

Shils, E. (1965) 'Demagogues and Cadres in the Political Development of the New States', in L. W. Pye, (ed.), *Communications and Political Development*, Princeton: Princeton University Press.

Singh, K. and Dhas, V. M. (1982) *Impact of Operation Flood I at the Village Level*, Monograph, 1, July, Anand: Institute of Rural Management Anand.

Slater, D. (1992) 'Theories of Development and Politics of the Post-modern: Exploring a Border Zone', *Development and Change*, 23 (3), pp. 283–319.

Somjee, A. H. and Somjee, G. (1978) 'Cooperative Dairying and the Profiles of Social Change in India', *Economic Development and Cultural Change*, 26 (3), pp. 577–90.

Sorensen, G. (ed.) (1993) *Political Conditionality*, London: Frank Cass.

Southall, A. W. (1956) *Alur Society: A Study in Processes and Types of Domination*, Cambridge: W. Heffer and Sons.

South Commission, The (1990) *The Challenge to the South*, London: Oxford University Press.

Stenning, D. J. (1958) 'Coral Tree Hill' (Preliminary Field Report of Land Tenure Enquiry in West Ankole District), EAISR Conference Paper, Kampala: East African Institute of Social Research.

Stockholm Initiative on Global Security and Governance (1991) *Common Responsibilities in the 1990s*, Stockholm: Prime Minister's Office.

Subramaniam, S., Mukunda Das, V. and Ghosh, S. R. (1989) 'Liquid Milk Marketing Strategies for Dairy Co-operatives', Workshop Report 2, Institute of Rural Management – Anand, (13–15 October 1988), Anand: Institute of Rural Management.

Terhal, P. and Doornbos, M. (1983) 'Operation Flood: Development and Commercialization', *Food Policy*, 8, August, pp. 235–239.

Turner, V. W. (1957) *Schism and Continuity in an African Society*, Manchester: Manchester University Press.

Uganda Argus, daily paper, Kampala.

Uganda News (1972) no. 4220, 24 August.

Uganda Protectorate (1939) *Native Administration*, Entebbe: Government Printer.

Uganda Protectorate (1955) *Land Tenure Proposals*, Entebbe: Government Printer.

Uganda Protectorate (1957) *Land Tenure in Uganda*, Entebbe: Government Printer.

Uganda Protectorate (1962) *Report of the Commissioner appointed to Inquire into the Operation of the Land Tenure Scheme in Ankole*, Entebbe: Government Printer.

United Nations Development Programme (1992) *Human Development Report 1992*, New York: UNDP.

United Nations Research Institute for Social Development (UNRISD) (1994) 'Rebuilding War-torn Societies: Problems of International Assistance in Conflict and Post-Conflict situations', Geneva, August.

USAID (1964) *The Ankole/Masaka Ranching Scheme*: Loan Application to USAID by the Government of Uganda, Appendix 9, 'A Brief Background on Tsetse Eradication in Ankole/Masaka', May.

USAID/Uganda Government (1966) 'Loan Agreement', 2 April, sect. 10th, 6.2.

Uvin, P. (1993) '"Do as I Say, Not as I Do": The Limits of Political Conditionality', in G. Sorensen, (ed.), *Political Conditionality*, London: Frank Cass.

Vaidyanathan, A., Nair, K. N. and Harris, M. (1982), 'Bovine Sex and Species Ratios in India', *Current Anthropology*, 23 (4), pp. 365–373.

van Binsbergen, W., Reyntjes, F. and Hesseling, G. (eds.) (1996) *State and Local Community in Africa*, Brussels: Studie- en Dokumentatiecentrum – ASDOC 1996.

van Dorsten, F. (1986) 'Operation Flood – the EEC Connection', The Hague: Institute of Social Studies ISS/IDPAD Working Paper no. 18.

van Thiel, P. (1968) 'The Music of the Kingdom of Ankole', *African Music*, 4 (1).

van Velsen, J. (1967) 'The Extended Case-Method and Situational Analysis', in A. L. Epstein, *The Craft of Social Anthropology*, London: Social Science Paperbacks.

Verhagen, M. (1990) 'Operation Flood and the Rural Poor', in Doornbos and Nair (eds.) *Resources, Institutions and Strategies: Operation Flood and Indian Dairying*, New Delhi: Sage.

Waterman, P. (1993) 'Globalisation, Civil Society, Solidarity: The Politics and Ethics of a World both Real and Universal', *ISS Working Paper*, 147, The Hague: Institute of Social Studies.

Wenger, G. C. (ed.) (1987) *The Research Relationship: Practice and Politics in Social Policy Research*, London: Allen & Unwin.

Wildawsky, A. (1972) 'The Self-Evaluating Organization', *Public Administration Review*, 32 (5), pp. 509–520.

Williamson, P. J. (1989) *Corporatism in Perspective: An Introductory Guide to Corporatist Theory*, London: Sage.

Willner, A. R. (1964) 'The Underdeveloped Study of Political Development', *World Politics*, 16 (3), pp. 468–482.

Wood, G. (ed.) (1986 *Labelling in Development Policy: Essays in Honour of Bernard Schaffer*, London, The Hague: Sage Publications and Institute of Social Studies.

World Bank, 1978, *India: National Dairy Project. Staff Appraisal Report*, Report No. 1964-IN, Washington, DC: World Bank.

World Bank, 1990, *The African Capacity Building Initiative: Towards Improved Policy Analysis and Development Management*, Washington DC: World Bank.

World Bank, 1997, 'The State in a Changing World', *World Development Report 1997*, World Bank/Oxford University Press.

Index